ARCADE

ARTISTS AND PLACE-MAKING

Edited by Rhona Warwick

Ronan,

Had you not taken a chance on a slightly mad art historian for the Urban Studies Fellowship, this chapter would never have been written — so this one's definitely for you!

With love

Vendakousi

Black Dog Publishing

CONTENTS

… the Arcade is a city, a world in miniature …
WALTER BENJAMIN, *THE ARCADES PROJECT*

THERE ARE few more emotive place-names than the Gorbals in Glasgow, Scotland. Since its establishment in the nineteenth century, it has fermented a reputation for chronic unemployment, slum housing and infamous razor gangs. Despite this and all its associated hyperbole, the Gorbals continues to reinvent, surprise and challenge interpretation. Whilst this book does not focus on the Gorbals specifically, its presence as the 'context' deserves special mention as it is key in appreciating and recognising some of the more idiosyncratic elements in *Arcade Artists and Place-making*. For the first time in the history of the Gorbals over 20 artists were commissioned by an artist-led initiative called The Artworks Programme to respond to the transitional stage of a wholesale urban redevelopment following the demolition of Sir Basil Spence's infamous, monolithic tower blocks of the 1960s. Now, at the tail end of this specific redevelopment, *Arcade* aims not only to survey and critically assess some of these projects, but to also raise wider questions about the role and impact artists have in the regeneration of urban spaces.

Arcade takes as its primary impetus the diversity of ideological approaches when interpreting notions of 'place'. To philosophers such as Walter Benjamin, Henri Lefebvre, or counter-culture visionaries such as Guy Debord, Archigram, and authors Thomas More or JG Ballard, the pursuit of a personal utopia reveals how unique and infinite the imagination can be when ideas of 'place' are meditated upon. Vital components to this enquiry though, are the inherent dichotomies manifested in this case by the idealised and the actual—lived and imagined. It is within this interstice from the 'masterplan' to 'everyday life', that we approach some of the following projects in the *New* Gorbals.

These themes are investigated in Moira Jeffrey's essay "Somewhere Nowhere: Monika Sosnowska's *Gorbals*". A ghost story in essence, Jeffrey weaves a compelling narrative around the subject of absence, finding focus in the ideological and political interplay between the given reality (is the Gorbals now "just a slab of urban real estate"?) and the spectacle of a past. Again we find the context of 'place' provides a significant

metaphor for this, however on this occasion it is not the Gorbals but the artist's home city of Warsaw.

The theme of spectacle is invariably touched on throughout *Arcade*. For example in John Calcutt's essay "Screening Off: Kenny Hunter's *Untitled. Girl With Rucksack*", his theoretical enquiry considers the historical conditions that gave rise to the abandonment of the figurative sculptural tradition in public space. Calcutt skilfully questions how this loss and devaluation impacts on the artist, implying that the salvaging of this medium points to a broader unresolved sense of loss of the 'real'. In response, the tradition of public statuary has been replaced by the kind of "spectacular imagery associated with mass media and the commodity".

In Simon Sadler's conversation with artist Ross Birrell, the recognition of a latent utopianism in regeneration programmes is initiated by Birrell's itinerant project in the Gorbals. Again the discussion focuses on the space between utopia and reality, with the conversation subsequently breaking down the boundaries between art, architecture and literature, and seeing these orthodoxies blur momentarily into one.

Anyone familiar with Gorbals history will be aware of the profound effect Sir Basil Spence had on the consciousness of most Glaswegians. Toby Paterson addresses the multiplicity of facts and myths surrounding the controversial architect in his essay "Basil Spence and the Creation of an After-Image". Paterson's reconnaissance of the infamous Queen Elizabeth Square high-rise development of 1965 not only surveys the cultural climate surrounding the conception and their spectacular demolition in 1993, but also provides an imaginative insight into Spence as an image-maker propelled by a romantic and utopian sensibility.

The high-rise also provides the setting for some of the more lyrical narratives in *Arcade*. Jim Colquhoun's pseudo-diaristic "Gorey-Bells" brings high-rise life into (sometimes uncomfortably) close proximity. Many essays in this book make reference to the literary legacy of the Gorbals and Colquhoun subverts the tradition of mythologising (especially where poverty and violence is involved) with a dark and acerbic humour. Another example of this emotive subject matter is Kirsty Williams' "*Highlights*", which recounts a temporary project centred around a high-rise block awaiting its demolition. A vertical excavation of sorts, Williams reveals a poignant portrayal of a new generation coming to terms with mass urban renewal and is made all the more profound by Scotland's recent Poet Laureate Edwin Morgan who collaborated in this project with his poem "Old Gorbals".

From the literary to the subject of language itself, Jordan Kaplan's "Deus ex Machina" charts the democratisation of the English language in relation to gentrification. Posited in this is the contentious subject of Glaswegian vernacular; Kaplan questions whether this will also be naturally homogenised by global standardisation. This enquiry is highlighted by David Cotterrell's project *The Debating Society* which, with the ingenuity of technology, celebrates the idiosyncrasies of language.

There are also essays by research academics specialising in Cultural and Human Geography. For example, Dr Venda Pollock, currently a research fellow in Urban Cultural Regeneration at the University of Glasgow, successfully tempts us to hang around street corners with the artist Stephen Hurrell; while human geographer Dr Nina Morris invites us to enjoy the fruits of Amanda Currie's *Orchard*, a project which is both literally and metaphorically rooted in the heart of the Gorbals—the former 'Old Burial Ground'. The public artwork most synonymous with this recent regeneration is most probably *The Gatekeeper*, as it was the first (and largest suspended sculpture in the UK) permanent work unveiled in the Gorbals. This work has attracted much attention since its installation in 2002 and in this instance cultural geographer Dr Julia Lossau, from the Humboldt University in Berlin, discusses *The Gatekeeper* in relation to the social function of thresholds and cultural landmarks.

It is possibly because the backdrop of mass demolition and redevelopment engenders a nurturing instinct that the subject matter of nature and its elements are a common motif throughout the projects in the Gorbals. Artist Christina McBride's *Source* is a subtle meditation on the civic fountain as a source for the wonder of water in a public space, and Ellie Herring's concise foray into the social significance of fountains makes their disappearance from our streets even more apparent.

These are just some examples of the essays in *Arcade*. There are others that offer insightful commentaries on specific projects. Caoimhin Mac Giolla Léith's essay "*Home Ornaments*", on Daphne Wright, looks at the imaginative space her project occupies between the tradition of story-telling and the material culture of domestic mementos. In "Boys and Girls Come Out to Play" Ray McKenzie discusses the work of community organisation Gorbals Arts Project (GAP) and reflects on the legacy of 'decisive moment' photography and its impact on collective memory and identity. Kathy Battista's taming of all things wild in "*Cultivated Wilderness*" examines issues of public and private boundaries highlighted by a collaboration project between Sans façon and Matt Baker.

Due to constrictions of space, not all the projects are featured as an essay. However, they are represented in synopses form, perceptively researched and written by Giles Bailey.

Topping and tailing *Arcade* is the Foreword by Piers Gough, the renowned architect who was personally involved in the masterplanning of the area where Spence's Queen Elizabeth Square once stood. From the systematic demolition of the tenements and more recently the high-rises, Gough expresses some of the ideas surrounding his involvement in this present redevelopment. As Lead Artist for The Artworks Programme, Matt Baker has the last word. Since 1999, Baker has been directly involved with the minutiae of the Gorbals regeneration where his enthusiasm for originality, experimentation and encouragement of sometimes little known artists is evident in every project. The Afterword offers his personal perspective but also reflects the wider issues facing artists working in the public realm today. Overall, each essay provides an engaging response to themes revealed by a place in transition. However, it is my hope that the intertextual exchange and diversity of perspectives expressed collectively reveals Arcade's uniqueness. Perhaps the reinvigoration of this discourse may serve to deterritorialise the subject of 'place' once again.

It only remains for me to express my sincerest thanks to each of the artists and writers for their contributions, also Matt Baker and Juliet Sebley, Project Manager of The Artworks Programme, Robert Johnston for designing this book, Duncan McCorquodale and Amy Sackville at Black Dog, Giles Bailey and Eddie Garscadden. •

FROM AN architectural perspective, the regeneration project in the Gorbals is simply a reassertion of the idea of classic tenemental street blocks as a reaction against the soulless inadequacies of the high and mid-rise tower blocks of the 1960s and 70s. At the time of the design competition, it seemed a very necessary move to rediscover a characteristic 'Glasgow street' quality to replace the alienating wasteland of so much semi public space left over between isolated buildings.

Good public art can only really be achieved in a milieu of passion and commitment ..."

In fact, the project is thoroughly postmodern, in so far as it has moved the game on from traditional grid, streets, ground floor flats and back courts with parking, to more imaginative ideas of responsive street layouts, ground and first floor maisonettes and residents' shared back gardens, with parking put back on the street. The overall aim has been to build a district which had an approachable, classless grandeur and that, socially, would bring family life back to the city centre. The incorporation of artworks into the scheme is another enrichment of the norm.

In the built masterplan the normal hierarchy of streets is reversed, so that the everyday residential living streets are wide and grand whilst the main shopping street is narrower and more intense. The extra width of the boulevards also allows space for cars to park, where they belong, in the street, rather than in tarmaced backland areas, so residents are not surrounded by the black stuff. The backland areas here are quiet gardens strictly reserved for the enjoyment of the residents who live around them (and inaccessible to others). Public space and play facilities are provided on a public park centred on a magnificently romantic view of the ruined Greek Thomson Caledonian Road Church.

CZWG also designed the recently completed Paragon building, when we were lucky to be able to work with the artist Daphne Wright; her idea to make household icons in lieu of the more usual public piece of work is typical of her lyrical but subversive approach to the commission. She worked incredibly hard on the project so as to relate it to Gorbals residents' memories—and equally hard to convince our slightly sceptical developer client. All we had to do was simply add to the design of each flat a display shelf in a rather recessive location above the back of each front door.

Alexander 'Greek' Thomson,
Caledonia Road Church,
1856. Photo Phil Sayer, 1999.
Licensor www.scran.ac.uk.

CZWG Architects, Paragon building, Queen Elizabeth Square, Gorbals.

Although I count a very great number of artists amongst my friends, in truth, after nearly 40 years of architectural practice, this is one of our first successful art and architecture projects. They so often flounder for a number of reasons that have made us quite reluctant to propose and put artists to work only to have the project not go ahead. This is not only due to cost-cutting by clients but by planners clawing back cash for other public goodies like bottle banks and play structures; or by the money being swallowed up by a landscape overspend.

The major issue seems to be that good public art can only really be achieved in a milieu of passion and commitment by the commissioning body or agent. A half-hearted obligation often flounders or finds excuses for inaction or cancellation.

In Gorbals, the genius was to make Heisenberg and subsequently The Artworks Programme agents for the whole project. Their passion and commitment infected the whole provision of the public art programme. As artists themselves they were at once supersensitive to the ideas and needs of the selected artists, as well as being enablers who nurtured the interest of the developers in those ideas through to fruition.

Indeed, one of my other forebodings is to expose an artist to the oppressive characteristics of our design and build world. Architecture is conceived in a heavily circumscribed world of planning, regulations, deadlines and commercial imperatives. It is bureaucratic and inimical to chance or change. It is obliged to be optimistic and not critical. Art, however, should be quite different; it should offer another take on our existence. A questioning, critical stance, which should certainly not be overburdened by the nature of procurement processes or artists becoming more like designers. They are at their most valuable

when making poetic propositions that are somehow realisable rather than just practically and spiritually comfortable additions to the building process.

The public artworks in the Gorbals have totally disproved my misgivings and proven thus far to have been a triumphant success. They crosscut the already exciting architecture of the area with emotionally resonant and rewarding ideas and images. I would like to take this opportunity to thank all the artists involved for the wonderful ideas and brilliant execution of their works. •

Daphne Wright, 'An Architect's Plan': one piece from a set of five artworks titled *Home Ornaments*, in collaboration with CZWG Architects and developers The Cruden Group. Courtesy the artist/Frith Street Gallery.

SOMEWHERE NOWHERE

Monika Sosnowska's *Gorbals*

SOMEWHERE

The action, which is about to start, takes place in Poland, which is to say, nowhere.[1]
ALFRED JARRY, *UBU ROI*, 1896

IT IS WINTER in Warsaw: soft sleet and rain. At The Foksal Gallery Foundation the artist Monika Sosnowska is talking to me about her solo show at the gallery and her forthcoming public art project in Glasgow. As we speak the weather is getting colder and the gallery is filling up with a frosty white light. In a couple of days Sosnowska will be leaving again, off to Spain to prepare a new show. I ask her for help with some shopping: she recommends her favourite chocolates in Warsaw. I have a Polish friend back home in Scotland to surprise .... I have kept the fact that I am coming here deliberately secret.

Sosnowska's exhibition *Display* is like a mini-retrospective: a series of models of her artworks from the last four years, each one a rigorous architectural installation designed for a specific place. There is *Corridor*, the shrinking and disorientating passageway made for the exhibition *Clandestine* at the 50th Venice Biennale in 2003; the dull pink maze of her installation at de Appel, Amsterdam in 2004; and the confusing brown labyrinth of her untitled exhibition at the Serpentine Gallery in London the same year. My panic, when I don't recognise all of them, is eased when the artist explains that the exhibition includes both completed and unrealised projects. Each model is pristine and delicate on its white plinth and has miraculously survived beer, small children and a particularly lively dog on the opening night.

The exhibition publication is an artist interview printed back to back with a photograph of a half-demolished building: all shattered plaster, exposed steel beams and fractured institutional walls of curdled buttermilk and pale blue. In one corner there's a poster still hanging on the wall. I can't quite make it out, but it looks like a picture of flowers, which incongruously seem to have grown teeth. This photograph of ruined domesticity is actually the view from the window of Sosnowska's apartment. Warsaw, a city entirely rebuilt after wartime obliteration, is once more in transition.

Looking out on to the city centre, we start talking about buildings and ideas, planning and power. Our talk is circling almost daintily around an inescapable presence outside. Stalin's Palace, now known as The Palace of Culture, is framed in the window directly above us. The socialist realist skyscraper took three years to construct between 1952 and 1955 and was made entirely with Soviet labour and materials: a 42-storey 'gift' from the Soviet leader to Poland. The building sucks up the oxygen around it like a vortex, it blocks out all the light. In its wake is a kind of dead zone, an empty plaza suitable only for parades and displays. These days it presents an unsolved challenge to contemporary planners: a monumental museum piece that is gradually shifting from ominous presence into the realm of historical kitsch. In December, an attempt to tame its dominating profile by appending strings of Christmas lights is a laughable failure. A corny old joke has it that the best view of Warsaw is from the terrace on the 35th floor. It's the only place in the city you can't see the building itself.

"The building occupies a key position described by the artist herself as 'on the border'."

All of this seems important. Not because Monika's Sosnowska's proposed artwork for Glasgow, entitled *Gorbals*, is somehow distinctively Varsovian, but because it touches directly on how one might navigate issues of planning and place, of architectural utopianism and of the layers of history embodied in our built environment, with a degree of imagination, inventiveness and freedom. Sosnowska's sculpture is for another city, another country, another time, but our conversation suggests it was conceived under the shadow of the architectural narrative that The Palace of Culture represents.

Gorbals is the final piece commissioned under The Artworks Programme. The artist's monumental corten steel sculpture will appear to be an integral part of the facade of the building known in development-speak as Phase G of Queen Elizabeth Square. The site is on Ballater Street, Glasgow, and the building has been designed by the architects Cooper Cromar for Bellway Homes.

Sosnowska's work may be read as an abstract metal sculpture, but will also spell out the word "Gorbals" in

[1] This famous stage direction to Jarry's play *Ubu Roi* not only sets its absurd tone, but reflects historical circumstances. Poland, partitioned between Russia, Prussia and the Austrian Empire in 1794, did not re-emerge as a nation state until 1918.

The Palace of Culture, Warsaw, Poland, viewed from the Foksal Gallery Foundation. Courtesy Monika Sosnowska.

Monika Sosnowska,
Preliminary maquette for
the *Gorbals* project, 2006.
Courtesy the artist.

relief against the sky or background artificial light. In an area where the developers and public agencies now use the preferred term "New Gorbals", Sosnowska is deliberately, gently—yet provocatively—dropping the "New". Her sculpture raises the spectre of the past through her appropriation of the history and identity of a name that has profound historical and cultural associations.

The building occupies a key position on the outward edge of the redevelopment area, facing both a public road and existing housing on a site described by the artist herself as "on the border". The commission has been described by the commissioners themselves, in their initial invitation to the artist, as "a signature piece for the Gorbals project". Thus Monika Sosnowska's *Gorbals* might be seen—in terms of both the timeline of the overall project and the work's physical location—as a pivotal piece, perhaps even a culmination of The Artworks Programme.

The problem for this essay is that at the time of going to press, it does not even exist as a fully realised artwork. *Gorbals* can currently be found in a number of forms: a piece of painted cardboard, a few centimetres high, photographed against a blue sky on the concrete balcony of the artist's home in Warsaw, an exchange of email correspondences, including the artist's own written proposal; a schedule to the contract negotiated between commissioner and artist.

In terms of location, *Gorbals* can currently be found in notebooks, files and computer memories in a handful of offices in Glasgow, belonging to the architects, the commissioners, the planning office and, of course, this writer. Perhaps its strongest presence is in the artist's own records and files: in Warsaw and in her laptop wherever she is working.

When you get down to it, though, perhaps, like the unrealised dreams in Sosnowska's exhibition at Foksal, this is not too much of a problem. For *Gorbals* is an ephemeral artwork: a work that, for all its proposed oxidised steel physicality, might be described as a ghost. It is a work that deals with 'spirit'. In terms of its geography it celebrates a place that perhaps no longer exists, in a slab of urban real estate beginning its third cycle in a 200-year-old story of development and demolition. In terms of form, *Gorbals* is a work that hangs between the abstract and the figurative. In the case of its construction Sosnowska has created the idea, the explanatory drawings and that modest little cardboard maquette. The rest will be left to experts: steel fabricators, architects, construction workers.

Perhaps *Gorbals* the artwork, like Alfred Jarry's Poland, is currently 'nowhere'. That is a very particular kind of somewhere, which is no less real for its lack of verifiable existence.

NOWHERE

I started my investigations … I saw the beautiful new houses. I walked around this area and saw that it's kind of boring. I couldn't understand on this first viewing why it was so famous and why it is so particular. And then … slowly, I started to learn.[2]
MONIKA SOSNOWSKA

Monika Sosnowska has reached international prominence early in her career for a series of complex sculptural environments, most usually in a gallery or site-specific exhibition setting. Her materials are usually familiar and readily available, including domestic flooring, MDF and household or industrial paints. Her work often makes reference to particular moments in architecture or interior history but her strategies depend on subverting or transforming these materials into experiences which have an immediate sensory impact on the viewer through strategies such as spatial disorientation, repetition or absurdity. Her characteristic form has been that of the labyrinthine or enclosed installation where the viewer finds themselves within the artwork, walking or crawling until they can go no further, opening successive doors until they reach a surprise dead end, or wrong-footed by meticulous fragmentations of light and space.

Sosnowska was born in Ryki, Poland, in 1972. She had a relatively peripatetic childhood as the daughter of

a pilot who, reflecting the geo-politics of the time, completed his postgraduate training in Moscow. Sosnowska attended a Polish high school specialising in art and design and underwent what was then a classical Polish art education, studying as a painter in Poznan. Between 1999 and 2000 she undertook postgraduate studies at the Rijksakademie in Amsterdam.

In subsequent years, as an emerging artist with a growing reputation founded on exposure on international platforms such as The Venice Biennale, Manifesta 4 and Art Basel, it would have been open to her to make her way in any of the obvious European art capitals. Instead, since 2001, she has made her home base in Warsaw, a city where a small but highly sophisticated contemporary art community faces both economic and cultural pressures during the country's continued political and financial transformation since the 1991 elections first heralded the post communist era.

Sosnowska's work is usually interpreted in two dominant ways: firstly in relation to Eastern Bloc aesthetics, secondly in terms of art historical Modernism including movements such as constructivism, minimalism and abstraction. These frames of reference are highly relevant for her works, but we should be cautious in approaching them as determining factors in her art.

Many of her works do, in fact, allude to Eastern Bloc architecture and social planning. *M10*, for example, refers to the Polish system for the allocation of housing according to defined amounts of space necessary. Historically, a single person might, for example, have been deemed to need ten square metres of space. But, as housing shortages bit deep, and apartments were subdivided, bureaucratic allowances were accordingly reduced. *M10* is a sequence of uniformly carpeted and wallpapered rooms, that according to a numerical formula, grow smaller and smaller as one moves through them. Eventually the viewer opens a door to be confronted with a space so small it would be impossible for an adult to stand in it.

M10 is a work about the failure of utopianism. It takes the bureaucratic aesthetic and amplifies it into sculptural absurdity. But despite its specific origins, the work's language is also highly mobile. Shown at the Glasgow International in 2004, *M10* was sited in a vacant space in the city's Briggait Centre, a former

2
Unless otherwise cited all quotes from Monika Sosnowska are from the artist in conversation with Moira Jeffrey, 18 December 2006, Warsaw.

Victorian Market that will shortly be redeveloped as part of Glasgow Sculpture Studios. The site, in its most recent occupation, had been a now long-abandoned Barcelona theme bar. As the art critic Adrian Searle pointed out, *M10* was "a fake inside a fake".[3]

In the heady days when Glasgow, confronted with long-term issues of post industrial decline, tried to reinvent itself as European City of Culture, Barcelona was developer shorthand for cultural vibrancy. For Catalonia, read an idealised new Caledonia where late licensing hours would not result in street violence but in street poetry, and where in a decade or so all of us Glaswegians would be web-designers wearing titanium-framed spectacles. The radical contrast in architectural aesthetic should not disguise that *M10*'s Glasgow setting was equally utopian.

Despite the clear historical sources in *M10*, Sosnowska's reference to actual architecture and interiors often has no clear narrative purpose. The visual information she provides is simply sufficient to bear some resemblance to real places or objects: a door handle, a skirting board, a shade of brown municipal paint. The intent is not historical recreation or storytelling, but a repeated insistence that the work has some relationship with the factual world, if only for the purpose of subverting or distorting it. "The idea is to question reality", says Sosnowska, "not simply to absorb it."

The artist's choice of materials may have some relationship with the context in which the work is being shown, or may be imported from other places or time periods. Often Sosnowska will work with what she calls non-materials: MDF, for example, which she likes because of its physical and conceptual malleability. Her use of colour, as a former painter, is particularly precise and evocative, but frequently confusing when it comes to descriptive terminology. I can't, for example, find any really accurate words to describe the shade of 'pink' used at de Appel, and press reviews of her Serpentine show described her painted labyrinth using a whole range of colours, from 'bronze' to 'mustard'.

In terms of art history the usual chronologies do not apply to the Eastern European context. In Poland, the tides of both literary and art historical Modernism washed up against the catastrophe of the Second World War and the brick wall of official culture and

socialist realism in the communist era. Under these circumstances Poland's avant-garde took a distinctive route. For Sosnowska, abstraction was a means of escape from her classical figurative education. Her technical skills, evident when it comes to her precise use of geometric forms and the hand-made typography utilised in *Gorbals*, are practical rather than programmatic and were largely acquired as a high school student, where she was trained according to the Russian school of design education.

To characterise her work with those of a number of contemporary artists whose subject is 'failed Modernism' assumes a joint history that doesn't exist. But the fact that Sosnoswska's work emerges from a historical time period, and from a social and educational system that is now deemed to have failed, is absolutely crucial. Her artistic practice, her decision to remain in Warsaw, and her response to the historical circumstances of the Gorbals district of Glasgow is inextricably bound up with this.

In the UK, the artist is probably best known for her solo show at the Serpentine Galley. Her work has been seen in Glasgow on a number of occasions including a solo show at her UK agents, the Modern Institute in 2004 and the work *M10* at the Glasgow International. Her invitation to participate in The Artworks Programme came against this background and in particular the context of the Modern Institute's profile as a phenomenally successful commercial gallery based in the city.

Sosnowska was invited for interview along with a number of other artists. It can be hard, in retrospect, to discern the chemistry of any such interview process, but in this case there was Sosnowska's high international reputation, her existing relationship through friendship and artistic practice with Glasgow and her interest in architecture, planning and bureaucracy. One participant commented on how swiftly, as an outsider, she seemed to grasp the situation she—and the Gorbals maybe—found themselves in. Perhaps sometimes these things are a matter of instinct rather than method.

In preparing her proposal, Sosnowska met with the architects, toured the area, and trawled through a reading list. The Gorbals has a rich representation in literature and drama, as location of or inspiration for plays like C P Taylor's *Bread and Butter*, Ena Lamont

3
Searle, Adrian, "I didn't laugh. I ran", *The Guardian*, 26 April 2005.

Stewart's *Men Should Weep* and Robert McLeish's *Gorbals Story*. There are a number of popular photographic histories of the Gorbals available on the market. The Gorbals is also the setting for a number of important published memoirs most notably those of Ralph Glasser, a Jewish Glaswegian who became an eminent economist and famously set out from the Gorbals on his pushbike to cycle to Oxford University.

Cultural representations of the Gorbals usually focus on either its role as the vibrant heart of Glasgow's working class and immigrant culture and, in particular, its place as the centre of the city's Jewish community in the first half of the twentieth century, or its subsequent tabloid reputation as place of unrelieved poverty and razor gangs.

The power of the Gorbals' name as linguistic shorthand for the latter is evident in the continual linking of the Gorbals with prominent public figures.

The eminent QC Helena Kennedy, who practises at the English Bar, for example, is always linked with the Gorbals, although she came from another working class neighbourhood nearby. When Michael Martin, a Roman Catholic Labour Member of Parliament whose constituency is in Springburn, an area of North Glasgow, some miles away, became the first working class speaker of the House of Commons, the right wing press in the UK began referring to him as Gorbals Mick: a nickname with no historical accuracy but a clearly understood attack on his elocution and humble origins.

A key moment for Sosnowska was meeting the local community and in her dawning understanding that the New Gorbals was only the most recent chapter in a sequence of utopian planning developments from nineteenth century tenement building to the social housing of 1960s tower blocks. Each of these building programmes had been understood by subsequent

Monika Sosnowska, No title, The Serpentine Gallery, 2004. MDF painted with high glossy enamel paint (DULUX S4050–Y20R). Courtesy Foksal Gallery Foundation/ kurimanzutto gallery.

Monika Sosnowska, *Rubin*,
Cieszyn, Poland, 2004.
Emulsion paint on wall.
Courtesy Foksal Gallery
Foundation.

4
Gilbert, Geoff, "Property: the
Pre-occupation of Modernism",
Before Modernism Was,
London: Palgrave Macmillan,
2004, p. 2

generations of planners and policy-makers to have failed when living conditions and the material fabric of dwellings deteriorated. Each was lamented by their inhabitants. Both 'slum clearance' and tower block demolition had resulted in relocation, and it was the fracturing of perceived community ties and social and cultural identity, rather than living conditions, that was regretted by those affected.

"I am only observing the situation", says Sosnowska. "I am not familiar with it. Whatever I learn about this area I can't know everything. I come from another country. I wanted to do something that was abstract in a way, but on the other hand, would also express my opinion on what is happening. I wanted to express the kind of spirit of the thing that happened. The

sculpture is a kind of monument for something that doesn't exist."

SOMEWHERE ELSE

In the case of houses, ghosts may make property more interesting and singular, attaching forgotten histories to the functional structure of the building, but they also disturb its market value.[4]
GEOFF GILBERT

In Warsaw, I ask Sosnowska where I should visit to get to grips with her work. She suggests I visit the Museum of Technology, which by no coincidence is housed in The Palace of Culture. It is a faded hymn to the future. An older man is talking to a clutch of acne-marked adolescents, explaining, I think, the process of iron smelting. A group of primary school children listen to a lecture on forestry.

I visit a room dedicated to astronomy, with a tiny planetarium. There are exhibits dedicated to Copernicus (a Pole), and to the Soyuz and Apollo spacecraft: these twin emblems of East and West are painted in a mural head to head. There is a life size model of Sputnik, a forlorn little thing with a serious dent in its side. My favourite room is dedicated to information technology. Banks of pioneering Polish computers give way to early Apple Macs. The room has a frieze around the walls: an image of a flint hammer whose handle transmutes into a ribbon of punched computer tape. The tape was once an emblem of progress, now it is just another quaint and dusty old technology.

In 2004, Sosnowska completed her own hymn to technological obsolescence: *Rubin*, a gable-end mural for the town of Cieszyn in Silesia. *Rubin* is, in many ways, the direct ancestor of *Gorbals*, a public artwork that is familiar but out of place both aesthetically and chronologically. The mural depicts a highly stylised image of a now outmoded Rubin television set, once made in the Soviet Union and the holy grail of modernity in communist Poland.

This is a found image. The artist sourced it in an advertisement for a Warsaw TV repair shop. The somewhat ham-fisted advert would have been hand-made in the early 1980s—when such commercial advertising was in its infancy—by cutting and pasting materials from other sources. Thus, in common with many of Sosnowska's works, it involves a process of distancing from source material, a process of extraction and abstraction from the familiar physical world.

Rubin emerged from a period when, on her return to Warsaw, the artist began to observe, collect and analyse the visual culture around her. "We all get used to many things", she says. "We accept them as normality. Because of my personal circumstances, I came back to Warsaw and saw them from a distance. I felt that I was coming from another planet. I tried to put myself in the position of being a stranger and look at everything as a stranger."

As a painting, *Rubin* bore no trace of the artist's hand and as an advert it bore no text or trace of what it might be selling. *Rubin* was instead a provocation to the emerging consumer culture. "I wanted to create an advertisement which wouldn't advertise anything but itself", says Sosnowska, "an advertisement for a product that doesn't exist anymore."

At a time when the local authorities in Cieszyn wanted to portray themselves as 'progressive', there were two options for visual culture: embracing new globalised imagery or returning to Polish folk art roots. Timed to coincide with a film festival, *Rubin* instead recalled a taboo period of communist culture and drew uncomfortable parallels between current Polish 'modernity' and the faith in the technological future that characterises the display in the Museum of Technology.

Like *Gorbals*, *Rubin* is essentially speculative, reliant on the experience and memory of its viewers. Like *Gorbals* its main call is for a renegotiation with the recent past. Like *Gorbals*, it relies on inserting an uncomfortable interruption into the apparently seamless facade of progress.

Sosnowska has used this tactic before in a much earlier work, *Women with Hens*, 2001, at Galeria Bielska BWA, in Bielsko-Biala, Poland. In this case she painted a large mural on the exterior glass and brickwork of the gallery facade, a traditional folk image which she had found in a book. *Women with Hens* was a response to the marginal position of contemporary art in Poland, a situation in which folk art has been seen as "representative" and has indeed represented Polish art activity in a number of international settings. Despite its historical "accuracy," *Women with Hens* decontextualised folk art to the dissatisfaction of both the traditionalist and contemporary art constituencies. "Everything was correct", says Sosnowska, "except the place and time and that's why this work was so controversial."

In the series of public works in which we might place *Gorbals*, Sosnowska's reference to the past is disruptive rather than nostalgic. Her historical ghosts are unwelcome visitors.

SOMETHING ELSE
Maybe it is not necessary to start the discussion of what is art, what is not, because we could not end this subject ....
MONIKA SOSNOWSKA, EMAIL TO COOPER CROMAR ARCHITECTS

So far the passage of Sosnowska's *Gorbals* commission has been remarkably smooth. In June 2005 the planners at Glasgow City Council wobbled a little, when one of their number suggested that the work was not in fact a monument but signage, and thus should be considered under a different aspect of the planning regime. There was some loose philosophical discussion about the nature of text in contemporary art, but eventually the proposal was accepted unhindered.

In fact, the doubt about what *Gorbals* might actually be goes to the heart of its fascination. In an email exchange with the artist, Matt Baker, then Lead Artist on the commissioning body, commented on the proposal: "I looked at the work initially as a piece of abstract sculpture and enjoyed it for what I read as Celtic/nautical references. Only on reading your explanation did I find the letters and thereafter it has been impossible for my eyes to see the abstraction again as I can now only see letters."

There have been, to date, a few practical changes. An illusionistic metal shadow beneath the 'letters' of the sculpture has been removed because of the likelihood of wind hazard, but essentially her conceit remains the same. It's a key aspect of the work that its monumentality is offset by its ephemerality, that the complex history it evokes appears as a visual joke.

It is a consistent aspect of Sosnowska's practice that her work only goes so far. In comparison with the elaborate work of installation artists like Mike Nelson or Gregor Schneider, her labyrinthine constructions take only a few steps towards confusing or 'irritating' their audience. Her sculpture is a game, a question of providing 'just enough', to transport her audience towards her conceptual intentions and no more. In *Gorbals*, for example, the broader impact of the artwork relies on the bundle of associations that residents and passers-by will attach to the name. Sosnowska is adamant that viewing her art is dependent on the imagination of the viewer as much as it is the sleight of hand of the artist.

In some senses, this would appear to be a considered rejection of the spectacular nature of both contemporary art and consumerism. But it also relates to her insistent engagement with the physical reality of a past in which spectacle was either unavailable or inextricably bound up with the public exercise of political power.

Sosnowska's emphasis on minimal means, her visual economy and her 'clean-edged' aesthetic also have other historical associations. In the summer of 2005, after she made her initial proposal for *Gorbals*, Sosnowska went on a short trip to the country of Belarus. 'White Russia', Polish territory between 1918 and 1939 and once the fount of much of Poland's cultural identity and a breeding ground for its military generals, is now an uncomfortable neighbour on the Polish borderlands: a firmly pro-Russian state, angered by the Polish government's recent public stance on the Ukrainian 'Orange Revolution'.

In Belarus, Sosnowska found indications of economic deprivation, but also great visual stimulation: hand-painted typography of the kind she had experienced when she was younger, an oddly pristine pre-consumerist streetscape and an excellence of design that wasn't diminished by poverty of materials. It was a reminder of her visual origins in communist era Poland.

At Fort Brest, where her own grandfather had once served as part of the garrison, she visited the complex now known as the Brest Hero Fortress. Unveiled in 1971, the complex was designed by Soviet and Belarusian architects and designers and includes a monumental memorial to the Red Army, a public 'Square of Ceremonies' and an 'Eternal Flame' accompanied by piped music.

The gate to the complex takes the form of a giant star shaped entrance, a negative shape, like the lettering reading Gorbals in her own sculpture. In the absence of the finished artwork, this image forms a coincidental visual unlocking of her proposal.

"It was not my inspiration," says Sosnowska,

I found it later, by accident, but it somehow refers to my work. It is maybe very handy for understanding the sculpture. When I look at this, I ignore the context. I am looking at the power, the means of expressing. This is what I wanted to achieve in the Gorbals, something monumental that would use similar language, but for another reason.

SOMEWHERE

The tower blocks built in the Gorbals in the 1960s were part of a great social experiment that swept across the UK, linked with post war readjustment, faith in the future and a programme intended to literally 'lift' communities out of poverty.

In Poland, similarly, building programmes of the early communist era were ideologically driven by ideas of collective living, but in the differing light of utter catastrophe. Nazi Germany invaded Poland in 1939. By the end of the war 1945 around a quarter of the country's population had died. Poland's Jewish community had been wiped out entirely, by conditions in the Warsaw Ghetto, by transportation to the death camps and by Nazi military action in the Ghetto Uprising in April 1943.

In Autumn 1944, in response to the Warsaw Uprising, Hitler ordered that the city be wiped off the map. Nazi demolition squads razed central Warsaw to the ground and more than 225,000 civilians died.

In the post war era, rebuilding soon became stymied by economic difficulties. "Architects and politicians wanted to create their own unique ideas for the shape of the city", says Sosnowska, "but very shortly, in the 60s, the basic economy started to collapse and these ideas couldn't be created in their ideal form. These realisations became more and more ridiculous." It is in this historical experience that you find the roots of the artist's interest in the absurd.

In the wake of such failures post communist redevelopment has been sporadic and largely unplanned. The city of Warsaw is only now beginning to re-address the question of coherent city planning. The historic buildings of central Warsaw these days are all post war reconstructions, its crumbling tower blocks and monolithic suburbs are in some sense its true heritage sights. In Glasgow some tower blocks remain, but the redevelopment of a site like Queen Elizabeth Square is a sure sign that architects, planners and social policy makers have deemed post war development a failure.

The idealism of Glasgow City Councillors like David Gibson, one of the great proponents of slum clearance, forms the factual backdrop for a recent work of fiction, Andrew O'Hagan's novel *Our Fathers*, published in 1999. In a newspaper article written on the eve of the publication of his novel, O'Hagan wrote of those who grew up in the tower blocks, "they grew up in the air, away from things, growing apart from

ABOVE AND OPPOSITE:
Entrance to Memorial at Brest,
Belarus. Research trip, 2005.
Courtesy Monika Sosnowska.

5
O'Hagan, Andrew, "Higher
Hopes", *The Guardian*,
13 March 1999.

memories of the war …. The generation who lived
at the centre of it have grown up different. In some
measure they have grown up remote. They lived in a
place that didn't work out." [5]

Sosnowska's *Gorbals*, obliquely, and with wit rather
than gravitas, draws attention to the generations
of distinctive experience that the New Gorbals is
built upon. In doing so she necessarily raises the
uncomfortable question of whether this current phase
of building is yet another utopian scheme doomed to
fail. For all its monumentality, there is an underlying
natural metaphor to her artwork. Her sculpture is
likened to a weed, a tuft of grass; something left over
from a previous time and place and pushed upwards
with the new building.

At Foksal it looks as though it might start snowing. I
have to go and buy the chocolates before I leave for
Glasgow. Monika Sosnowska has things to do. I ask her
how it feels to position herself as an artist in a period
when the city around her is changing so rapidly, when
the values she was brought up with have eroded or
disappeared. "I feel lucky that somehow, as an artist, I
cannot serve the process", she says;

Many people are in a very difficult situation, especially
for people of my generation who grew up in one
system and must now live in another. We were trained
as something else; we knew the history of something
else, a world which didn't exist. I think for our
generation it's very important to stand back. It is a very
rich subject. •

In 1975, Raivo Puusemp ran for mayor of Rosendale, New York, a small town of 1,500 people. His campaign for election rested on offering realisable solutions to problems, which had badly effected and demoralised the community. Because of this, he was successfully elected to office. During the next two years, he governed the town taking it from extreme financial troubles to positive wealth. He co-ordinated the repair and maintenance of long term water supply and sewage problems. He was personally responsible for developing highly participatory community groups to address problematic social and local community issues. At the height of his success and increasing popularity, he resigned from post for reasons due to family health. His resignation was received sadly in the town, and he left the post with praise and genuine thanks from the local community.[1]

AT NO STAGE in the two years that Puusemp held office did anybody know that this was a work of 'fine art'. He stood down only when his task was accomplished; the artwork was complete. Puusemp later maintained that it had been essential to remain covert, so as not to hinder the success of the project with public awareness, scepticism or even justified anger at his actions. With no intention of publishing details of the experience, preferring to keep the whole event secret, Puusemp was only persuaded to reveal the artwork (and agreed to its publication) several years later in the belief that other artists might benefit from it. Whilst purists would critique Puusemp's temerity in calling his work 'fine art', on the grounds that it lacked an aesthetic object traditionally recognised as 'art', what was evident was its power to effect real positive change politically, socially, and communally.[2]

There is much dissimilarity between Amanda Currie's recent work in the Gorbals and the activities of Raivo Puusemp in Rosendale, not least the fact that the work of the former has been widely publicised, the scale of the work is far smaller, and she has continued to work on other projects since the project's inception four years ago. Yet, it is clear to see why Currie cites this example as a key influence in her work. The Gorbals *Orchard* does not immediately appear to be an 'artwork' in any conventional sense; incorporating 75 native fruit trees, it is a 'living thing' which will grow, die back and regenerate itself with the passing seasons, a poetic metaphor indeed, for the actions, events and operations of everyday life

in the Gorbals. Currie has intentionally tried to blur the boundaries between the suppositions of 'art' and lived experience, weaving into the very fabric of the neighbourhood, its people, its place, its purpose; merging into this fabric and its surroundings, this artwork does not exist by itself.[3]

"Beneath the surface of the regenerative activity there lay a deeply established network of neighbourhood life."

Like Rosendale, the Gorbals was an area trapped in a degenerative cycle of decline and despite many regenerative activities over the years, for the residents, promised improvements in quality of life have often been short-lived or have not materialised at all. For Currie, this situation resonated strongly with that of ancient Rome and the ways in which successive 'authorities' (the emperors) had managed to violate parts of the city through fickle development programmes.[4] Centrally located and dating back to the eighteenth century, the Old Burial Ground on Old Rutherglen Road was one of the few spaces in the Gorbals to have 'survived' the dramatic changes the area had experienced over the last 200 years. Although it had been cleared of burials and landscaped in the 1960s, the site had retained a presence of the past through the many headstones that remained around the boundary wall. In recent years, however, it had begun to lose its purpose and was viewed by many as nothing more than a sterile patch of grassland, stripped of its character and favoured by drug users. The cultivation of an orchard was an opportunity to revitalise this important local landmark with a thoughtfulness and significance that it had previously been denied. Social history has played a large role in shaping the community of the Gorbals and locating *The Orchard* on the site of the former burial ground would ensure that it would be both literally and metaphorically 'rooted' in the past.

An important element to this project was also the appeal of infiltrating, and perhaps subverting, institutional authority along the way (something of a recurring theme in Currie's work).[5] That the Burial Ground was owned by Glasgow City Council was not a deterrent; on the contrary, it was a pull. Currie notes

1
Kaprow, Allan, "The Real Experiment (1983)", in *Essays on The Blurring of Art and Life*, Jeff Kelly ed., Berkeley, CA: University of California Press, 1996, pp. 201–218, p. 201.

2
Webster, Andy and Jon Bird, "Celebrating the Streets", http://www.andywebster.info/texts/atruestoryramble.doc.

3
Webster and Bird, "Celebrating the Streets".

4
Sennett, Richard, *Flesh and Stone*, London: Penguin Books, 2003.

5
Recent examples include video works *HMS Victorious* and *Base Station, Arada*, and *GIEM (Good Intent Emergency Morse—A Code of Signals Manual)*.

Before *The Orchard*, 2004.
Photo: Anthony O'Doibhailein.

A plan of the Fruit trees planted in the old burial ground, Gorbals 2004

Old Rutherglen Rd

Cooking Apple ~ CA
Eating Apple ~ EA
Damson ~ D
Quince ~ Q

By each tree are 4-6 fruit bushes....& 2-4 wild plants

1.	GRENADIER	CA
2.	SHROPSHIRE PRUNE	D
3.	SHROPSHIRE PRUNE	D
4.	GALLOWAY PIPPIN	CA
5.	FARLEIGH	D
6.	MAGGIE SINCLAIR	CA
7.	CAMBUSNETHAN PIPPIN	EA
8.	MEECHES PROLIFIC	D
9.	SCOTCH DUMPLING	CA
10.	FARLEIGH	D
11.	SCOTCH BRIDGET	CA
12.	HAWTHORNDEN	CA
13.	4 BUSHES	
14.	STIRLING CASTLE	CA
15.	LONGSTART	CA
16.	JAMES GRIEVE	EA
17.	SHROPSHIRE PRUNE	D
18.	MERRY WEATHER	D
19.	SHROPSHIRE PRUNE	D
20.	THORLE PIPPIN	EA
21.	FARLEIGH	D
22.	VERANIA	Q
23.	KESTON PIPPIN	D
24.	SHROPSHIRE PRUNE	D
25.	FARLEIGH	D
26.	BEAUTY OF MORAY	D
27.	BEAUTY OF MORAY	D
28.	LAXTONS FORTUNE	EA
29.	MERRY WEATHER	D
30.	SHROPSHIRE PRUNE	D
31.	LORD DERBY	CA
32.	GALLOWAY PIPPIN	CA
33.	EAST LOTHIAN PIPPIN	CA
34.	SHROPSHIRE PRUNE	D
35.	GRENADIER	CA
36.	3 BUSHES	
37.	MANKS CODLIN	CA
38.	MERRY WEATHER	D
39.	EAST LOTHIAN PIPPIN	CA
40.	FARLEIGH	D
41.	MAGGIE SINCLAIR	CA
42.	BEAUTY OF BATH	EA
43.	STOBO CASTLE	D
44.	MERRY WEATHER	D
45.	LADY SUDLEY	EA
46.	SHROPSHIRE PRUNE	D
47.	MERRY WEATHER	D
48.	KESWICK CODLIN	EA
49.	EMNETH EARLY	CA
50.	WHITE MELROSE	CA
51.	3 BUSHES	
52.	MEECHES PROLIFIC	Q
53.	MERRY WEATHER	D
54.	SHROPSHIRE PRUNE	D
55.	MEECHES PROLIFIC	D
56.	STIRLING CASTLE	CA
57.	ADAMS PEARMAIN	CA
58.	ELLISONS ORANGE	EA
59.	TAM MONTGOMERY	EA
60.	FARLEIGH	D
61.	ARTHUR TURNER	CA
62.	HAWTHORNDEN	CA
63.	SHROPSHIRE PRUNE	D
64.	BEAUTY OF MORAY	D
65.	STOBO CASTLE	D
66.	MANKS CODLIN	CA
67.	MERRY WEATHER	D
68.	MERRY WEATHER	D
69.	HOWGATE WONDER	CA
70.	CAMBUSNETHAN PIPPIN	CA
71.	SCOTCH BRIDGET	CA
72.	WHITE MELROSE	CA
73.	LONGSTART	CA
74.	KESWICK CODLIN	EA
75.	SHROPSHIRE PRUNE	D
76.	MANKS CODLIN	CA

Gooseberries ~ 10 Invicta, 5 Whinhams Industry, 5 Leveller, 5 Careless, 5 Greenfinch, 5 London, 5 Warrington, 5 Freedom, 5 Blotcher, 5 White Lion, 5 May Duke, 5 Langley Gage, 5 Ashton Red, 5 Gunner
Raspberries ~ 10 Glen Moy, 10 Glen Lyon, 10 Glen Prosen, 10 Glen Magna, 10 Glen Ample
Blackcurrants ~ 10 Ben Nevis, 10 Ben Gairn, 10 Ben Hope, 10 Ben Tiran, 10 Ben Sarek

Blackberries ~ 5 Ashton Cross, 3 Tummelberry, 3 Silvanberry, 5 Bedford Giant, 4 Himalayan Giant. Redcurrants ~ 16 Laxton No1, 24 Jk Van Tet, 25 Red Lake, 10 Redstart. Whitecurrants ~ 20 White Grape, 55 White Versailles

Wild Plants ~ Red Campion, Tufted vetch, Common valerian, Cat mint, Sage, Lavender, Ox eye daisy, Field Scabious, Lemon balm, Common thyme, Chicory, Bugle, Yarrow, Bizort, Travellers Joy, Meadow cranesbill, Knapweed, Chives, Ragged Robin.

A Currie

ABOVE AND OPPOSITE:
Amanda Currie, *The Orchard*, working plan, 2003. Courtesy the artist.

6
Kaprow, "The Real Experiment (1983)"; Carey, Phil and Sue Sutton, "Community Development through Participatory Arts: Lessons Learned from a Community Arts and Regeneration Project in South Liverpool", *Community Development Journal*, vol. 2, no. 39, 2004, pp.123–134.

that she was particularly interested in Glasgow as a 'council-run' city and, in particular, its self-defined image as the 'people's city'. Keen to infiltrate into the realm of municipal planning, she saw the opportunity to influence the planning and development of a public resource with the aim of producing something not only of social interest but actually useful to the people who lived and worked in the area. Although Currie would be the first to note the obvious differences, she saw *The Orchard* as a chance to play with authority in a way in which was not dissimilar to the actions of Puusemp.

The success in Rosendale was due, in large part, to Puusemp's knowledge of group dynamics and predictive behaviour, but one of the most important things he did was to get the residents involved as partners in the planning process.[6] Although sceptical at first, it soon became clear that by joining together to solve the village's problems the residents had spent more time together and assumed a more conscious responsibility for their 'community'. Currie is hesitant to use the word 'community' in connection with her work as (whilst appreciating the irony) she feels that the term can be exclusive: "there are always people on the outside". Yet, resident participation has been integral throughout the project and will be a crucial factor in its future success. By August 2004 *The Orchard* was 'complete' and although Currie has continued to play an active role in the project, co-ordinating a number of informal gardening sessions since the final planting, like Puusemp she will eventually pull back completely. Responsibility for *The Orchard* was handed over to

oster and Bird, "Celebrating
Streets".

ane, Kevin, "Urban
hards", *Reforesting
tland*, no. 18, 1998.

er, Irene, "Glasgow's Public
ks and Community 1950–
", *Urban History*, vol. 3,
25, 1998, pp. 323–347.

er, "Glasgow's Public Parks
Community 1950–1914",
28.

Glasgow City Council in October 2004 and its success will be determined in large part by the efforts of Council employees to maintain and improve channels of communication amongst those responsible for the area's preservation. In keeping with the ethos of the project, however, the Council has recognised the involvement of, and the importance of working in partnership with, local residents. For this relationship to be successful, stakeholders have agreed that a formal interest group must be established with whom the Council and, in particular, the Parks Development Officer, can communicate. Currie admits that this has perhaps been the "trickiest" part of the project to organise, as future commitment will only depend on one thing, namely the sustained involvement of key individuals over time and a genuine interest in the orchard as it develops.

Whilst the connections between Currie's work and that of Puusemp are important, it would be wrong to assume that *The Orchard* was inspired entirely by this one artistic experiment. In actual fact Currie's work falls at the crux of a series of debates relating to the role of the arts in community regeneration, the nature of contemporary art and the presence of nature in the urban environment. These themes all inter-connect in some way; however, for clarity I will consider each of them separately in the remainder of this essay.

THE ROLE OF THE ARTS IN COMMUNITY REGENERATION

When considering an artwork such as *The Orchard* it is crucial to address the following questions: "what does art in this context actually achieve?" and "who does it propose to communicate with, how, and why?" [7] Although an orchard in the Gorbals might seem odd to the contemporary observer, the concept of urban orchards is not new and it is not so long ago that there were many in and around Glasgow. [8] The majority of these orchards, however, were private or commercial, established by the tobacco lords to disguise the smell of the city and to act as living status symbols—the more exotic the fruit or flower, the more cultured and well-travelled the individual. In this sense, Currie's orchard perhaps has more common ground with the Glasgow Green, part of the city's "Common Good", gifted to the city in the fifteenth century and officially made into a Park in 1957. Responsibility for the Green lay with the City Council; however, following the flight of the wealthier classes to the West End, by the mid-nineteenth century it had acquired an "ambiguous reputation". [9] In addition to its proximity to, and use by, the dubious denizens of the slums, the factories and workshops in the industrial East End "meant that its potency as a reservoir of fresh air was seriously dissipated". [10] Yet the Green had an enduring popularity amongst the masses and when it was threatened (by coal extraction) the people protested

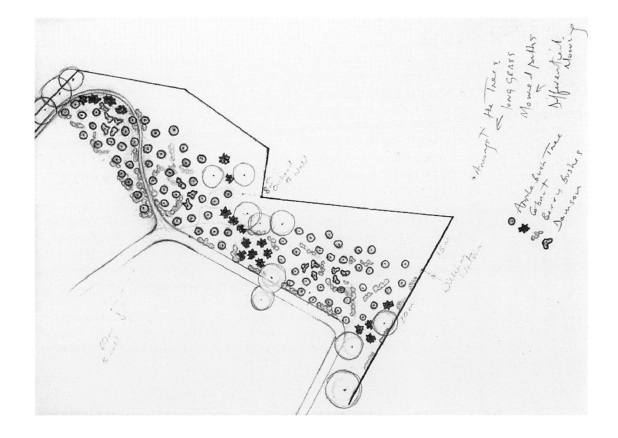

Correspondence/idea in development, 2002–2004. Courtesy Amanda Currie.

23rd Septemi

14th March 2002
Jim Byrne
Hutchesontown Community Council
Glasgow

Dear Jim,

Enclosed is a proposal fo
Local involvement is crucial to the
heart of my proposal. The Comm
know the committee's opinion of
stage), how do they think we ca
care? And finally, what is their v

At this stage, how this
with an organisation called Gr
Council they specialise in enc
my proposal. I would like them

There are plans a f
development. Crown St Reg
be approaching the Glasgo
difficult, I personally canno
document I have sent you
Therefore, I would appre
committee members and

My intention with
than just a park. It will be
it will be the start of a ne

I look forward to your re

ng the meeting o
an orchard in the
e main questions r
ths I will try to ga
ing the primary sc
d care organisatio
other people who
ntinue with the des
ct and Glasgow Cit
rom the meeting
very generously o
every hour giver
how Time Bank op
rt for the Orchard.
ow will be for me t
ments for the Orcha

ng to the meeting,

Councillor James Mutter
Glasgow City Council
City Chambers
Glasgow, G2 1DU

Dear Councillor,
On the '
Garden was discussed at t
spoken with Jim Bryne and
Committee backs the proje
the matter of there poss
you mentioning this to m
hopefully we will be ab!

At the moment Cro
Fiona Plumtree of the L
take on the project. Al
negotiations, I am in
crucial local involvem
already doing a relate
are keen on the idea
The idea has material
into the history, the
spent several months
people like and feel
was popular, sociall
the infrastructure.
heritage of the loc
functional Orchard

I would like
your support to Tol
produce a place th
simply an attracti
that within whate'
I am writin
next Wednesday ar
you could let me

Thankyou for you
Regards

Amanda Currie

Orchard in th
next meeting - Tulip Inn coffee

16.01.04

Dear All, ... Happy New Year !

We are
mid Feb. to mid March. I would like to hold a
everyone about the planting and find out who wa
the future role of this interest group. As you know
maintenance of the orchard. However, to establish
upkeep of the orchard, we need to set up a fo
council.

I have had meetings with the city council and they a
being involved in the upkeep of the orchard. The p
would like to attend a meeting after the planting to di
the group could do to compliment their maintenance
Norman Fitzjpatrick from New Gorbals Housing Asso
of their offices as a possible meeting point and photo

The meeting on the 7th February is important as we v
nominate a group representative and a correspondenc
the planting please attend the meeting or let me know.

I look forward to seeing you,

Regards,

and won. Whether the Green will remain a truly people's place (as it's now subject to a "beautifying" programme with the landmark Doulton Fountain) is a question that is yet to be settled; however, my emphasis here is on its role as a public space in which local people invested time and energy. *The Orchard* is designed to be similarly 'public'; although it will reestablish a way from 'a bygone era' it will do so with a renewed outlook and purpose.

Arts and cultural activities have a growing profile in community development and urban regeneration; however, there is a danger that new initiatives meet with cynicism from the people whom they are directed at.[11] Such projects are often accused of being elitist and failing to reflect the reality of residents' lives or aspirations. As a consequence there is increasing interest in, and demand for, participatory arts programmes that are flexible and responsive to local needs.[12] Rather than simply delivering a finished product, participatory arts engage the community and can encourage personal development as well as social cohesion by providing a means for people to express their relationship with their social and physical environment. Above all, Currie intended to instil a local sense of ownership of,

and involvement in, what could otherwise have been a meaningless piece of planning.

In order to generate ideas that were both popular and socially relevant, during the summer of 2001 Currie spent several months getting a sense of the area. She met local people, talked to them about their everyday lives, observed current local situations, read the local newspapers, and even stayed for a while in a caravan in the grounds of a local primary school. The area looked very different during this period; the high-rise flats were still being demolished and many of the new developments were yet to be built. Currie recalls that at first, it seemed as though the only activity in the area was along the brand new shopping street, but it soon became clear as she moved around the neighbourhood and became less of an 'outsider', that beneath the surface of the regenerative activity there lay a deeply established network of neighbourhood life. Working with the idea of initiating a new annual event in the Gorbals that would look to the future but was also rooted firmly in the past, Currie undertook research on the development of 'traditions'. In the process she realised that nearly all customs stem from one of a few sources—a political event, religion, a local phenomenon or a natural resource.

11
Carey and Sutton, "Community Development through Participatory Arts".

12
Carey and Sutton, "Community Development through Participatory Arts".

rdsley, John, "Beyond
thworks: the New Urban
dscape", *Earthworks*
Beyond (Third Edition),
v York: Abbeville Press,
127–158.

rdsley, "Beyond
thworks", p.127.

rdsley, "Beyond
thworks", p.127.

rdsley, "Beyond
thworks", p.129.

Aware that politics and religion were likely to spark divisions in the Gorbals rather than create something that was accessible to everyone, Currie was drawn to nature. During her stay in the Gorbals, she recalls that she had noticed a relative absence of wildlife in the area and imagined the sudden appearance of unusual migrating birds on the rooftops of Cumberland Street; a phenomenon which would undoubtedly have ignited local curiosity. Thinking about the ways in which animals of various kinds might be attracted into the area more permanently, she concluded that it would be necessary to first provide food and a habitat. It was when she combined this with the idea of creating a natural resource that people might also be able to use (and the potential gains of readily accessible fruit and wild edible plants in an age of imported fruit and supermarket selection) that she struck on the idea of planting a community orchard.

THE NATURE OF CONTEMPORARY ART

Beardsley notes that as environmental art (including sited sculpture) has increasingly become the focus of public commissions, more and more of these have been for inner city locations.[13] This "paradigmatic shift" in both location and intention reflects the changing attitudes of both artists and patrons. Among artists,

… the antagonistic posture that prevailed at the end of the 1960s has given way to a more cooperative stance. Many environmental artists now desire not merely an audience for their work but a *public* with whom they can correspond about the meaning and purpose of their art. […] Moreover they have recovered the idea that art can attempt to determine its own social function and thereby attain a prominent position in public discourse.[14]

Concurrently, "the sponsors of public art projects have increasingly turned to environmental art as a way of resolving the many difficulties caused by installing sculpture in public space".[15] Schemes such as 'per cent for art' fulfil many criteria—they can be educational, provide opportunities for artists, stimulate tourism and economic development, even help to promote civic identification and pride. Yet, if public art programs are to succeed, some effort must be made "to develop a language—either in the art or its explication—that is intelligible to at least some of those unfamiliar with contemporary art".[16]

The involvement of artists in the design of public space has required some modification in their working methods. Many of these projects, like *The Orchard*, are public not only in their setting but also in their execution. Jacob notes that "When art moves

t public meeting with
artist. Courtesy Amanda
rie.

outside studio production and becomes a process of community or institutional negotiation, when it must be responsive to a social dynamic and address the needs of others, when it is collaborative by nature, or when it draws upon the expertise of other fields, it becomes a more open-ended and fluid process." [17] Although collaborative work with communities can be a rewarding and genuine way of developing ideas and often provide a life enhancing experience (both for the artist and for the people involved), it is a process in which the artist must welcome participation and discussion, developing a depth of understanding about the public who will interact with the work. Many artists are unfamiliar with this way of working and it is by no means always easy. Collaboration thrives on a diverse range of perspectives and on constructive dialogues between individuals who negotiate their differences while creating a shared voice and vision.[18] Currie's collaboration with Glasgow City Council has, at times, not been an easy one to manage, requiring perseverance from both sides. Perhaps the most difficult stage in the process was when the proposal was first presented to Glasgow City Council Land Services and Hutchesontown Community Council in 2002. It soon became clear that *The Orchard* was enmeshed in political debates that were to a large extent 'unknown', especially to those who did not have full access to Council affairs. Regulations dictated that the plans could only be presented to the Council by representatives of the Crown Street Regeneration

Project. Prevented from taking part in these 'official' dialogues for herself, Currie was restricted to covertly lobbying and eliciting support from as many people as possible. She was aware, however, that key members of the City Council were uncomfortable with the idea and that they had the power to veto the whole project; the correspondence from this period shows Currie's frustration at being prevented from taking part in these sensitive discussions. The documentation from these exchanges provides a revealing element to this project, where bureaucratic systems constrict development—an anathema to entropic natural growth and indeed *The Orchard*.

Some artists have spurned the opportunity to work in the public sphere because they find it too restrictive. However, in Currie's case, she was eager to develop a new role, moving away from the traditional stereotype of the solitary artist towards an image of the artist as collaborator in civic projects.[19] This methodology rejects the long-established qualities, which emphasise 'separate-ness' and 'special-ness' (in which there can only be a one-way message between the artist and their audience), valuing instead a non-linear process.[20] As a result, the concern with process rather than with product often leads artists practising this approach to relinquish some control over the development of their artwork. Beardsley feels that great advances have been achieved by the involvement of artists in shaping the public landscape:

17
Jacob, Mary Jane, "An Unfashionable Audience", in Lacey, Suzanne ed., *Mapping the Terrain*, Washington: Ba Press, 1995, p. 57; John-Stei Vera, *Creative Collaboratio*, Oxford: Oxford University Press, 2000.

18
John-Steiner, *Creative Collaboration*.

19
Beardsley, "Beyond Earthworks".

20
Kaprow, "The Real Experime (1983)".

Councillor Mutter planting 'the last apple tree' in *The Orchard* 2005. Photo: Anthe O'Doibhailein.

The *Orchard*'s first summer, 2005. Courtesy Amanda Currie.

There is no question that art, as it has become more responsive to its physical setting and its cultural context, has gained an important element of public relevance. There is little doubt [...] that this art has had a beneficial impact on the public space. Environmental art has taken the lead not only in making those spaces more satisfying visually, but also in restoring some element of public meaning to them.[21]

PRESENCE OF NATURE IN THE URBAN ENVIRONMENT

In recent years increasing attention has been focused on green spaces in urban areas and the fact that investment in and appropriate management of, local green space can bring wide-ranging social, economic and health benefits to an area. Having green space 'nearby' (be it a local park, a road-side verge, a flower box perched high on the windowsill of a tower bock, or a view towards distant trees) is highly valued by urban residents regardless of whether they visit it or not.[22] Fruit trees and orchards are an important part of Britain's cultural heritage, with more than 40 known varieties in Scotland alone, and again there is increasing recognition across Britain that urban orchards can play an important part in regeneration,

encompassing a variety of areas such as environmental awareness, education, and health.[23]

Another key influence cited by Currie is environmental philosopher Andrew Light's concept of "faked nature", and what he has referred to as the "urban blind spot" in environmental ethics.[24] According to Light, "much of contemporary environmental ethics distinguishes itself from more traditional ethics by setting for itself the goal of articulation of the value of nature in terms independent of the human attribution of that value".[25] As a result, environmental philosophers (and, in particular, those in the wilderness-abundant areas of North America and Australia) have spent the last three decades pursuing various forms of non-anthropocentrism. What these individuals have in common is "a unified belief that the inspiration for extending moral consideration beyond the boundaries of the human community will come from connection with those spaces unsullied by humans, especially wild areas, or at least vast tracts of otherwise protected land".[26] Accordingly, Light states that the vast majority of environmental philosophers have assumed some kind of opposition between culture and nature, the city and the countryside, urbanity and wilderness.

21
Beardsley, "Beyond Earthworks", p. 156.

22
Bell, Simon, Nina Morris, Catherine Findlay, Penny Travlou, Alicia Montarzino, Georgina Gooch, Gemma Gregory and Catharine Ward-Thompson, *Nature for People: The Importance of Green Spaces to East Midlands Communities*, English Nature Research Report, no. 567, 2004; Price, Richard and Jane Stoneham, *Making Connections: A Guide to Accessible Greenspace*, The Sensory Trust, 2001.

23
O'Kane, Kevin, "Urban Orchards"; Central Core Orchard and Apple Network, http://bcehive·thisisnorthscotland.co.uk/default.asp?WCI=SiteHome&ID=8951&PageID=48869, 8 March 2003, site accessed 21 December 2005.

24
Light, Andrew, "The Urban Blind Spot in Environmental Ethics", *Environmental Politics*, vol. 1, no. 10, 2001, pp. 7–35.

25
Light, Andrew, "Elegy for a Garden", *Terrain.org: A Journal of the Built & Natural Environments*, no. 13, Fall/Winter 2003, 5 pages, p. 2.

26
Light, Andrew, "Elegy for a Garden", p. 2.

27
Light, "The Urban Blind Spot in Environmental Ethics".

28
Light, "Elegy for a Garden", pp. 3 and 5.

29
Light, "Elegy for a Garden", pp. 3 and 5.

30
Light, "Elegy for a Garden", p. 3.

31
Light, "Elegy for a Garden", p. 5.

32
Light, "The Urban Blind Spot in Environmental Ethics".

33
Elliot, Robert, *Faking Nature*, London: Routledge, 1997.

34
Light, Andrew, "'Faking nature' revisited", *The Beauty Around Us: Environmental Aesthetics in the Scenic Landscape and Beyond*, D Michelfelder and B Wilcox eds, Albany, NY: SUNY Press, 2003; Light, Andrew, "Restorative relationships", *Healing Nature, Repairing Relationships: Landscape Architecture and the Restoration of Ecological Spaces*, R France ed., Cambridge, MA: MIT Press, 2004; Light, Andrew, "Restoration of art and restoration of nature".

35
Light, Andrew, "Restoration or domination? A reply to Katz", *Environmental Restoration: Ethics, Theory, and Practice*, William Throop ed., New York: Humanity Books, 2000, pp. 95–111, p. 108.

36
Light, "Restoration or domination? A reply to Katz", p. 108.

37
Light, "The Urban Blind Spot in Environmental Ethics".

This conceptual division between nature and culture as "divided spheres of moral and political concern" has resulted in a tendency to devalue the urban as the "source of all environmental ills covered only by a thin veneer of cultural accomplishment".[27] Either that, or environmental ethicists have tended to be largely silent on the matter of urban environmental issues. Whilst Light appreciates the sentiments of fellow theorists such as Robert Elliot and Holmes Rolston III, and agrees that the preservation of statutorily designated wild areas and the issues involving species preservation and biodiversity loss are important, he feels that there is much more at stake under the umbrella of environmental philosophy than seems to be getting attention and, as far as he is concerned, the reasons for this predicament simply don't ring true.

From a non-anthropocentric perspective it would seem that "only certain kinds of places count as acceptable spaces for forming moral bonds with nature". Whilst Light agrees that if humans are "fortunate enough to survive it will come from recognising our relationship with nature as residents of the natural world", he argues that it is not only in the wilderness that we might regain our connections with nature.[28] In the city "there are environments well worth engagement and deserving of responsibility—not just green 'spaces' such as large parks but also the 'brown space' such as sidewalks, buildings and places in between".[29] Light stresses that the city is "not just the background that urban inhabitants move through, it is the foreground of most everyday conversations".[30] He uses as his example the urban garden Esperanza in New York, and although *The Orchard* is not threatened in the same way, one can see how it might become a similar symbol of urban green space and community empowerment. These small areas of green space have the potential to connect people to their everyday environment in tangible, rather than abstract ways. And it is for this reason that a "fully environmental ethic ought to include all environments, not for theoretical reasons, but because urban spaces […] can and do represent an important connection between humans and the natural world".[31]

One of the aims of an environmental ethic sensitive to urban issues would be the development of a sense of ecological citizenship and, according to Light, the first and most important goal of this should be to stimulate public participation in the maintenance of natural processes.[32] Evidence suggests that individuals involved in restoration projects are more likely to adopt a benign attitude of stewardship and responsibility toward nature as a result of such interactions. This is as much about a restoration of nature as it is about the restoration of the human cultural relationship with it. Whilst not strictly concerned with environmental 'restoration' *per se*, Currie highlights Light's critique of the work of Robert Elliot as particularly interesting.[33] Although I simplify, the premise of Elliot's argument is that restoring nature is akin to faking a work of art; it is fraudulent or deceptive and, while it can have value, it will never have the same value as an original nature that has evolved over time independent of human artifice.[34] Light disagrees with this view, stating: "even if we admit that restored nature is an artefact and not real nature, restored nature can […] act as a conduit for real nature to free itself from the shackles we have previously placed upon it. Restoration can allow nature to engage in its own autonomous restitution".[35]

Light recognises that restoration should perhaps be seen as an "aid to nature" rather than a creation of new nature, and even if restoration is the production of an artefact it still presents an opportunity to interact with flora and fauna and can increase the bonds of care that people feel for non-restored nature.

… restoration of an inner-city lot will give people a better appreciation of the fragility and complexity of the natural processes of nature itself should they encounter them. The fact that restorationists are engaged in a technological process does not necessarily mean that their practices do not serve the broader purpose of restoring a relationship with nature.[36]

Light admits that large restoration projects are difficult to manage in a voluntary capacity and this is why smaller sites, such as *The Orchard*, may be best suited to fulfilling the full normative value of restoration, creating an opportunity for citizens to form relationships with their local environments. For him there will only be a fully environmental ethic, which covers all environments, when we turn our attention to the preservation of richly textured urban spaces as often as we do to wilderness areas.[37]

As noted above, local people (including pupils from nearby primary schools) were encouraged to participate on a practical level throughout the orchard's development (marking out where the trees would be planted, nurturing seedlings, assisting with planting, etc.) and updated plans/work schedules were regularly posted on the park notice board. From the outset Currie was keen for something unusual and undetermined to stem from *The Orchard*—a new species in the area or the development of a fruit picking tradition. Whilst she admits that the former is slightly more difficult to instigate and the trees will take time to mature, the fruit bushes are already producing fruit.

Over 20 years ago, Kaprow argued that Puusemp's intervention wasn't simply a "novel art event"; its genre (the village and its survival problems) was unusual, but so were its frame (the geographical place), its public (the townspeople, mayor, county officials, lawyers, local newspapers and readers) and its purpose (therapeutic). He states:

these four characteristics of lifelike art—the what, where, who, and why—make up what [he calls] the whole situation, or as much of it as can be identified at present. Anyone can see that the four parts merge and that the artist merges with the artwork and those who participate in it. And the 'work'—the 'work' merges with its surroundings and doesn't really exist by itself.[38]

Despite the obvious differences between the two projects, I believe that Kaprow's assertion about what the 'work' is, still today provides a useful starting point when attempting to summarise what Currie has achieved in the Gorbals.

The ultimate form of *The Orchard* will develop naturally and, in a sense, its physical shape and local significance will remain undetermined for a number of years to come. This particular orchard is undoubtedly the sum of its parts; the result of a great many strategic but also creative partnerships. It demonstrates the ways in which residents can be actively enlisted to help shape the development of their immediate area and provides an effective example of how a benevolent culture of respect and stewardship (as emphasised by Light) might be established within inner-city neighbourhoods. As Beardsley states, "Every work that engages the landscape underscores the crucial connection between culture and nature and helps to revitalise—and with any luck improve—that relationship."[39] The artwork's participatory approach also demonstrates how a more collaborative and open

Apple tree in *The Orchard*, 2005. Courtesy Amanda Currie.

artistic process can help to break down or blur the barriers between art and life. *The Orchard* is not an 'art object' with the conventional associations attributed to public art; instead it merges into the fabric of the neighbourhood. It is also not just a patch of green in an urban landscape or a clever bit of utopian art; it will be a place where the generations can remember and learn about environmental traditions, their past, and also their aspirations for the future.[40]

Arts projects are increasingly being implemented as a way a celebrating people's possession of the local environment, increasing interest in, and creating a sense of ownership and pride for particular green space environments. At this stage it is impossible to come to any firm conclusions regarding the influence that Currie's artwork will exert in the Gorbals, although *The Orchard* is already being used to illustrate the significant contribution that quality green space can make to communities across urban Scotland and has been 'case-studied' in the Greenspace publication *Making the Links: Greenspace and the Partnership Agreement*. There is a sense that this is the beginning rather than the end of the project. ●

38
Kaprow, "The Real Experiment (1983)", p. 211.

39
Beardsley, "Beyond Earthworks", p. 201.

40
Light, "Elegy for a Garden".

SCREENING OFF

Kenny Hunter's *Untitled. Girl with Rucksack*

As a practice within the built environment, public art participates in the production of meanings, uses, and forms for the city. In this capacity, it can help secure consent to redevelopment and to the restructuring that constitutes the historical form of advanced capitalist urbanization. But like other institutions that mediate perceptions of the city's economic and political operations—architecture, urban planning, urban design—it can also question and resist those operations, revealing the suppressed contradictions within urban processes.[1]

IN THE following pages I hope to expand upon and add to these issues raised by Rosalyn Deutsche. My ultimate aim will be to suggest ways in which the reader/viewer might understand Kenny Hunter's *Untitled. Girl With Rucksack* as an invitation to engage imaginatively and critically with the challenge they offer to contemporary publicly sited art, especially within the context of a programme of urban regeneration. It is not my intention to offer a detailed interpretation of the work itself, merely to suggest connections and possible patterns of significance within the historical and contemporary pressures that enfold and inform it. Contradiction is at the heart of this exploratory enterprise, and in keeping with the nature of my subject matter and method I leave the final work of interpretation and evaluation to the reader/viewer.

That is not to say that I begin with no agenda, or that my motivations are not tendentious. My principal concern is with those material and social conditions in which the meanings of a publicly sited work might be made and understood today. Inevitably, certain aspects of *Untitled. Girl With Rucksack* strike me with greater force than others. In approaching this work I am, after all, a member of the public, and as such I am interested in trying to understand how the work addresses me, how it 'constructs' me as a member of its public. In that sense I am in agreement with Leo Steinberg when he states:

… my notion of the public is functional. The word 'public' for me does not designate any particular people; it refers to a role played by people, or to a role into which people are thrust or forced by a given experience. And only those who are beyond experience should be exempt from the charge of belonging to the public.[2]

Kenny Hunter, *Untitled.*
Girl With Rucksack, in situ,
Cumberland Street and Jane
Place, Gorbals, 2004. Photo
Alan Dimmick.

This statement appears in Steinberg's 1962 essay "Contemporary Art and the Plight of its Public". More than 40 years have since passed, but many, if not all, of Steinberg's observations still resonate:

"How do I come to terms with my sense that this figure resists my best efforts to fix a meaning upon it?"

I know [he continues] that there are people enough who are genuinely troubled over certain shifts as they occur in art. And this ought to give what I call 'The Plight of the Public' a certain dignity. There is a sense of loss, of sudden exile, of something willfully denied—sometimes a feeling that one's accumulated culture or experience is hopelessly devalued, leaving one exposed to spiritual destitution.[3]

The following material is thus partially directed towards questions of loss, exile, denial and devaluation, but it also hopes to at least imply salvage, if not exactly salvation.

I am interested, for example, in Hunter's seemingly anachronistic reference to a European, pre-modern, classicising tradition of public statuary (key features of the pose of *Untitled. Girl With Rucksack* seems to derive directly from Michelangelo's *David*, for example), whilst simultaneously alluding to the seamless, fluent surfaces of industrially produced, plastic commodities. (This is a central and recurrent feature of Hunter's work throughout the last 15 years or so.) I am also struck by certain ambiguities that pervade the semantic aspects of the work: Is the girl arriving, or is she leaving?[4] Is it possible to determine the meaning of her facial expression? To me she appears 'lost' in thought, mentally 'withdrawn', and otherwise psychologically 'absent' or disengaged from her surroundings. Furthermore, how am I meant to read the work in relation to its various contexts: geographically, in terms of its physical location, and culturally, in terms of its relation to other competing representations? Where should I be looking to find appropriate comparisons and reference points? Other works of art, certainly, but should I also turn to the fields of mass culture, to the world of toys and commodity styling in general, to teenage fashion and

1
Deutsche, Rosalyn, *Evictions. Art and Spatial Politics*, Cambridge, MA: MIT Press, 1996, p. 56.

2
Steinberg, Leo, "Contemporary Art and the Plight of its Public", in Gregory Battcock ed., *The New Art*, New York: Dutton, 1966, pp. 208–9.

3
Steinberg, "Contemporary Art and the Plight of its Public", p. 211.

4
To avoid typographic awkwardness, inverted commas will not be used at every reference to the sculpture as 'her', 'she', 'girl', etc.. It is nonetheless important to maintain a distance between the physical actuality of the sculpture and its supposed referent. This element of self-consciousness about the relation between representation and reality is unavoidable within the circumstances I try to characterise in the essay.

culture, to comic books, to TV and movies (I detect and suspect various such references in the work, but many of these areas lie beyond my own cultural experience and competence)? And how, finally, do I come to terms with my overwhelming sense that this figure resists my best efforts to fix a meaning upon it? It is paradoxical and elusive in that it seems to be a permanent monument to transience, migration and other modes of impermanence. The work incorporates a prominent base but, unlike the function of a base in a traditional sculptural monument, this base does not establish a signifying unity between a specific representation and a specific place. This figure is in this place, certainly, but her presence here seems almost accidental and contingent. There is a strong sense that she has only paused momentarily and that she is, anyway, mentally elsewhere. Aloft on this towering column, I also find that to engage with her—to look at her—I have to direct my eyes and my attention away from the physical circumstances that surround me, the actual location that the work has brought me to, and view her against the virtual placelessness of an open sky. In other words, the work seems to demand of me two irreconcilable modes of attention. One of these modes is diffuse, attuned to the local environmental ambience and 'framed' by the site (here the sculpture appears one 'thing' among others). The other mode demands a focused attentiveness and occurs within an 'open', apparently limitless field (here the sculpture appears alone and in a more symbolic guise). And why, I wonder, does the work have this curiously contradictory title: both 'Untitled' (as if to suggest a distancing from any external claims upon it by the world of natural appearances and commonly understood meanings); and, in its subsequent part, literally descriptive of what it invites us to look at? Given such wavering uncertainties, to what extent can I—or any one of us—think of this work as occupying the common physical and conceptual space of conventional public art, and as articulating a set of widely shared social and cultural meanings and values? What conceptions of art and of the public must we call upon, and what understanding of the urban conditions in which they meet, in order that we might speak meaningfully of *Untitled. Girl With Rucksack* as public art?

Suffice it to say that, if it is not to be read as an exercise in mere nostalgia, Hunter's characteristic return to apparently outmoded representational conventions must be understood as a motivated

response to current circumstances. Perhaps our best way to make sense of this seeming revival—or could it be survival?—of the outmoded is to consider some of those historical conditions of the modern period that gave rise to its abandonment. In so doing I hope to at least suggest that Hunter's work turns us towards our still unresolved relation to that past, the better to understand the limits and possibilities of our present condition. As Freud suggested, there are several ways in which we may manage our responses to a significant loss. In failing to accurately identify the lost object (the sufferer does not know what has been lost, thus the object-loss remains unconscious), the melancholic finds it difficult to consign this loss to the past and thus return to immediate reality. Those who mourn, however, are fully conscious of what has been lost, work through the attendant pain, and successfully leave the object of loss in the past, the sooner to return to reality.[5] The response of the fetishist is different again. In such cases, an excessively high evaluation will be placed upon an object associated with the moment immediately before a momentous loss is experienced, in an attempt to disavow or deny that loss.[6] In considering certain aspects of Robert Longo's work of the early 1980s, Hal Foster notes the artist's fascination—a fascination that we might liken to Hunter's—with the forms and the rhetoric of earlier public representations (monuments, statues, relief sculptures, etc.). But it is, Foster observes, a fascination with these forms precisely at a time when they have lost their currency and have been emptied of their previous significance. Why, he asks, should Longo rework the now meaningless rhetoric of such public representations? In reply to his own question Foster offers the following:

One answer seems evident: in the authority of these representations is concealed a fear—about a lack of authority, a loss of reality. Faced with this loss, our culture resurrects—morbidly, hysterically—archaic forms … in order to recover at least the image of authority or a sense of the real. For 'it is no longer a question of a false representation of reality (ideology), it is a question of concealing that the real is no longer the real, and thus of saving the principle of reality'.[7] It is this fetishism—of the real as well as the commodity image—that Longo explores ….[8]

Two central issues are raised here that will continue to echo throughout this discussion of *Untitled. Girl With Rucksack*; namely, a supposed loss of the real (of

5
Freud, Sigmund, "Mourning and Melancholia", in *The Pelican Freud Library, Volume 11, On Metapsychology. The Theory of Psychoanalysis*, London: Penguin Books, 1987, pp. 247–268.

6
Freud, Sigmund, "Fetishism", in *The Pelican Freud Library, Volume 7, On Sexuality*, London: Penguin Books, 1977, pp. 351–357.

7
Here Foster quotes Jean Baudrillard, *Simulacres et simulation*, Paris: Editions Galilée, 1981, p. 26.

8
Foster, Hal, *Recodings. Art, Spectacle and Cultural Politics*, Seattle: Bay Press, 1985, pp. 84–86.

9
Debord, Guy, *Society of the Spectacle*, Exeter: Rebel Press, 1987, Section 34 and Section 4 respectively (unpaginated publication).

10
Berman, Marshall, *All That Is Solid Melts Into Air. The Experience of Modernity*, London: Verso, 1983, p. 15.

the social and the public as sites of direct exchange between individuals), and its replacement by the kind of 'spectacular' imagery associated with mass media and the commodity. Key to much of what follows will be Guy Debord's definition of the spectacle as "capital to such a degree of accumulation that it becomes an image", and his additional claim that it "is not a collection of images, but a social relation among people, mediated by images".[9] Both, it would appear, have profound implications for any serious attempt to enter the territory of contemporary public representations in an urban context.

Hunter's own intellectual stance towards the historical question of modernity and its legacy of socio-cultural effects (including the spectacle) has been shaped to a degree by his reading of Marshall Berman's *All That Is Solid Melts Into Air. The Experience of Modernity*. To live in the modern, Berman writes, is to live—for better or for worse—under the signs of perpetual change, constant flux, permanent fluidity, endless migration: "it pours us all", he writes, "into a maelstrom of perpetual disintegration and renewal, of struggle and contradiction, of ambiguity and anguish. To be modern is to be part of a universe in which, as Marx said, 'all that is solid melts into air'."[10] Driven by the imperatives of ever-expanding capital, nothing in this modern world must remain fixed and immutable: within this environment, to stagnate is to die. Whilst this extraordinary historical revolution releases unforeseen creative energies, the only value cherished by its instigators—the bourgeoisie—is monetary. The law of profit prevails. The consequences for art, for the city, for the social and the private are broad and profound. This is so because within the processes of modernisation, capital transforms the city into an accumulation of visual signs, a spectacle. Paris provides the historical model here, especially as it underwent its dramatic transfiguration at the hands of Baron Haussmann from the later 1850s onwards. A massive programme of expansion, demolition, building and rebuilding witnessed the operations of speculative capitalism at full tilt. Plate glass windows and gas lighting turned street-level shopping into a novel experience, one based primarily upon looking and desiring, rather than negotiating and needing. Tree-lined boulevards offered framed perspectival vistas culminating in architectural set pieces, such the Opera and L'Arc de Triomphe. The consequence of the spectacle, according to Guy Debord, "is *affirmation* of appearance and affirmation of all human life,

Artist unknown, Five and a half metre (18 foot) replica of Michelangelo's *David* on the roof of a ceramics outlet, Gorbals.

Kenny Hunter, *Untitled. Girl With Rucksack.*

namely social life, as mere appearance".[11] This new urban environment, in fact, now 'appears' as a kind of image—a spectacle—in its own right. As TJ Clark notes, Paris was not simply a capital city, it was a city of capital. But how would this new city *look*, how could capital be *read* from its new lines, surfaces and spaces?

One might even say that capital preferred the city not to be an image—not to have form, not to be accessible to the imagination, to readings and misreadings, to a conflict of claims on its space—in order that it might mass-produce an image of its own to put in place of those it destroyed. On the face of things, the new image did not look entirely different from the old ones. It still seemed to propose that the city was one place, in some sense still belonging to those who lived in it. But it belonged to them now simply *as an image*, something occasionally and casually consumed in spaces expressly designed for the purpose—promenades, panoramas, outings on Sundays, great exhibitions, and official parades. It could not be had elsewhere, apparently; it was no longer part of those patterns of action and appropriation which made up the spectators' everyday lives.[12]

In considering the city as a representation in its own right we also confront the realisation that the city is not a given, but a particular kind of 'product'. Furthermore, it is a product whose production and uses are sites of conflict and contest. The more we explore these sites, the more we will find continuing evidence of that "maelstrom of perpetual disintegration and renewal, of struggle and contradiction, of ambiguity and anguish" identified by Berman as fundamental to the modern experience. As Clark insists, "The spectacle is never an image mounted securely and finally in place; it is always an account of the world competing with others, and meeting the resistance of different, sometimes tenacious forms of social practice."[13] According to Henri Lefebvre, for example, there are three, possibly incommensurate, ways of experiencing and imagining the city's existence. These "three moments of social space", as Lefebvre calls them, are "the perceived, the conceived and the lived". As far as "the perceived" is concerned, its identity is determined by "spatial practice": in other words, by the social activities which occur therein (shopping, walking, eating, sight-seeing, and so on). "The conceived", by contrast, is a conceptual abstraction; an image or a "representation of space". This is space as mapped by planners and

architects, according to the laws and conventions of geometry, linear perspective, cartography and other such graphic systems. Lefebvre's third term, "lived space", draws attention to the ways in which space may be *appropriated by the imagination*. Such "representational space" is harder to define because it is essentially non-verbal, but it nevertheless "overlays physical space, making symbolic use of its objects".[14] The questions then arise; is it possible for a symbolic representation such *Untitled. Girl With Rucksack* to help us reconfigure the relations between the "conceived", the "perceived" and the "lived" aspects of our experiences of the urban environment?

In order to pursue these lines of enquiry it will be necessary to propose connections between seemingly disparate areas. Initially, however, we should make it clear that to speak of representation is to enter the realms of the political and the ideological. Three statements by various writers will serve as a condensed summary of the claims involved here: "Representation … is not … neutral; it is an act … of power in our culture."[15] "Images change us as we change them; they are part of the contest that is social change, the contest of differing histories and ideas."[16] The "'political' and the 'aesthetic' are the inseparable, simultaneously present, faces of the postmodern problematic."[17] The city-as-representation, then, has a force; it is productive of, it intervenes in, and acts upon a situation.

Among the figures whom Berman chooses to exemplify the experience of urban modernity in post war America is Robert Moses, the creative and organisational force behind the sweeping highways, expressways and parkways that cut aggressively through many cities during this period. But, as Berman notes, a new, disastrous element enters into the dynamic with Moses. "Throughout this book", he writes, "I have tried to show a dialectical interplay between unfolding modernization of the environment—particularly the urban environment—and the development of modernist art and thought."[18] However, the lack of concern for the urban environment and its inhabitants displayed by Moses' projects marked a new attitude. Oblivious to the tremendous destruction and ruthless displacement of communities caused in the late 1950s and early 1960s by his Cross-Bronx Expressway, Moses merely observed, "When you operate in an overcrowded metropolis, you have to hack your

11
Debord, *Society of the Spectacle*, Section 10.

12
Clark, TJ, *The Painting of Modern Life. Paris in the Art of Manet and his Followers*, London: Thames & Hudson, 1984, p. 36.

13
Clark, *The Painting of Modern Life*, p. 36.

14
Lefebvre, Henri, *The Production of Space*, Oxford: Blackwell, 1991.

15
Owens, Craig, "Representation, Appropriation, and Power", in *Beyond Recognition*, Berkeley, CA: University of California Press, 1992, p. 91.

16
Nairne, Sandy, *State of the Art. Ideas & Images in the 1980s*, London: Chatto & Windus, p. 20.

17
Burgin, Victor, *The End Of Art Theory*, London: Macmillan, pp. 163–164.

18
Berman, *All That Is Solid Melts Into Air*, p. 309.

19
Quoted in Berman, *All That Is Solid Melts Into* Air, pp. 293–294.

20
Berman, *All That Is Solid Melts Into Air*, p. 305.

21
Deutsche, *Evictions*, p. 58.

22
Deutsche, *Evictions*, pp. 58–59.

23
Owens, "The Yen for Art", in *Beyond Recognition*, p. 318.

24
Owens, "The Yen for Art", in *Beyond Recognition*, p. 323.

25
All quotations from Walter Benjamin, "The Work of Art in the Age of Mechanical Reproduction", *Illuminations*, London: Fontana, 1973, pp. 219–253.

26
Burgin, Victor, *In/Different Spaces*, London: University of California Press, 1996, p. 34.

27
Jameson, Fredric, *Postmodernism, Or, The Cultural Logic of Late Capitalism*, London: Verso, 1991, p. 14.

28
Jameson, *Postmodernism, Or, The Cultural Logic of Late Capitalism*, p. 42.

29
Jameson, *Postmodernism, Or, The Cultural Logic of Late Capitalism*, p. 44.

30
From here it is a short technical and conceptual step to the memorable shot in Ridley Scott's futuristic movie *BladeRunner* where the (dystopian) Los Angeles of 2019 is dominated by a huge electronic advertisement. The gigantic screen that carries this moving image is not an independent advertising hoarding: it is the architectural fabric of a towering building.

way with a meat ax." [19] Such stupendous lack of concern for the physical environment was matched by supercilious disdain for the public and for public accountability. In the latter part of his career Moses funded his grandiose projects by "the creation of a network of enormous, interlocking 'public authorities', capable of raising virtually unlimited sums of money to build with". But, as Berman is at pains to point out, such "public authorities" as those developed by Moses took on an independent life of their own, and were "accountable to no executive, legislative or judicial power". [20]

Moses' aggressive 'sculptural' remodelling of parts of New York City serves to focus our attention upon a crucial moment of "disintegration and renewal, of struggle and contradiction, of ambiguity and anguish". The city, we tend to believe, belongs to the public domain; it is common property. The public unaccountability of Moses' financial arrangements, however, tells a different story. It exposes a fundamental contradiction at the ideological heart of the public sphere as it is commonly understood. According to Alexander Kluge and Oskar Negt, this public sphere is in fact—and always has been—a "pseudo-public sphere". As Rosalyn Deutsche explains:

Although idealized by Habermas as a spatiotemporal terrain where citizens participate in political dialogue and decision making, the bourgeois sphere for Negt and Kluge actually represses debate. This repression originates in the strict demarcation drawn in bourgeois society between the private and public realms. Because economic gain, protected from public accountability by its seclusion within the private domain, actually depends on publicly provided conditions, the bourgeois public sphere was instituted as a means for private interests to control public activity. [21]

In order to overcome any potential conflict arising from this invasion of the public realm by private interests, it was necessary, Kluge and Negt argued, to organise its perception and reception in such a way that dissenting perspectives were disqualified. Thus this pseudo-public sphere "only represents parts of reality, selectively and according to certain value systems". Consequently, "the pseudo-public sphere has yielded to a public sphere that is privately owned, determined by profit motives, and ... 'the public' is defined as a mass of consumers and spectators". [22] The effect of capital, therefore, is not simply to restructure the city in its own image, but to simultaneously define its ideal 'public' as—rather unsurprisingly, perhaps—consumers, both of the spectacle and commodities. As Craig Owens noted: "'the public' is a discursive formation susceptible to appropriation by the most diverse—indeed, opposed—ideological interests; and ... it has little to do with actually existing publics or constituencies". [23] Moreover, according to Owens, "the question of who is to define, manipulate and profit from 'the public' is, I believe, the central issue of any discussion of the public function of art today." [24] Our next step, therefore, will be to consider how the city-as-spectacle was organised so as to provide an environment conducive to consumerism.

The results of radical transformations to the city's fabric offered a new kind of representational experience, one that demanded new practices of interpretation, new forms of engagement, new modes of attention. Old communities and old meanings had been swept aside, communities and meanings that had slowly emerged from gradual accumulations of habit, memory and history. Whereas the pre-modern urban environment could be read as a coherent narrative directly related to one's own immediate experience, it was now fragmented into a series of disconnected episodes. Typically, the modern city would be zonal in its organisation, with 'specialist' districts: financial, entertainment, residential, administration, etc.. By thus transposing the city into the registers of the episodic and the visual, it was now necessary to inhabit this revised urban environment in different ways. The only way to navigate the kaleidoscopic image that the city had become was to retreat into a state of relative inattentiveness, a state defined by Walter Benjamin as "absent-minded" and "distracted". Our relation to architecture offers a model here in so far as, Benjamin suggested, buildings become so assimilated into our lives that habit alone determines our relation to them. Moreover, "habit determines to a large extent even optical reception. The latter, too, occurs much less through rapt attention than by noticing the object in incidental fashion." Significantly, Benjamin also noted that, "Reception in a state of distraction ... finds in the film its true means of exercise." [25] Both the viewer of the film and the inhabitant of the city, then, are encouraged to inadvertently absorb the spectacle, rather than subject it to critical reflection. Active engagement is displaced by passive consumption.

Benjamin offered this insight in 1936, before the days of television and video. The advent of these newer media has, however, only served to further enforce his point. Whereas film may elicit modern forms of distraction and inattentiveness from its audience, many of its structures remain traditional. In a pre-TV age, for example, films are firmly located in time and space (they are shown in a certain place at a certain time; they last for a certain amount of time). Television, on the other hand, is ubiquitous; it is always available in countless locations. Television is thus ambient; it constitutes an environment. Unlike a film, television has no beginning, has no end. Furthermore, the 'contents' of television are discontinuous and fragmentary: drama/news/ documentary/sport/comedy/soaps/arts/etc.. The fact that films themselves are incorporated into television's scheduling is further indication of the latter's omnipresence. "Television", as Victor Burgin claimed, "presents itself as if it 'covers' life itself." [26]

I am aware that this approximation of the contemporary urban experience to TV may seem far-fetched, but the point I wish to suggest is that in the figure of the screen they share certain common formal features that tend to evoke a particular receptive mode of inattentive fascination. Thus, as the light transparency of glass sheets replaced the heavy materiality of carved masonry a development occurred within the modern architectural environment that led increasingly to facades being treated as screens. Fredric Jameson points to the "depthlessness" of such architecture, "whose ... surface renders our older perception of the city somehow archaic and aimless". [27] At its extreme, in cases where such facades are mirror-like, "the glass skin achieves a peculiar and placeless dissociation of the [building] from its neighborhood: it is not even an exterior, in as much as when you seek to look at the ... outer walls you cannot see the [building] itself but only the distorted images of everything that surrounds it." [28] As a consequence, "the individual human body" loses its capacity "to locate itself, to organize its immediate surroundings perceptually, and cognitively to map its position in a mappable external world". [29]

An architecture of screens is tantamount to a public space delimited and defined by screens. [30] The metaphor and the reality of screens extend beyond the architectural and invade virtually all aspects of

Kenny Hunter, *Gate of the West*, 2004. Courtesy the artist.

Kenny Hunter, *3ft Thatcher*,
2003. Courtesy the artist.

present life: TV and video screens, cinema screens, computer screens. The ubiquity of the screen undermines the differences between public and private experiences. Screens become the interface between individual and world not only in the home, but also in the workplace, and the public spaces of the world outside. How many first-time visitors to New York feel they have been there before? The image of the city is so sharply defined in movies and TV series that the actual city is virtually inseparable from this image. Visiting the city merely confirms the image (which it never fails to do). Image-screens and screen-images: they tend to be bright, thin, temporary, highly sensory and fast. But the very intensity of the screen image also produces, paradoxically, a kind of de-realisation within the representation, a heightened artificiality of surface and colour, not unlike the appearance of plastic and other industrially produced synthetic substances.

In an interview with WJT Mitchell, Barbara Kruger claimed that the modern mass media—film, advertising and, especially, television—are not in the business of making meaning. On the contrary, she claimed, their effect is to dissolve meaning. They construct a "space of fascination rather than the space of reading". The content of television is "not made to be read or seen, or really it's made to be seen but not watched".[31] In a similar vein, Fredric Jameson has argued that the "informational function of the media would be to help us forget, to be the very agents and mechanisms for our historical amnesia".[32] Thus, as the urban environment is increasingly given over to the fascinating appeal of the mediated spectacle and the depthlessness of the screen, so it enters a zone of comparative meaninglessness. History is eradicated, the body is disoriented, and a state of ambient distraction and amnesia is induced. It is at this point that public art is often called upon to reinstate meaning, location and attentiveness, but here we encounter yet another paradox.

The commercial development of the city—its exploitation as a source of ever increasing profits, its conversion into spectacle—demands, as we have seen, a constant cycle of destruction and regeneration. This is not part of any 'natural' rhythm to the city's life; it is planned and orchestrated to maximise commercial and property values. The fate of those many members of the Bronx community forced to quit the area to make way for Moses'

Expressway is far from unusual, and yet such severe disruption and devastation of established communities often provide, paradoxically, the pretext for the recuperation of community by means of public art projects. Thus a state-sponsored and/or privately-funded public art project may well be initiated to restore the identity of a community that has been destroyed by a state-sponsored and/or privately-funded urban 'regeneration' project. But this identity itself may be 'mythical', less than 'authentic', as much externally imposed as internally generated by the site and the community, and serving primarily to endow identity by means of those same processes of visual differentiation that endow commodities with their distinctive identity in a competitive and overcrowded marketplace. Perhaps, however, this is not such a bad thing. Perhaps the very notion of an authentic 'essence' or set of 'eternal' meanings inhabiting a place, site or community is, as Miwon Kwon suggests, "ideologically suspect … out of sync with the prevalent description of contemporary life as a network of unanchored flows".[33] The movements of capital are now global rather than local or regional, and the imperatives of universal mobility affect all our lives. One of the generally recognised effects of multinational capitalism is the international homogenisation of the urban spectacle, leading to what Deleuze and Guattari identify as a "dynamics of deterritorialization", or Marc Augé characterises as the "non-places of supermodernity".[34]

Indeed the deterritorialization of the site has produced liberatory effects, displacing the strictures of fixed place-bound identities with the fluidity of a migratory model, introducing the possibilities for the production of multiple identities, allegiances and meanings, based not on normative conformities but on the nonrational convergences forged by chance encounters and circumstances. The fluidity of subjectivity, identity, and spatiality described by Gilles Deleuze and Félix Guattari in their rhizomic nomadism, for example, is a powerful theoretical tool for the dismantling of traditional orthodoxies that would suppress differences, sometimes violently.[35]

Yet what this view ignores, as Kwon acknowledges, is that, whilst we may all be subject to the "unanchoring" effects of globalisation, we are so to varying degrees of consent and control. Economic migrants, for example, may often be unwilling migrants.

31
In WJT Mitchell ed., *Art and the Public Sphere*, Chicago: University of Chicago Press, 1992, p. 247.

32
Jameson , Fredric, "Postmodernism and Consumer Society", in *Postmodern Culture*, Hal Foster ed., London: Pluto, 1985, p.125.

33
Kwon, Miwon, "One Place After Another", in Erika Suderberg ed., *Space, Site, Intervention. Situating Installation Art*, Minnesota: University of Minnesota Press, 2000, p. 56.

34
Deleuze, Gilles and Félix Guattari, *A Thousand Plateaus: Capitalism and Schizophrenia*, Brian Massumi trans., Minnesota: University of Minnesota Press, 1987; Augé, Marc, *Non-Places. Introduction to an Anthropology of Supermodernity*, John Howe trans., London: Verso, 1995.

35
Kwon, "One Place After Another", p. 57.

Untitled. Girl With Rucksack stands high on a cylindrical column at the corner of Cumberland Street and Jane Place in the Gorbals. Casually dressed in a 'tracky' top, loose jeans and plain shoes, the young woman's gaze seems directed over the adjacent Blackfriars Primary School towards the distant southwest. Her hair is tied back in a simple ponytail. In her left hand she carries a book. On the ground between her feet sits a duffel bag, while the rucksack on her back sags with the weight of its contents. She appears to be travelling; she appears to be waiting. Fundamental though it may be, this brief sketch has already exceeded mere description, has begun the process of speculation, and invites a series of questions. What is the book that she has been so recently reading? Where has she arrived from, or where is she travelling to? What is she thinking? What does she see from her lofty vantage point? These questions, it will be noted, concern a set of imagined intentions and mental states that we ascribe to the figure. And they are impossible to answer with certainty. But it is too late: we have already entered into an empathetic relationship with a representation. We have begun to respond to this sculpted figure as if 'it' were really 'her'. Whether wisely or not, we have made an imaginary leap from surface appearance to inner thoughts. We are engaged.

All representations demand a response from us, be it engagement or refusal, but at a cost. All representations invite us to occupy a position in relation to them, but that position has been prepared for us in advance. Every act of representation might be thought of as an utterance that wishes, more or less consciously, to 'say' something (even if this utterance concerns a refusal to speak). In so doing it anticipates a response. Moreover, it attempts to impose the very terms of reference within which such a response must be framed. But the utterance, by means of which it attempts to elicit this response, is frequently directed towards a potentially hostile situation. Such an utterance, according to Bakhtin, enters a context that is

… already as it were overlain with qualifications, open to dispute, charged with value, already enveloped in an obscuring mist—or, on the contrary, by the 'light' of alien words that have already been spoken about it. It is entangled, shot through with shared thoughts, points of view, alien value judgements and accents. […] Discourse lives, as it were, on the boundary between its context and another, alien context.[36]

Such utterances anticipate us, and they address us as a certain 'kind' of person (a mother, a teenager, an intellectual, a liberal, a consumer, etc.). If we recognise ourselves, our values, our fantasies in any of those representations—if we each think as an individual that it is really 'me' who is being addressed—we may say, according to Althusser, that we have been successfully hailed, or "interpellated", by that representation.

I shall then suggest that ideology 'acts' or functions' in such a way that it recruits subjects among the individuals … or 'transforms' the individuals into subjects … by that very precise operation which I have called interpellation or hailing, and which can be imagined along the lines of the most commonplace everyday police (or other) hailing: 'Hey, you there!'[37]

The effect of such an act of interpellation performed by a representation, then, is to 'transform', or 'turn', the individual into a subject—a subject of ideology. We may be reminded here of Steinberg's views on the 'functional' aspect of the public: "The word 'public' for me does not designate any particular people; it refers to a role played by people, or to a role into which people are thrust or forced by a given experience." And, at the risk of tautology, we would have to reaffirm that in a consumer society we are interpellated within representation as 'subject to' the ideological imperatives of consumerism—the role of consumer being 'thrust or forced' upon us. With the final usurpation of the public sphere by private interests, even art cannot occupy a space beyond this ideological coercion. As Owens observes, "It is clear that, at least in the 1980s, museums regard 'the public' as a mass of (potential) consumers."[38] Should art attempt to address itself to some contemplative realm of absolute, eternal and disinterested values beyond the reach of self-interested consumerism (that is to say, to that ideological space cleared by the bourgeoisie in earlier times to accommodate and promulgate its own cultural values), it will find that the citizens of this mythical realm have either died or moved away. Consequently, as Benjamin Buchloh has claimed,

All sculptural production since the last thirty years finds itself knowingly or naively suspended between two realms and registers of articulation: on the one hand it is positioned within the institutions of the public sphere …. On the other, [it] is positioned within the equally mythical but more powerfully 'real' dimensions of the culture industry and of spectacle.[39]

36
Bakhtin, Mikhail, *The Dialogic Imagination*, Austin: University of Texas Press, 1981, p. 276 and p. 284. These comments on Bakhtin's notion of "utterance" in relation to painting borrow from TJ Clark, "Jackson Pollock's Abstraction", in *Reconstructing Modernism*, Serge Guilbaut ed., Cambridge, MA: MIT Press, 1990, p. 177.

37
Althusser, Louis, "Ideology and Ideological State Apparatuses", *Lenin and Philosophy and Other Essays*, Ben Brewster trans, London: New Left Books, 1971, pp. 162–163.

38
Owens, "The Yen for Art", in *Beyond Recognition*, p. 317.

39
Buchloh, Benjamin HD, *Gabriel Orozco*, London: ICA, 1996, p. 43.

hloh, *Gabriel Orozco*, p. 46.

usser, "Ideology and
ological State Apparatuses",
53.

In the first of these realms it may be asked to operate in that "mythical domain of 'public space'" (here we might think of that contradictory space defined by Kluge and Negt as the pseudo-public sphere), but in such a location it can only pretend to "enable acts of simultaneous collective reception and historical commemoration". In the second of these realms, it fares no better, operating alongside "industrially-produced 'objects' and 'signs'… in the field of ideological interpellation". This leaves Buchloh wondering,

to which other forms of object- and image-relations could sculptural production take recourse in order to communicate at all with its presumed spectators? In what way could sculpture provide the innate resources of critical opposition against the universality of the reign of the commodity object and the sign of interpellation without relapsing into a claim for a purely phenomenological object or without claiming a discursive specificity and autonomy for sculpture? And lastly, more difficult yet: in which institutional space and in which discursive register could the sculptural object articulate critical opposition to these universally valid principles without reclaiming a mythical sphere of a 'naturally' given public space?[40]

Our discussion of Hunter's *Untitled. Girl With Rucksack* has finally brought us to the question of ideology and ideological interpellation. The task of ideology, as it is understood by Althusser, is to "represent the imaginary relationship of individuals to their real conditions of existence".[41] In so doing, it must mask those contradictions that lie at the heart of the "real conditions of existence". The task of any critical project thus becomes precisely to unmask and expose those same fundamental contradictions. In focusing upon those aspects of the contradictory and divided that seem to pervade Hunter's work (contemporary versus historical modes of representation; a simultaneous appeal to the incommensurate modes of attention demanded by the urban/commodity spectacle on the one hand, and by art in the bourgeois public sphere on the other; a series of doubts concerning the reliable interpretation of the work's semantic aspects—what is the girl 'doing', what is she 'thinking'—and so on), I hope to suggest that *Untitled. Girl With Rucksack* manages to thematise these issues as they recur within various levels or registers of representation. The question still to be answered, however, is whether the work simply repeats the logic of contradiction that supports it (whether it represents contradiction), or whether it acts as a support for further critical reappraisal (whether it performs that contradiction). •

ny Hunter, *Skull*, 1997, Tron
atre, Glasgow. Courtesy
artist.

THE GATEKEEPER

Urban landscape and public art

ACCORDING TO cultural geographer Denis Cosgrove, "landscape is not merely the world we see, it is a construction, a composition of that world".[1] Therefore, when I came to Glasgow, to conduct research on landscape, urban regeneration and public art, I was interested not only in the social and spatial structure of the city I could physically observe. I was equally trying to explore the various memories, narratives and myths that have come to—and continue to—symbolically shape the contemporary urban fabric.

LANDSCAPE, ART AND SOCIAL SPACE

There has always been a strong relationship between art and landscape. Not only has the meaning of the term landscape itself, in the seventeenth century, developed under the influence of Dutch *landschap* painting, referring until today to the visual or representational aspects of territory. More materially speaking, art can be a powerful medium of forming our images and associations of a given landscape. Accordingly, the power of art to inform our imagery of an area, to literally produce places, is used in very different contexts. With public art programmes becoming more and more popular strategies of contemporary cultural politics, artistic practices play an important role in the process of urban regeneration. While an artwork might not be as decisive as, say, a prestigious shopping arcade or another so-called flagship development, it greatly matters when it comes to reinforcing the identity of a specific area or replacing an old image with a new one. This is due to the fact that, by definition, artists are used to working with the imaginative, seriously playing with and sometimes distorting our accounts of reality.

The ways in which art can influence our 'geographical imaginations' stand at the heart of one the first artworks realised as part of the Crown Street Regeneration Project.[2] *The Gatekeeper* is located on the southern corner of the New Gorbals and is composed of three elements: a suspended sculpture, a framed photograph and a small crypt in the foundation underneath the photograph. At night, the photograph is illuminated from the back, highlighting the sculpture from below. Given its prestigious location and superhuman scale, the artwork's unveiling in April 2002 was reported in both local and national newspapers.[3] The media's interest in the public monument was mirrored on the more everyday level, where the artwork was widely debated by locals and guided bus tourists alike, soon becoming a new Glasgow, or at least a New Gorbals landmark.

"Only one year after the installation of the artwork, the value of the adjacent flats had doubled."

The Gatekeeper is the product of Heisenberg—a partnership between two artists, Dan Dubovitz and Matt Baker, which dissolved in 2002 after five years of close collaboration. In 2002 and 2003, I had the chance to interview Matt Baker several times for my research project, asking him questions about his accounts of the process of interpretation or 'consumption' of public artworks, about his understanding of the relations between public art and its place in the city and, last but not least, about the social role of the artist. As I learned from the interviews, Heisenberg's engagement was characterised by an interest in the idea of 'social space', thus reflecting the same enthusiasm for space and the social production of meaning that drove my research on art and landscape.

Others might define it as 'public space', we call it social space because public space tends to have echoes of civic grandeur. We are interested in how art can be a way of affecting social space. It might be a mechanism for people who live around or have an interest in that space to become involved in the future of it. Or we might take on the remit of looking at that space, what its future might be and what its past has been and in some way represent its identity back to the people who are around it.[4]

ON A THRESHOLD

According to Baker, *The Gatekeeper* represents the Gorbals as a place "on a threshold"—on a threshold between coming and going, between demolition and reconstruction, between past and future. Not only do all formal elements of the artwork relate to the notion of change, the name of the artwork itself—*The Gatekeeper*—refers to a threshold between two time-spaces, i.e. to a transition to another time or/in another space:

1
Cosgrove, Denis, *Social Formation and Symbolic Landscape*, London: Croom Helm, 1984, p. 13.

2
Following Derek Gregory, *Geographical Imaginations*, Oxford: Blackwell, 1994, I use the term 'geographical imaginations' to refer to the—often contested—social and cultural meanings making up the realities of specific places, spaces and landscapes.

3
McCormack, Gillian, "Gorbals gets a big lift from new artwork", http://scotlandonsunday. scotsman.com/scotland. cfm?id=321572002, accessed 25 March 2006; "Biggest artwork ever for Glasgow", http://news.bbc.co.uk/ hi/scotland/1897521.stm, accessed 15 March 2004.

4
Matt Baker in conversation with Julia Lossau, 17 May 2002.

Unveiling *The Gatekeeper*.
Photo: Anthony O'Doibhailein.

Our approach to the brief was to create a free standing piece of sculpture worked around the idea of a threshold. We were very interested in the fact that the Gorbals itself currently stood at a place of a threshold from being demolished and being rebuilt. This was a new vision of the Gorbals, and it was another time when the Gorbals was standing on a threshold, looking forward and looking back. So we wanted to make something that embodied that condition.[5]

Being one of Glasgow's oldest and best-known districts, the Gorbals has, over the past 200 years, experienced radical transformations. The repeated changes to the area—from a respectable Victorian neighbourhood to a notorious slum in the inter war and post war years, from a comprehensive redevelopment 'showcase' of the functional phase of urban planning to a well-designed contemporary urban village—made it one of the most popular communities in Britain and beyond. Against this background, there is a myriad of representations of the area, subjective and individual, as well as symbolic and social.

An important element in the symbolic narrative of the area is its history of immigration. Immigrants and refugees, particularly from Ireland, the Scottish Highlands and Eastern Europe "… found the Gorbals a convenient location, given its proximity to the city centre and river, with their attendant employment opportunities, and given its reasonable accommodation costs".[6]

What appealed to us was that the Gorbals has this amazing history of being the first port of call for immigrants coming into Scotland. It was somewhere that is integrally about transition and change and new life, with a constantly shifting, constantly changing community… there was a restlessness to it.[7]

It is in this sense that the woman in the photograph mirrors the emotions of somebody "coming to the Gorbals for the first time full of hope, fear, expectation".[8] The way in which the photograph is presented, i.e. the sublime position and the dark frame that is illuminated at night, resembles the style of a public artwork in Berlin. Located at Checkpoint Charlie, the untitled piece by German artist Frank Thiel shows portraits of a Russian and, on the reverse side, of an American soldier. Part of a series of public artworks located at former Berlin checkpoints, Thiel's

t Baker in conversation
h Julia Lossau, 17 May 2002.

mpson-Fawcett, Michelle,
inventing the tenement:
sformation of Crown
eet in the Gorbals Glasgow",
rnal of Urban Design, no. 9,
4, p. 183.

t Baker in conversation
h Julia Lossau, 27 May 2002.

t Baker in conversation
h Julia Lossau, 27 May 2002.

overview of the Berlin
es of public artworks is
n in KunstStadtRaum.
Kunstprojekte im
liner Stadtraum, Berlin:
atsverwaltung für
dtentwicklung, Kunst im
dtraum, 2002.

t Baker in conversation
h Julia Lossau, 17 May 2002.

Eric Eunson, The
bals—An Illustrated
tory, Ayrshire: Stenlake,
6.

piece is necessarily embedded in a very different historical and cultural context.[9] Nevertheless, it speaks about transition—or, indeed, about the dangers, if not the impossibilities of being on a threshold. As such, it influenced Heisenberg in creating a photograph which, in turn represents the feelings of sorrow and alienation as they relate to the consequences of displacement and migration.

The theme of the sculpture stands in contrast to—or rather complements—the restlessness of the photograph. While the latter stands for the vulnerabilities and insecurities of migrants, the sculpture's intention is to protect and shelter those who are on their way. Influenced by Ernst Barlach's *Der Schwebende Engel*, it addresses questions on the universal or essential, if not metaphysical conditions of human existence, of being in the world. The sculpture embodies a sense of protection, safety and trust which, in turn, reverberates with the symbolic power of the Gorbals and its specific 'sense of place'.

A sense of belonging is very common in Scottish culture. Where do you come from, is the first question … and the Gorbals has this very strongly. The number of people that you meet who have a relationship to that place

through a member of their family is just incredible. It really is, all over the world people know the place. And (…) the figure above was to show a sense of protection, guardianship, the power of the place.[10]

The overall framing of transition and change is mirrored by the third element, a small crypt in the fundament underneath the photograph. However, unlike the sculpture and photograph, the crypt does not speak so much of the old times when the Gorbals used to be a rapidly growing community with a strong sense of identity, serving as chief port of entry for immigrants. Rather, it alludes to a more recent phase of transition. In the 1960s and 70s the traditional tenements which used to symbolise the social life of the Gorbals were demolished and replaced by modern and functional high-rise and deck-access blocks.[11] The construction and fabric of the new buildings, however, were so poor that the blocks soon became infamous and finally had to be demolished after only ten or 20 years of occupation. Against this background, the area is again subject to redevelopment, presently turning from a failed modernist housing utopia into a new 'urban village'. The crypt depicts the change of the 'New Gorbals', however it does so not in concrete terms—as in passage or migration—but in an

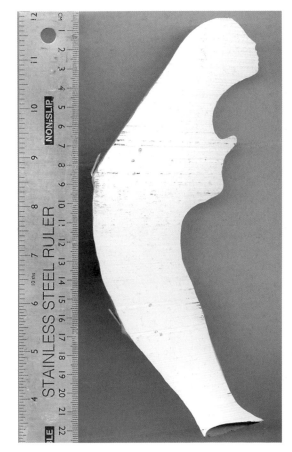

HT: Matt Baker, Early clay
del for suspended figure;
Gatekeeper.

RIGHT: Matt Baker, Cross-
tion of The Gatekeeper
quette used to construct
ature for full-size clay
sion.

tos: Matt Baker.

abstract, transcendental way. The crypt contains the remnants of a bonfire to which Heisenberg had invited local residents:

We asked them all to bring something that they wanted to leave behind from the old Gorbals [i.e. the Gorbals of comprehensive redevelopment], and we had a big bonfire, and over the course of an evening we did some drinking and did some burning … everybody did their private ritual.[12]

INVENTING THE 'TRUE' GORBALS
One year after being unveiled, the sculpture developed a quaint and non-intended feature which awarded it the reputation of a mystery. After rainfall, reddish water drips out from one of the sculpture's hands through a crack in the bronze. As a consequence, the figure has been dubbed "the angel with the bleeding hand" and was listed as a mysterious object on the internet.[13] Considering the subtext of the artwork and the symbolism of its

elements, it is not without irony that the sculpture is regarded as mystic in esoteric circles. Although the crack occurred unintentionally, the 'bleeding hand' turns the sculpture—a mere icon of protection—into a guardian angel. As such, it can connect easily to the spiritual iconography of the other elements. Especially the crypt with its history of burning souvenirs refers rather unambiguously to the religious themes of birth, death and reincarnation. The photograph, too, can be interpreted in this light. The walking woman, a 'simple' icon of passage, is then turned into a biblically vested figure who reverentially walks down a cloister. Against such a background, *The Gatekeeper* speaks about leave and resurrection, about reverence and purgation, about devotion and commemoration for something that is past recovery but somehow still there.

What is this transcendental condition that is to be commemorated? Put differently, what images are central in the artistic remaking of the landscape? The interplay between what the photograph (fear) and sculpture (protection) represents is intended by the

12
Matt Baker in conversation with Julia Lossau, 27 May 2[...]

13
Matt Baker, 28 July 2003; Gallacher, Pauline, "Accompanying text", in *The Gatekeeper. A public artwo[...] by Heisenberg*, p. II.

14
For a more detailed accoun[...] this imagination see Micha[...] J Miller, "Conflict in the soci[...] representation of place: the cases of Gorbals and Alma-Gare", in *Myth and memory the construction of commu[...] historical patterns in Europ[...] and beyond*, Bo Stråth ed., Bruxelles: PIE Lang, 2000, pp. 115–135.

15
Watts, Stephen, "New mira[...] in the Gorbals", *The New Yorker Magazine*, reprinted in *Evening Times*, 11 January 1960, p. 5.

16
McArthur, Alexander and H Kingsley Long, *No Mean City*, London: Corgi Adult Paperback, 1992 (first editi[...] 1935).

17
Miller, Michael J, "Conflict i[...] the social representation of place", p. 119.

18
Embedded in specific powe[...] knowledge systems, the essentialist view succeeds in producing a supposedly natural meaning of a certai[...] place. Although this meani[...] is constructed from a speci[...] observation or vantage point and, therefore, has only partial relevance, it ca[...] gain hegemony and then marginalise alternative interpretations (see e.g. Rosalyn Deutsche, "Boys town", *Environment and Planning D*, no. 9, 1991, pp. 5–30).

'Crypt-ritual' event, 2002.
Photo: Dan Dubowitz.

artists to allude to the Victorian era of immigration, i.e. to the old Gorbals, where people of different origin met and lived, door to door, their everyday and sometimes laborious lives. Indeed, the geographical imaginations of the old Gorbals are characterised by close social bonds and mutual aid, often represented as a hard but good life in the tenements. Epitomised as a cultural melting pot, the old Gorbals was regarded as a vital and bustling, decisively homely place where people chatted from their windows, gossiped at street corners and debated things of public relevance.[14] By choosing the good old times of the Gorbals as reference point, the artists actively partake in the nostalgic invention of the 'true' Gorbals.

Calling the hard but good times of the old-Gorbals-as-the-true-Gorbals an 'invention' is not to say that the community had never seen such things as close social bonds, social reciprocity or solidarity. It is rather to say that the history of the old Gorbals was as much about the dark sides of the industrial era—slum-like housing conditions, high infant mortality rates, and crime—as it was about solidarity and social reciprocity. We should not forget that, against the background of miserable social conditions in the area and with the housing conditions further deteriorating in the inter war years, the Gorbals was described, in an article of 1959, as "the most notorious single slum area in the British Isles, and among the most notorious in the world".[15] Of some importance to this image was the novel *No Mean City* by Alexander McArthur and H Kingsley Long.[16] Telling the story of street fighter Johnnie Stark, 'Razor King'[17] of the Gorbals of his time, the popularity of the book "sealed the fate of the Gorbals which, to this day, bears the scars inflicted by the Razor King". Until today, the area is famous for its history as a notoriously rough neighbourhood, associated not only with bad living conditions but also with alcoholic excess, gang violence and what is known more recently as 'anti-social behaviour'.

During the last decades, however, the reverse imagination—i.e. the imagination of the Gorbals as a place of social cohesion, solidarity and respectfulness—has become more dominant. Conveying an essentialist view of the area, it has superseded, if not gradually replaced, the negative image of the inter and post war years.[18] Representing the other of Johnnie Stark's miserable slums and reflecting the good old Victorian times, the image of the 'hard but good' Gorbals seems to be of some

STIGMATA: Locals say angel statue seems to be 'bleeding' from its hand

RIDDLE: mechanic Andy Cosh looks up at mystery angel

vintage. However, it only came into being in the 1970s, when the failure of the modernist high-rise experiment, i.e. bad physical fabric and social isolation in the newly built blocks, had become apparent.[19] Fuelled by a profound sentiment of loss, the respective narrative romanticises the life on the streets and in the traditional tenements as a vital part of the area's culture. The shift in the local memory—from 'slum' to 'community'—was, in turn, taken up in the attempts to once again revitalise the area. Not surprisingly, therefore, the 1980s and 90s witnessed the re-implementation of the tenement block, albeit in a somehow privatised form, as a liveable urban environment.[20]

Against this background it can be argued that *The Gatekeeper* is part of the new hegemonic imagination. Privileging good memories over bad ones, the artists reproduce the presently powerful image of the 'true' Gorbals as a self-confident community which is about integration and collaborative life. The artwork can thus serve as an example of how the new identity of an

"Miracle in the Gorbals—Angel statue's hand 'bleeds'." James Mulholland, *News of the World*, 29 September 2002.

19
See Michael J Miller, "Conflict in the social representation of place", pp. 115–135. For an account of the social consequences of the modernisation process see Nick Fyfe, "Contested Visions of a Modern City: Planning and Poetry in Post-War Glasgow", *Environment and Planning A*, no. 28, 1996, pp. 387–407.

20
Thompson-Fawcett, Michelle, "Reinventing the tenement", pp. 177–203.

Matt Baker, *The Gatekeeper*, low view. Photo: Anthony O'Doibhailein.

[We hoped] that it [*The Gatekeeper*] would in some way become a totem for people to talk about their history. There have been meeting places in the past in the Gorbals, where people just came to debate things. Those have gone, they have been demolished. So our hope was to try and make another one.[21]

This hope is somehow undermined, however, by the fact that the site of the artwork is non-public in juridical terms. Put differently, *The Gatekeeper* is situated on the property of a new private residence building. While it is still possible to go round the fence and have a closer look at the artwork, the residents have been discussing ways of restricting the public's access. On the one hand they would like to keep 'their' artwork under their hat, not least in order to protect it from vandalism. On the other hand, they are disinclined to barricade their property.

There is a big debate at the moment about whether they should put a screen across it…. The people there are looking after it and they have come down on a number of occasions to stop kids throwing stones. There have been some incidences with graffiti down there. So they are really thinking hard about how they want that space. Because they are so proud of the thing, and they really want to show it to people. But on the other hand, they don't want to spend their whole lives policing the space either.[22]

As an attempt to find a compromise between public access, on the one hand, and exclusion of the public on the other, the residents finally decided to put up a small, additional wall between the fence and the artwork. The purpose of the wall is to underline the private character of the site in a rather subtle way, without closing the territory off completely.

area is retroactively invented by a particular reading of history—a reading of history that brings some myths to the fore while other memories are excluded from the history of that area.

A MEETING PLACE?
The interplay between inclusion and exclusion can also be observed on a more material level. *The Gatekeeper*'s popularity was soon reflected in the house prices. Only one year after the installation of the artwork, the value of the adjacent flats had doubled. While Matt Baker admits to be happy with the increase, the artists' intentions were far from simply producing a popular, prestigious and marketable landmark. Heisenberg aimed rather at creating a meeting point in the sense of a genuine public space, where people could commemorate the old Gorbals and where locals could discuss matters of public concern:

The discussions about safety and control of access, about the prevention of graffiti and vandalism, remind us that the Gorbals regeneration and, as a consequence, The Artworks Programme as the commissioning body are embedded in the context of economic restructuring, both on a local and on a global level. Due to their structural crisis, former industrial cities in particular are forced to reinvent themselves by culturally upgrading their urban landscape. As French sociologist Pierre Bourdieu notes, related development strategies aim at transforming cultural capital into economic capital, thus increasing urban surplus in the face of an ever intensifying

21
Matt Baker in conversation with Julia Lossau, 27 May 2002.

22
Matt Baker in conversation with Julia Lossau, 27 May 2002.

competition.[23] The increasing intermingling of economy and culture, not least in urban planning, has been conceptualised as the symbolic economy of the entrepreneurial city.[24]

After all, the social orientation of European urban development changed radically during the 1980s: it was no longer resistance against the ousting of the poorer classes from the inner city … that was in the foreground, but rather the struggle to enable the higher-income classes to either stay or to return. The middle classes were courted by the sirens of urban redevelopment—as residents, consumers and visitors. This transformation was expressed in new alliances and interests, the artistic architect celebrated his comeback at the cost of the participation architect and urban planner.[25]

The same exclusive process of implementing a new and more attractive city image can be observed in the Gorbals. If we are to take up an instrumental perspective, the current revitalisation of the Gorbals represents nothing less than the attempt to strengthen Glasgow's position as a prosperous and attractive location, aimed at transforming the Gorbals into a socially and economically dynamic area.[26] It is against this background that *The Gatekeeper*, itself being part of the development process, becomes suspect of materially excluding those who are not part of the new corporate identity. Not only is the artwork installed on private property, but the discussions about control of access that are led by the residents are contradictory to the ideal of social inclusion that the artists intended when they created the artwork. After all, fences and access restrictions seem to be more important than the inclusion of those who do not fit the new imagery of the area. As a result, is it only a slight exaggeration to say that the site of *The Gatekeeper* resembles a gated community rather than a place of public exchange.

AMBIGUITY

This instrumental or strategic reading of the artwork is probably not completely wrong, and maybe it is even the most compelling. Assessing *The Gatekeeper* only from this perspective and, thereby, reducing it to a purely economic icon in the context of urban redevelopment, however, would be too simple an interpretation. It would obliterate what *The Gatekeeper* provoked, and continues to provoke; that is, all sorts of interpretations and reflections.

The most interesting discussions and forms of appropriation, however, take place on the local level. At first sight the ongoing discussions about access control and regimentation underpin the powerful perspective of urban redevelopment according to which the revitalisation of the Gorbals is predominantly about upgrading and exclusion. Yet a second look reveals that the discussions are the result of very different ideas of what *The Gatekeeper* is or can be about. Many residents, on the one hand, are proud of 'their' piece of art, they want to look after and care for it. Some of the younger members of the community, on the other hand, mainly regard it as an object they can turn their aggressions to or at least their aerosols. Nevertheless, the residents do not treat lightly the question of how The Gatekeeper should be regulated. Although their strategy of adding another wall to further protect the artwork does not conform to Heisenberg's intention of creating a public place, it is not condemned by Baker. On the contrary, he asserts that it is the residents who have to live with the artwork and who should decide about its regulation accordingly:

It's really interesting to see what happens in the way those decisions get made now…. And it's interesting for me to see how people get empowered into a situation where they are taking control over their space.[27]

In acknowledging this, Baker addresses the significance of the processes of negotiation, thus highlighting that the use and appropriation of spaces and places is not fully determined by their (juridical, spatial, economic, administrative etc.) structures. The same is true, I would argue, for *The Gatekeeper* itself. Taking into account the various and contradictory ways that it is negotiated and appropriated on different scales; "In revisiting the figurative tradition, the artists have created a work that is at once accessible and subversive, posing more questions than it answers about the nature of art in the city. And that is how it should be." [28] •

ACKNOWLEDGEMENTS: This essay was supported through a European Commission Marie Curie Fellowship. I would like to thank Matt Baker for sharing his thoughts and the staff members of the Department of Geography and Topographic Science (now Department of Geographical and Earth Sciences), University of Glasgow, for their hospitality and support.

23
Bourdieu, Pierre, *Distinction: A Social Critique of the Judgement of Taste*, Richard Nice trans., Cambridge, MA: Havard University Press, 1984.

24
See, for example, David Harvey, "From managerialism to entrepreneurialism. The transformation in urban governance in late capitalism", *Geografiska Annaler* no. 71B, 1989, pp. 3–17; Sorkin, Michael ed., *Variations on a Theme Park. The New American City and the End of Public Space*, New York: Noonday, 1992; Zukin, Sharon, *The Cultures of Cities*, Oxford: Blackwell, 1995.

25
Bodenschatz, Harald, "Urban conversion—concepts and perspectives", in *Urban conversion. Recent international examples*, Matthias Boeckl ed., Vienna, New York: Springer, 2002, p. 16

26
See *Crown Street Regeneration Project, Past, present and future*, Glasgow: Crown Street Regeneration Project, 1992.

27
Matt Baker in conversation with Julia Lossau, 27 May 2002.

28
Gallacher, "Accompanying text", p. II.

1960. 20 December. 8.15 pm. Amsterdam. A packed room in the Stedelijk Museum waits for the 40-year-old artist Constant Nieuwenhuys. A slide projector and a large tape recorder sit behind the audience. Constant enters, stands by the machines, and delivers a half-hour statement about 'Unitary Urbanism'. The tone is militant.[1]

IN JANUARY 2005, I received the last 'Itinerant' commission by The Artworks Programme: Gorbals to make a temporary artwork in response to the current programme of redevelopment in the area. For this I worked on two very different but related works that sought to respond to the latent utopianism of regeneration programmes, of community-building through architecture, and how this might relate to utopian architectural projects of the past and present.

First I flew to Florida to make a short video, *Looking Backward*, filmed in Market Street, Celebration. Founded by the Disney Corporation in 1995 but sold on recently to a developer, Celebration was, in my view, an attempt to realise a late capitalist utopia, a space where people could live out a particular version of the American dream, just so long as they didn't contravene the edicts of The Celebration Corporation's 70 page Pattern Book (a revival of the eighteenth and nineteenth century illustrated pattern book, which had provided "architectural instruction to builders about how to maintain proportion and unity in the design of a town"). As the Scottish academic Andrew Ross (who lived for a year in Celebration) noted in his *The Celebration Chronicles*, 2000:

Celebration's Pattern Book is a comprehensive volume of recommendations for the placement and design of houses within streetscapes. The community patterns establish 'correct' proportions for everything from massing and setbacks to the height and opacity of fences…, the depth of porches, and the recommended facade material and colour, each laid out according to the size and lot of the house. Landscaping is also strictly regulated: precise percentages are decreed for the appropriate mix of grass, hedges, shrubs, and trees…. The architectural patterns are addressed to the integral unity of the house, and govern such matters as the spacing between its elements (dormers, doors, porches, columns, and bays), laying down additional rulings about the colour of cladding material and other facade

features for each of the six prescribed housing styles. For the Coastal style, for example, all windows, trim boards, columns and railing should be white, but they are to be brown in the Mediterranean; pale green, pale ochre, or pale blue in the French; and a 'deeper shade of the body colour' in the Victorian.[2]

"Architecture, built, drawn and theorised, is a projection of the social imaginary—of how we would really like to live and to be."

Surrounded by the pale shades of neo-traditionalist, Victorian architecture in downtown Celebration's Market Street, I sat myself on a rocking chair to read silently a passage from Edward Bellamy's *Looking Backward: 2000–1887*, an important and influential utopian novel which helped to start a utopian socialist movement in America. The novel envisions a harmonious, rationally designed city and American nation in the year 2000. The city is full of high-rise buildings and supermarkets where money is replaced by credit cards. The city and the nation are run by a largely anonymous but benign 'Administration'. It is also a vision of a technological utopia where surround sound comes effortlessly from the walls of your home. This was echoed in Celebration where they pipe muzak into the streets from speakers which mushroom from the ground. The video was first screened in the Gorbals Library on the tenth anniversary of Celebration, on 18 November 2005. The intention in this work was to establish a critical relation between two very different designed environments in terms of community and aspiration.

At the same time I had been working on *Legend*—a large neon sign for the gable-end wall of the last remaining tenement block in Ballater Street in the Gorbals. The sign read "keep true to the dreams of thy youth" in handwritten, lower case blue neon lettering. It was a quotation from the German Romantic writer Schiller which I had come across on a website dedicated to the Gorbals-born boxer Benny Lynch.[3] 2005 was the 75th anniversary of Lynch becoming the World Flyweight Champion. Lynch was a legend in the Gorbals not only for becoming World Champion, and representing a kind of triumph of the spirit in the face of economic adversity, but

1
Wigley, Mark, *Constant's New Babylon: The Hyper-Architecture of Desire*, Rotterdam: Witte de With, 1998, p. 9.

2
Ross, Andrew, *The Celebration Chronicles: Life, Liberty, and the Pursuit of Property Values in Disney's New Town*, London: Verso, 2000, pp. 87–88.

3
A modified version of Schiller's line appears in Robert David MacDonald's translation for the production of *Don Carlos* at the Citizens Theatre in the Gorbals, Glasgow, 1–23 September 1995: "Posa: … Tell him, when he becomes a man he must/still hold his youthful visions in esteem,/and not allow the deadly parasite/of vaunted, far superior Reason to/gnaw at his heart's divine, but fragile flower./Nor must he let the Wisdom of the Dust/perplex him, when it utters blasphemy/against Idealism, Heaven's daughter." Friedrich Schiller, *Don Carlos*, Robert David MacDonald trans., London: Oberon Books, 1995, p. 187. Importantly, Walter Benjamin also cites this line in his short text "Experience", *Selected Writings Volume 1, 1913–1926*, Marcus Bullock and Michael W Jennings eds, Cambridge, MA: Belknap Press of Harvard University Press, 1996, p. 4.

Ross Birrell, *Looking Backwards*, Celebration, Florida, 2005.

also for dying at the age of 33 of illness related to his alcoholism. But the text was not simply a reference to Lynch and the Gorbals past. The reading of the text is open enough to refer to anyone's dreams, young and old alike. To me it related to my recent reading of Alain Badiou's *Ethics*, which talks about fidelity to the truth of love, art or revolution, and concludes with the ethic of 'keep going', like the final line from Beckett's trilogy of novels: "I can't go on I'll go on." The neon was placed high, overlooking the final stage in the redevelopment programme and the building of an up-to-date version of the Glasgow tenement. This new tenement would gradually obscure the gable-end wall and the neon sign with it. I liked the poetic element of this work becoming gradually obscured, to the point that only a slight glow from the resultant side alley would remain.

During this same period I was commissioned to make two new public works as part of *Adam*, an exhibition of site-specific work in Amsterdam organised by Smart Projects. I decided to use the same structure for both projects, that is a neon sign in public space and a site-specific reading on video to be screened in a different location. The Amsterdam neon sign read "eternal now" (a reference among other things to the constant transformation and renewal of a city) and was rendered in similar lower case handwritten neon letters, this time in white, located under a canal bridge in the red light district. The video was titled *Homo Ludens* and was shot on the roof of the temporary Stedelijk Museum and screened in Sjakoo, an anarchist bookshop in Amsterdam.

Johan Huizinga's *Homo Ludens*, 1938, was a key reference for Constant, and inspired the production of the large-scale, unrealised (unrealisable?) architectural project of New Babylon (Constant even published a collection of essays with the title *Opstand van de Homo Ludens*, 1969—which translates as *Uprising of Homo Ludens*). In the series of drawings, paintings, collages, lithographs, maps, manifestos and architectural models, which span almost two decades from 1956–1974, Constant envisioned New Babylon as a dynamic, labyrinthine city, spreading above the surface of the earth, a space of constantly changing ambiances and experiences in an environment designed in such a manner that it was possible for inhabitants to transform the fabric of the unfolding city according to the situation and the free-play of their desires. As Mark Wigley writes: "New Babylon

constitutes the last comprehensive formulation of an idea of the new man, or better, of a social space that allows for the emergence of an other man, of a new way of living in community, in society." [4] Although Wigley reminds us that Constant refused to use the term 'utopia' in relation to the New Babylon project—"New Babylon was not an abstract model, but an assertion about a plausible reality"—as Simon Sadler indicates below, architectural projects are always at work somewhere in the space between utopia and reality. [5]

Homo Ludens became the title of my recent solo exhibition of works from the Envoy series in the Fries Museum, Leeuwarden, 24 September 2005–29 January 2006, which included prints from *New Babylon* from their collection and the maquette of the *Hanging Sector of New Babylon* borrowed from the Gemeentemuseum in the Hague. Originally, I had intended to interview Constant for the *Adam* project and for this show, but unfortunately, his health was already in decline. Instead, I decided to make a new video piece and dedicate it to Constant. Sadly, when I had finished editing the video back in Glasgow and was about to send it to Constant, I got a telephone call from Rudy Hodel, the curator at the Fries Museum who had put me in touch with Constant's wife Trudy, to tell me that Constant had died.

Constant was the catalyst for my approaching the architectural historian Simon Sadler after I heard about Basil Spence's reference to Babylon in the design principle for the Hutchesontown blocks in the Gorbals, that the skyline should resemble the Hanging Gardens of Babylon. I had met Simon and invited him to Glasgow School of Art around the time of his publication *The Situationist City*, 1998, which included a chapter on Constant and New Babylon. I suspected that it was the libertarian aspects of these works which attracted him and, given his other publications on radical architecture and his move to California—that other utopian space which conjures visions of a libertarian America—I thought that Simon might be the perfect person to address some of the utopian themes in my work as it moved towards specific architectural contexts. I also hoped that these utopian themes might, in turn, open up the political dimension of his architectural research. This is one of those rare occasions where one's hopes are not dashed but surpassed. I thank him here for his commitment, patience and generosity.

4
Wigley, *Constant's New Babylon*, p. 5.

5
Wigley, *Constant's New Babylon*, p. 5.

keep true to the dreams of thy youth

NEW GORBALS, NEW BABYLON: ROSS BIRRELL IN CONVERSATION WITH SIMON SADLER

A dialogue between artist Ross Birrell and Simon Sadler, Professor of Architectural and Urban History at the University of California, Davis.

Sadler is the author of two important studies on experimental architecture of the 1960s, *The Situationist City*, 1998, and *Archigram: Architecture Without Architecture*, 2005, and is co-editor with Jonathan Hughes of *Non-Plan: Essays on Freedom, Participation and Change in Modern Architecture and Urbanism*, 2000.

ROSS BIRRELL: How did you get interested in utopian architectural projects like Constant's New Babylon or groups like Archigram?

SIMON SADLER: In 1989 I was at Birmingham Polytechnic wondering about a topic for a Masters thesis, and my old friend Ben Franks (now a political philosopher and the author of *Rebel Alliances*), suggested looking at the Situationist International. Ben put me in touch with Sadie Plant, who was writing *The Most Radical Gesture*, a book that was pivotal for English-language readers. Peter Wollen's essay in the 1989 I C A catalogue on the SI was also very useful.

Ross Birrell, *Legend: keep true to the dreams of thy youth.*

But at that time it was hard to locate much material on Situationist architectures, so I spent some time in Britain, France and The Netherlands tracing material on Constant, slowly reading COBRA's journals, *Potlatch* and *Internationale Situationniste* (very little had been translated at the time), and walking around Paris with another old friend, Alexis Lachèze-Beer.

In my late teens I started to encounter situations very different to those of my suburban upbringing, which made me acutely aware of the variability of social geography. For example, I had a job working in public libraries around the massive 1960s–70s housing estate of Chelmsley Wood. This was the first time I'd met people with no telephones. At one library, the windows had been strengthened so that bricks bounced off, and at another branch part of my job was persuading kids not to cycle inside the library. These libraries were nonetheless important social centres for their users even if they were 'reading' them, in a somewhat inventive fashion. As a student, I became a cycle courier and got completely absorbed by cycling subculture, which immersed me in a sort of liminal, mobile city, populated by seemingly classless, bicycle-bound, self-invented people. London, with which I had been in love since I was a child, proved to have an existence separate to the monumental and the privileged. A little later, in the 1990s, my slight familiarity with the newly Ecstasy-driven club scene (nothing like the lager-and-fight Birmingham clubs of the 80s I knew as a teenager), and anarcho street politics also made an impression on me.

These shaped me in a strange way ideologically: as the title of my co-edited collection with Jonathan Hughes puts it, I am drawn to 'Non-Plan', but to the extent that the non-planned is dependent upon its opposite, the planned. The tension between the spontaneous and the contained strikes me as recurrent within architecture, within personal lives, and within society. If emancipation is to be equitable, it has to be grounded in rationality, which is a structure of sorts. I was intensely curious, then, what role architecture might play as a mediator between freedom and order. Architecture has always imposed order—monumental, geometric, social. Assembled as cities, nevertheless, it has provided the setting for projects of emancipation—Greek democracy, the Enlightenment, Marxism, anarchism, and to some extent feminism and the civil rights movement. So, I wondered whether Situationist architectures would accelerate emancipation. My

interest in Archigram grew concurrently. But what really caught my imagination was the degree to which architecture, built, drawn and theorised, is a projection of the social imaginary—of how we would really like to live and to be. The Situationists and to a lesser extent Archigram show us an alternative built reality, and in this they function in the best traditional of utopianism—or indeed psychotherapy—by showing us possibilities and inviting us to consider whether we will choose to live like that.

As a student I realised that the spatial development of society and desire was being explored by geographers in the wake of David Harvey, Doreen Massey and Edward Soja, apparent more marginally in the short-lived but intriguing journal *Transgressions* and in the quixotic resurrection of the London Psychogeographical Association (LPA). Such lines of enquiry were being adopted by architectural historians around the Bartlett School of Architecture in London, and resonated with postmodern architectural theory, where architecture has been put on the psychoanalytic couch, so to speak, its languages and presuppositions interrogated.

But I've always worried that avant-gardism is an onanistic area of the arts, a field for hobbyists with little relation to the body politic, and since the 70s it's been customary to note that utopianism is the preserve primarily of bourgeois intellectuals. And I am personally no exemplar of the style of life that I have researched.

RB: Apparently, when Basil Spence was designing the Hutchesontown redevelopment in the Gorbals in 1965, he envisioned the skyline to be like the Hanging Gardens of Babylon. In *The Situationist City* you note that the Babylon myth inspired many utopian architects and in particular the Situationist architect, Constant and his project New Babylon. Do you see any relationship between the work of Constant and Spence, who designed his tower blocks in the Gorbals in the years following Constant's designing New Babylon, from 1958 onwards?

SS: This takes us to the relationship between realism and the utopian. The two are peculiarly intertwined. I am susceptible to a nostalgia for Modernism, especially of the post war, British Welfare State ilk, partly because that dialectic between the utopian and real is so tangible in it. The road to hell is paved with good intentions, but it is also paved with indifferent, amoral ones, and I can't help but feel forgiving about a generation of British architects who kept a liberal-left social project in mind. It was hubristic of course—the notion that architecture could intervene in inequitable political economies or, for that matter, the hope that mixed-economy, centrist politicians could pull off the job of attaining universal social justice. But at least Spence, for example, hoped to provide decent, affordable housing, and at the same time to point the social imaginary towards the Hanging Gardens of Babylon. 1960s Gorbals was of course a typically tragic failure to communicate with the client, but then again, I grew up in an 80s Britain that had regressed to allowing people to beg from street shelters of cardboard. Was this meant to pass as social realism? It is little wonder that many young architects were driven to look, of all things, at the ultra-left, at the S I and so forth.

Speaking as an historian, the point that I was trying to make in the books *The Situationist City* and *Archigram: Architecture without Architecture* is that realism and the utopian know each other very well indeed. Archigram's most bizarre projects were only ever extrapolations of things read in newspapers. The Situationists worked with the material of Paris as found, and Constant read architectural periodicals with projects like Spence's in them. From Town and Country Planning back to Futurism and Expressionism, the entire tradition of Modernism rested upon utopianism—Reyner Banham

and Peter Collins eloquently explained this in the 1960s. I don't have the detailed knowledge of Spence's archives to be definitive, but in Spence's mind, I am prepared to bet, was the thought that if the Mesopotamians could have the hanging gardens, then why not working class Glaswegians? The relationship between the real and ideal, by the way, is never, ever done with—neither in the strictest Modernist rationalism, nor in ashlar-veneered postmodernism, nor in the micro-piazzas of out-of-town retail parks. Your neon sign in the Gorbals makes this point better than I can here.

RB: In Amsterdam this year I made a video on the roof of the temporary Stedelijk Museum (the museum which first exhibited Constant's New Babylon project), called *Homo Ludens*. I had originally intended to do an interview with Constant but he was too ill, so instead I dedicated the work to him, just before he died. It was screened in Sjakoo, the libertarian bookshop I had visited on my first trip to Amsterdam 12 years earlier. Do you think either Constant's New Babylon or Huizinga's work, *Homo Ludens*, which influenced Constant and the Situationists, is still relevant today?

ss: Peering at this video, I think I recognised the cover of *Homo Ludens* in your hands, the same copy with the De Chirico painting on it that I ploughed through as a student trying to fathom its intellectual resonance

ss Birrell, *Homo Ludens,*
delijk Museum, 2005.

with anarchists. Beyond the radicalism of its thesis (that human culture is motivated by the instinct to play), it's an endearingly traditional piece of scholarship.

By its very production and consumption, history is inevitably relevant to the present, and the fact that you and I are having this conversation, and that the publishers of this exchange conceive of a market for it, indicates some continued relevance for Constant and Huizinga. Really though it's my job to be asking you—what are you doing filming yourself on the roof of the Stedelijk reading Huizinga? I have always been uncertain about the relevance of my research to 'things happening now'. As an architectural historian I hoped to find out why so many architects and artists think that art and architecture can or should be a means of transgression or festal release, instead of being merely mono-functional or didactic or commodified or edifying, and I wondered what the linkage between architecture and life was thought to be. Huizinga remains quite a good place to start answering these questions. And in turn I think there are good reasons for art and architecture to serve as a social event or condenser, as Huizinga and Constant urged, just as there are good reasons for humans to attend to community and the pursuit of happiness.

What though of New Babylon specifically—does it show a solution to a problem? I was shocked when as a student I found the 1974 Hague Museum catalogue, buried deep in the collection of

Birmingham Public Library, and first saw in detail Constant's New Babylon—the illusionistic quality of its photomontages, as though the future had actually happened; its relationship to other architectural modernities; its ambition (should that be megalomania?); its hint of menace as well as joy. I was not sure what it solved, either; Constant presented it as though it was a solution, whereas I felt it worked better as a provocation (a word chosen by my colleagues from Delft for the subtitle of their major new collection *Exit Utopia: Architectural Provocations*). Where would the money and the technology for New Babylon come from? In other words, was this a prelude to revolution, or its product? Why leave nature? Why abandon the domestic so completely?

So here we are asking one another what we're doing looking at Constant's work and reading Huizinga and mulling over utopia, that most hackneyed of concepts. My personal reading of your Stedelijk film would be precisely this—what we are doing decade after decade, cogitating upon a more fully lived culture from within its perpetually disappointing realisation. Someone else you could ask about this is Mark Wigley, a prominent commentator whose handsome volume about New Babylon appeared just after *The Situationist City* came out. I am unsure why New Babylon is relevant to architectural practice once, as Wigley insisted we do (at a 2000 conference in Delft), we disregard its utopianism as being without interest. I wondered: should we then approach New Babylon as

Constant, *Large Yellow Sector*, 1969, Haags Gemeentemuseum. Courtesy Victor Nieuwenhuys.

a precursor to Deconstructivism, the last Modernist style of the twentieth century (which Wigley brought to the Museum of Modern Art in New York in 1988)? Or was Wigley attracted by Constant's superlative mode of architectural rendering?

In retrospect I don't think that was what most excited Mark Wigley about New Babylon. At about this time, he was also researching the history of architectural interest in networks (for instance via Constantin Doxiadis's Ekistics), a very pressing matter because in theory our 'network society' hasn't much use for buildings. New Babylon was invented as an open-ended network with extensive cybernetic control systems. But to invert Professor Wigley's comment at the time, I confess that it's the utopian aspect that most interests me in New Babylon, a little less so its pertinence to what is being, or could be, built now. This is because New Babylon strikes me not so much as the thesis of an architecture of information technology, but its antithesis. New Babylon depends on real space, shaped communally through physical switches, not on the virtual space of password protected electronic command-control systems. True, we can build real, push-button spaces, but to build New Babylon today would be to erect a parody of the actual, neoliberal political economy that is largely indifferent to social development (unless one thinks of capital growth as equivalent with social development). To best observe the architecture of the network society, take a drive through suburban sprawl. This is the reality that implies that remarkable architectural interventions into it are the *greater* fantasy. The most exciting built interpretations of the space of flows, by designers like Zaha Hadid, Rem Koolhaas, and Frank Gehry, are showpieces impressive for the fact that they were built in the face of the banalising force of neoliberalism—cosseted by metropolitan benefactors with the resources to rise above the strict limitations of the market and, thankfully, with the acumen to do something tasteful with this power.

Culturally, too, this approach will struggle to gain traction as long as suburban sprawl itself manages to project fantasies of freedom and autonomy and even community. Celebration, the Disney operated small town that you depict in your film, is only the tip of the iceberg for a new generation of private planned communities in the US. Moreover for middle class occupants, and likely for swathes of the aspirational working classes riding low interest rates and ready

credit, there is no contest between sprawl and the downtown. Even as a member of the middle classes, I see no prospect of being able to return to the metropolitan existence for which I yearn and from which I am financially compelled to retreat.

Architectural training is bereft of the ideological guidance (read, the utopian projections) which rationalised not just Modernism, but, in different ways, the architecture of Victorianism, or French and American Republicanism, or of the Renaissance, the Gothic, and so we go on. In the 1980s and 1990s, 'architectural theory' concentrated on admittedly fascinating questions relating architecture to language and the psyche, but many on the left found such theory irritatingly remote from the socio-economic, and still more middle ground architects argued that theory was irrelevant to everyday practice. By the late 90s some architectural seminarians were themselves calling for a 'post Ωtheory' moratorium and a concentration on building itself. What, then, guides the ideology of design—and there has to be one, whether or not it's explicit—in the early twenty-first century? I guess this is one of the motifs in your projects: whither the principle for our built space? Elsewhere I've argued that the failure of Britain's Millennium Dome summarises this malaise. The Dome was not even postmodern, which in its refutation of ideology was committedly ideological; it was simply the state's shabby attempt to show that Britain was open for transnational business. The present compromise within architecture seems to be (and I wonder whether this coincides with the reemployment of architects as the economy picked up) to build what you can, and build as well as you can. This is not so different from the attitude which gave us postmodern property development in the 1980s, and redeveloped city centres in the 1960s, which are not encouraging precedents. In any case, architecture is going to have to take account soon of the Spengler-esque turn in contemporary culture, with people and their buildings and spaces divided and under attack along racial/cultural lines, and the related return of interest in energy efficiency. Constant and Huizinga might not be the obvious resources for addressing this situation, though it would certainly do no harm to retain their basic presupposition, that culture is for living by, not dying by.

RB: I was struck recently by the reproduction in *Situationist City* of an engraving after John Martin's *Belshazzar's Feast*, 1820, with the Hanging Gardens of Babylon in the background, although Martin's real Babylon is the redevelopment and industrialisation of London. What struck me in the painting was the luminous lettering shining from the wall, it reminded me of the neon sign high on the gable-end wall of the last remaining occupied tenement in the Gorbals, which reads "keep true to the dreams of thy youth"—it beams like those letters as a warning from a disembodied voice. I suppose the connection I am attempting to draw here between Martin, Constant and my work is to do with atmosphere and the sublime. Is architecture always approaching the sublime? Can you see a role for the sublime in social housing?

SS: Attending the increased interest in Situationism in the 1980s and 1990s was a greater attentiveness to the everyday. On the one hand, the Situationist 'drift' invited us to contemplate the sublime as a way of thinking ourselves beyond everyday life in the modern world, a world which is shy of anything (death, the past, the future, the cosmos, desire, etc.) that might interrupt business as usual. At the same time situationism, and the accompanying philosophy of Henri Lefebvre, drew our attention back to the possibility of critique, cleaving open the prospect of difference and change starting, precisely, with everyday life. So the everyday and sublime might well be part and parcel of the same project of enlarging lived experience—much as architecture simultaneously projects images of fact and fantasy.

Contemporary architecture sometimes seems insistent that it is essentially practical, of the here and now. Curiously, this is the tenor adopted by supposedly opposite tendencies—say, the currents originating out of an avowed, phenomenological interest in materials and ordinary spaces on the one hand, and on the other, out of late Deconstructivist streams shy of grand, universalising abstractions. Both suppose to be revelatory of the here and now, the moment, as opposed to some larger (utopian) vision or project. Revelatory, though, of what aspect of the moment? One detects something metaphysical and Heideggerian amongst the architectural materialists; and amongst Deconstructivists, one senses a fantasy of the sublime cosmopolis, by which architecture places us at the thrilling precipice of a technocultural complex bigger than any of us and inaccessible to mundane reason. Speaking as a middle aged man living in the provinces and trying to juggle work, childcare, money, and his horror at the rise of the right,

I have to tell you that these modes of contemporary architectural sublimity are revelatory to me of very little. Lower Manhattan is now reduced to a metropolitan theme park for the so-called creative classes that bears an ever more distant relationship to the city its residents think it is. Meantime though the hold upon my imagination of death, the past, the future, the cosmos, desire, etc. (basically, the sublimity of a mortality that seems so proximate in architecture), shows no sign of weakening.

As regards social housing, it seems to me that Modernism instilled the nineteenth century tenement and row house with the sublime when it started to stretch it and stack it to extraordinary heights. When I first saw Trellick Tower and Park Hill, I was stunned (somewhat as I was when I read the 1974 *New Babylon* catalogue); it was like looking at a Piranesi print. If principally the effort here was toward form and image, it also represented the heroism of (ordinary, everyday) working class life. We tend now not to talk about the working classes—such, I suppose, is the ideological restructuring enacted by Thatcherism and Reaganism—and we tend not to build social housing, as though it is not needed, such again being the long reach of the 1980s. But as Hardt and Negri's books suggest, we do still have a 'multitudinal' social connection that is reminiscent of sublime infinitude, so perhaps the challenge of housing the world's population satisfactorily could be the source for our meditations upon the sublime. Sooner that than the ongoing portrayal of information technology networks, and of globalisation itself, as sources of a contemporary sublime, which merely mystifies the production of power and knowledge (Cisco Systems knows exactly how to build routers that control the flows of electronic information, and manufacture them as instruments of censorship).

RB: Do you agree with Tafuri when he suggests that a purely architectural solution to planning (perhaps along the lines of Le Corbusier and Celebration) is insufficient and that we must necessarily find a political solution?

SS: Of course. So rudimentary is Tafuri's observation that it is no wonder architects have since disavowed an interest between architecture and utopia (i.e. architecture and universal environmental justice), otherwise design would come to a halt, or be deeply depressing, or fall ever further into the hands of the talentless and the drones of property development.

Tafuri was correct to no less an extent than Marx, upon which his observation was based, or likewise Adorno on the culture industry more generally.

There are some complications to adhering to a Tafurian position unyieldingly, however. The process of living, of getting up, drawing social security, going to work, and consuming makes us all complicit in capitalism, and makes us all party to the deferment of utopia, and so, logically, do the built containers that we occupy, and the makers of those containers. But it would be nuts to denounce every survivor and every moment of life and indeed every moment of consumption as inimical to utopia. Likewise with architecture: I see plenty to admire, as I stand before an architectural history survey class, in the buildings of regimes that had no right to exist, even as the buildings effectively translated nonsensical and outright malevolent ideologies. I see both sides of the argument to demolish Notre-Dame during the Paris Commune, and overall I'm happy that the building survived. As well as being prisons for our behaviour and thinking, buildings are also the traces of our lives. Use them, and evaluate them critically, or we risk censoring ourselves and abolishing memory; I am not of the school that sees Pol Pot's return to the year zero as utopian. This is an old debate in any case amongst historians and cultural commentators, that split between vulgar Marxism and neo-Marxism. Art may be false consciousness, but then it might also contain, as Marcuse and Bloch contended, signals of the utopian, or at the very least information that

may be critical to change. Even as Walter Benjamin's research deconstructed Paris, he deepened for us the city's mystery and interest and the critical theory that accompanies that mystery and interest.

Architecture is unusually plagued by its bad conscience, so it's understandable, if not quite forgivable, that architects started to disavow the utopian content of their art. When I read a novel, I rarely berate it for its diffidence to social justice, so it would behove me to bring the same tolerance to architecture. Architecture's problem stems from that fact that it represents uneven development more explicitly than any other artform; it is more deeply complicit in the economy (at this stage in history, capitalism) than any other artform; it physically disciplines more directly than any other artform. However these facts can be used to argue in favour of building *better* architecture, even in—perhaps *especially* in—the absence of a reformist or revolutionary political program. And if the architecture is bad, what should I blame, the architecture, or the political and economic effluent that made it grow? The extraordinary thing is that *any* architecture is *any* good.

What I'm wary of, though, is the possibility that disavowing utopia is the architect's disingenuous shorthand for disavowing politics, for feigning apolitical status. This will give us architecture that is in some way mindless. It does architectural students

Martin, *Belshazzar's*
t, 1821, engraving after
ainting of 1820. Private
ction.

no favours either—if in the process of avoiding giving them guilty consciences you tell them not to worry about politics, you'll also be giving them none of the political *savoir-faire* necessary for getting things built. More seriously, *everything* is political, and to the degree to which politics takes as its reference the ideal, and thus the utopian, everything is related to utopia; and since architecture is historically the principle technology of community building, architecture ranks as extraordinarily proximate to the political.

Now on the one hand, this is not to say that the architect *is* a politician, nor that her or his buildings are conduits for wholly political processes—doubtless architects wish they had this degree of power, and there have been times (such as Britain in the 1950s and 60s) when architecture has been virtually a branch of central government. But certainly the architect is, like everyone else, a political being and her or his work is related to their political existence. I can imagine there are things I would not do as an academic because it would be too much in conflict with my values, and I would have the same expectations of the designer. Most important, I'd like to think that all political subjects—all subjects of architecture—are cognisant of their relationship to the architectural-political process. It's not all the responsibility of the designer and teacher; it's mostly about joint social responsibility, and the more power one has, the more responsibility one has. And I guess this is one of the values of your work, as you show yourself sitting there within the 'real world' cramming on utopia, history, politics.

RB: During the talk you gave in Glasgow on your book *The Situationist City*, I remember that you remarked that it must be awful to be old in New Babylon—where were the places to sit down? Does this observation point to what you perceive to be a failing of utopian dreams in terms of architectural projects, that they impose an unlivable plan (or even non-plan—e.g. Constant's 'dynamic labyrinth') upon inhabitants? or even that idealised architectural projects are always in some way uninhabited, unlived spaces? or does it simply point to a 1960s emphasis upon 'youth' and the dreams of a new generation at the expense of the elderly (which is ironic in this instance, as Constant lived to be 85)?

SS: Constant, we might recall, occupied an historic canalside building in an historic city, not New Babylon. Anyway, only since about the 1920s, with Le Corbusier's urbanism, or a little before that with the Futurists, has the idea of utopia been so caught up with movement and change. In other words, utopia began to embrace modernity, whereas in the nineteenth century it offered an enclave in which the onslaught of industrialisation and the mercantile economy could be managed. And in its origin with Thomas More, it was simply a model of rationality.

You could say that your various recent projects address different models of utopia, and their disjointed relationship to the contemporary world. When at the Friesmuseum you announced your donation of utopian texts to political institutions, you drew a contrast with twenty-first century politics and More's standard of political rationality. With your Celebration piece, you film an emanation of the nineteenth century village utopia but, by reading Bellamy there, make its seeming pleasantness dystopian because of its absolute rejection of the utopian redistribution of wealth. Atop the Stedelijk, we have a trickier problem, because it's unclear that Situationist physical mobility would have correlated with social emancipation.

The end of the subjugation of one human to another—surely the purest form of utopia—would be a political process first, and then a cultural and spatial one. It would not have us all floating in ether and playing games around the clock. It would respect the occasional need for privacy, silence, introversion, and a connection to place. The utopia that I have in mind here would be one in which pockets of individual space are respected as necessary, just as the right to movement and assembly would be respected. In other words, it would look a little like the spatial conditions imposed by the free market. Pay your money and take your choice, the crowd or the mountaintop, the free market invites. It is little wonder that neoliberalism, in which 'the world is flat', has been able to assume a utopian dimension. Indeed, it has to, for reasons of legitimisation—without the promise of emancipation, our submission to the exchange economy would be an act of insanity, or would have to be forced upon us violently, and indeed violence and insanity are doubtless present in our 'flat' world. As it happens, neoliberalism is *truly* utopian in the pejorative sense, because it implies an impossible set of conditions—equal access to economic opportunity, for a start—that are prohibited under the very processes of neoliberalism (by preserving, for example, inherited wealth.) But like all stages in capitalist development, neoliberalism feigns a naturalness to which any opposition, however mild, is made to appear at odds with reality. Still, that flat world of neoliberalism looks a lot like the utopia-scapes of high Modernism, which is why we should never forget the attendant political projects of Modernism, underpinning which was Marxism. And for the time being neoliberalism is held up as fully functional because it is cheap and easy and facilitated by political apathy.

Also underpinning high Modernism was the dogma of progress, which was conflated with change, movement and the annihilation of tradition; and this dogma was in turn linked to youth (to humans in which habit was not yet fully formed). By the 1950s and 60s the emphasis upon youth had assumed the aspect of cultishness, threatening to occlude the complications of class, race, gender, age. Youth, in turn, has been defined by its aptitude with electronics and drugs, and that leads us to the likes of Archigram (which was of course wholly modern behind its iconography of youth and play because it believed unflinchingly in progress). Electronics and drugs did not exert *that* great a fascination for me even as a youth, and as I get older the podded world leaves me modestly entertained but uninspired, so I find myself more interested in places, history, boundaries, and nature. You can put this down to parenthood and the onset of conservatism, but it means that plenty of utopianism still works for me, not least the basic Situationist conception of the city as it emerged in the first editions of *Internationale Situationniste*. Paris combined places to sit down with spaces to move through. It had a spatial memory but it also had live culture. It had amusing reconstructions of nature in its parks. And these properties were not unique to Paris, but were familiar to metropolitanism generally. Nor am I averse to the promise of green, suburban utopia.

We're not short of design concepts for a better world. We are short of fun, transparent, inclusive political processes, and of discourses that value humanity over sectarianism, masculinity and property. We are short of public arenas, and the education to use them. We're short of universal housing, sanitation, healthcare. Architecture *per se* doesn't enthuse me nearly as much as the possibility of these 'utopian' institutions. Designing them on paper, or marking their absence as you seem to do in your art, is one way of keeping them in mind. I would have to agree with those who may say, "humanity has never attained such institutions, they represent utopia", but then I'd ask whether we should

be concerned that, to my perception, we are actually *further* from this utopia in the early twenty-first century than we were in the late twentieth century. That we can *regress* proves that utopia *is* related to our lived institutions—their making and their withering.

I am an architectural historian, though, whereas your questions, Ross, have eked out the political subject in me, which is a still less complete aspect of me than my scholarship. Thank you for asking me though. •

BIBLIOGRAPHICAL REFERENCES:

Bellamy, Edward, *Looking Backward, 2000–1887*, New York: Buccaneer Books, 1994

Bloch, Ernst, *The Principle of Hope*, 3 vols, Cambridge, MA: MIT Press, 1995

Franks, Ben, *Rebel Alliances The Means and Ends of Contemporary British Anarchisms*, Oakland, CA: AK Press, 2006.

Hardt, Michael and Antonio Negri, *Empire*, Cambridge, MA: Harvard University Press, 2000.

Plant, Sadie, *The Most Radical Gesture: Situationist International in a Postmodern Age*, London: Routledge, 1992.

Marcuse, Herbert, *The Aesthetic Dimension*, Boston: Beacon Press, 1978.

More, Thomas, *Utopia*, London: Penguin, 2003.

Nieuwenhuys, Constant, *Opstand van de Homo Ludens*, Bussum: Paul Brand, 1969.

Sadler, Simon and Jonathan Hughes, eds, *Non-Plan: Essays on Freedom, Participation and Change in Modern Architecture and Urbanism*, Oxford: Architectural Press, 2000.

Sadler, Simon, *The Situationist City*, Cambridge, MA: MIT Press, 1998.

Sadler, Simon, *Archigram: Architecture without Architecture*, Cambridge, MA: MIT Press, 2005.

Tafuri, Manfredo, *Architecture and Utopia: Design and Capitalist Development*, Cambridge, MA: MIT Press, 1979

Van Schaik, Martin, and Otakar Macel, eds, *Exit Utopia: Architectural Provocations 1956–1976*, Munich and London: Prestel, 2005.

Wherever he looked, vegetation was rampant. Cucumbers 'came scrolloping across the grass to his feet'. Giant cauliflowers towered deck above deck till they rivalled, to his disordered imagination, the elm trees themselves. Hens laid incessantly eggs of no special tint. Then, remembering with a sigh of his own fecundity and his poor wife Jane, now in the throes of her fifteenth confinement indoors, how, he asked himself, could he blame the fowls?

ORLANDO, VIRGINIA WOOLF

THE NINETEENTH century witnessed a period of unprecedented change in this country, not least in the area of sanitary reform. Urban life had developed at such a speed that not only were the streets overburdened with a population intent on insatiably reproducing itself, but the antiquated water systems were simply unable to cope. In response, a combination of Victorian evangelical piety and moral crusade stopped up wells and pumps across the country which had been identified as purveyors of impurities, installing drinking fountains in their place. The proliferation of fountains saved many lives from the frequent outbreaks of disease, yet for many of those responsible for sanitary reform, such as the Temperance movement, this was a moral crusade, for fountains were an easy way to extend their influence over the 'lower sort'. Likewise, what underpinned the cultivation of parks were clear ideas regarding 'appropriate' recreation for all sections of society, which in turn influenced the design of the parks themselves. And while it would be misleading to suggest that all fountains were located within parks, for clearly this was not the case, rarely was a park considered complete without a fountain.

As a metaphor for the nineteenth century, the park and the fountain serve to highlight the plight of the Victorian idealist, vainly bathing the landscape in the limpid clarity of order and reason. This era, at once so prim in its habits, and so unbuttoned in its momentary enthusiasms and fantasies, struggled to come to terms with its inherent contradictions. While the Victorians may have expressed the formal order of objects, it was conveniently bound within demarcated space to suppress and ignore the disorder of man. These tensions, so implicit in the nineteenth century social project, may still resonate today; thus it is to the Gorbals, a century later, that we now turn.

Christina McBride as a young child in the Gorbals with her mother, brother and sister, 1968.

In 2006, another round of park and fountain building is taking place, and like the people of the nineteenth century, the residents have lately witnessed great changes to their environment. From the demolition of those infamous tower blocks to the regeneration project gathering pace, issues concerning the nature of reform and who it benefits abound. Having grown up in the area, the issues may be especially pertinent for Christina McBride, whose proposal to build a fountain in a reclaimed park will inevitably touch on, most notably, the issue of territory. Past lessons point to the danger of installing heavily loaded objects into public places, of trying sanitise the only space available for dissent; however, McBride seeks to transcend the differences between people through what she feels is common to us all: water. From the medieval well to the urban fountain, it is water that ties us to place.

"From the medieval well to the urban fountain, it is water that ties us to place."

Fountains instil a sense of magic in our urban landscapes, as well as simultaneously providing an important decorative element and focal point, and a natural balance to our technologically dominated environment. Not only this, but they counter the predominantly visual qualities of our cities by producing sound, an altogether more holistic approach to sensory experience. Delivering any one of these qualities can only serve to benefit Hallside Place, the proposed site for the fountain, which is a little park built in the 1960s having sadly fallen victim to neglect. Currently many people pass through on a regular basis but few seek it out as a destination, for 'lingering' has in the past been rephrased as 'loitering'. Instead, the park acts as a transitory passageway connecting the older houses with the newer developments of the Gorbals, an interface between past and present. Yet it may be worthwhile remembering that objects signify the spaces they inhabit, therefore building outwards from this fountain may also activate the surrounding park landscape. In other words, space is not just a place where things happen, but where things can make space happen.

While urban projects such as these should by now have departed from the notion that space is something to be shaped for overarching moral purposes, should space just be shaped according to aesthetic aims and principles which have nothing necessarily to do with social objectives? Clearly much has changed since fountains were weighted down with morality and inserted into a controlled pseudo-public arena; nevertheless, social projects, of the type that McBride's fountain belongs to, should not be stigmatised. Reform and regeneration are essentially optimistic social goals, something which both examples may be proud of. Social purpose, not through control but through agency and communication, may instead be a more appropriate theme for today's practices of urban intervention. For in a climate when clarity is appreciated above all else in the circulation of signs, the public realm and its objects must communicate transparently, otherwise, by mistakenly lending themselves to the communication of morality, they have effectively sentenced themselves to their own decay. •

Christina McBride, *Source*, digital line drawing, 2005.

Christina McBride, *Loch Katrine: water supply to the City of Glasgow*, silver gelatin print, 2005.

OLD GORBALS

Old Gorbals in his long black coat
muttered and stalked from room to room.
He kicked up dust, dead flies, newspapers,
a crumpled envelope or two.
There was no news, there was no message
in the stillness, no cat, no dog,
no voice to his 'Anybody there?'.
Of course not, they've all gone, gone where?
He'll never know, the thread is snapped
that he held fiercely all these years.
He shakes his head, crosses a window
like a shadow. There was so much life!
He can't believe it has disappeared:
he hears the children running, shrieking,
sees the TVs glowing blue,
marvels at the rows, the language,
crash of bottles, slam of doors,
car-doors too, oh yes, look down
at taxi after taxi, all piled full
with the raucous hopes of a Saturday.
The lamplight in the street looked up
at many windows bright at midnight,
and even when curtains were snatched tight
you felt hearts beating and lips meeting
as private twenty storeys up
as in any cottage by the sea.
Old Gorbals flicked dust from his sleeve,
sighed a bit and swore a bit,
made for the stairs, out, looked back
at the grand tower, gave a growl,
and in a spirit of something or other
sprayed a wall with DON'T FORGET.

EDWIN MORGAN, 2003

VIEWS FROM WITHIN

487 Cumberland Street is a 23-storey tower block. It houses 138 flats, six per floor. Each flat has a bathroom, a kitchen, a living room, one or two bedrooms and a balcony. It took over five years to depopulate it, turning it from a living space to a place waiting to disappear.

It's cold inside the building—the dampness echoes through corridor after corridor of abandoned, grey concrete. The only thing to break up its uniformity is coloured doors and graffiti—and, when the sun's

Highlights—light installation celebrating the life of a Gorbals towerblock, 2004. Photo: Anthony O'Doibhailen.

setting, the quick and definite shafts of light that flicker and change as you walk up or down the 23 storeys through the sky.

"The concept of belonging is essentially illusory; regeneration reminds us of that."

You go into one house—kicking aside the piles of junk mail still dropped through the letter box months after there's nobody to receive it (once you've been in three, maybe four houses, this ritual sweeping aside of yellow and red shiny paper reminds you of walking through wet and heavy autumn leaves). And you find yourself in another barren corridor. This time it's colourful throughout: the wallpaper, the kitchen units. All that remains.

Then you move up a storey or two, and you walk into a flat that smells like freshly opened chocolate bars—rich cocoa and vanilla soaks up the atmosphere, as if the inhabitant, expecting guests, refreshed the air on hearing footsteps in the corridor. After perhaps a year of emptiness, this sweet homeliness at once both warms and chills you.

Another house and the wallpaper's peeling back—the dampness prising it from the walls. Layer upon layer of paper is slowly stripped back, like a palimpsest that's gradually returning to its original form—a concrete body written over by family after family.

Always you gravitate towards the windows, soaking up the sunset that drapes over you, the wind that buffets you and the dark that encircles you 20 storeys away from streetlights and pedestrians. And the magnetic force of the view never weakens, different from every window: beyond the manmade structures to the hills that embrace this city sprawl. A pocket of isolation in a bustling city. You'd give everything to live encircled by these sights. But you can't: they'll disappear with the building that lifts you to them now.

And then there's the haunted house—not haunted as much as wailing. Each flat has a balcony—small and rectangular with high glass panels that separates you from the sky. This one catches the wind in its keyhole, and whoops it up and through the rooms. Imagine a foghorn personified—that's the sound of this house:

a mournful, incessant lamentation. Like the voice of the high-rise itself: on death row, decaying, marking time. On its balcony you see a solitary Timberland boot lying on its side next to three decomposing pigeons. No foxes here to save us from the sight, their puffed out bodies are beginning to flatten as they slowly fade into the concrete. There they'll not return to regenerate the land, but disappear in a puff of smoke with all that remains.

A bedroom that tells the story of a childhood. The small wooden plaque on the wall with letters burnt into it signifying its belonging: "David's room". The room where David grew from the little boy who played at being a Teenage Mutant Ninja Turtle, to the young man who dreamed of busty blondes and listened to the legend himself. Mister Bob Marley. You know all this definitively. You know because his wallpaper (mutant turtles) and the posters that begin to cover it (torn-out pages from *FHM*, a hand drawn Marley) tell you.

Then it's the boy David's living room. High up in the empty concrete block—a space that shouts at you. Written on the wall in thick black ink, a final goodbye:

JIMMY
ISABEL
DAVID
BUTCH (PAW PRINTS)
STAYED HERE
AND LOVED THIS HOUSE
WE LEFT 9/11/00

From the outside the building dies. First the curtains disappear one by one and week on week the evening glow the building beams across the city slowly wanes until there's nothing but darkness. And the structure becomes a hollow space that sits and waits to disappear.

In 1999 Peter Smith began a series of explorations pivoting around the demise of 487 Cumberland Street: this culminated in illuminating one face of the building using 220 spotlamps in 2004, but the concept began with a simple toothbrush.

Studying for his postgraduate diploma in architecture, he was given a metre square piece of plastic and asked to make a memorial to something. Living in the Gorbals and knowing the high-rise was to be demolished, he'd begun thinking about the lives within it. As a massive homogeneous grid, 487 Cumberland Street lacked the freedom of expression that houses and tenements offer their residents. Where garden gnomes, flowers and window pots tell us something about the owners of houses and tenements, the exterior world is only offered curtains and blinds from the high-rise. So, as a symbol of the dwellers' self-expression and freedom of choice, he collected old toothbrushes from the building's residents. As little icons of design, they're chosen on the basis of colour and style, and disregarded when their functional performance is past its peak. As discriminate objects, they are a window to the owner. Mounted onto his metre square board, they became a memorial to both their design and to their owners. Inadvertently, they became a memorial to the high-rise as a living space.

Later Peter noticed a single flat that framed its windows with fairy lights, and began to think about how illuminating the entire building would change its aesthetic quality. But before then, he designed a memorial park. During this process, Peter moved into one of the condemned tower blocks to experience life from within. As an architect in the making, he recognised the need for regeneration, but not the desire to wipe the slate clean. With no trace or physical memory of the Gorbals' tenements, Peter began searching for the history of this space in old archives and maps (manor houses and farmland preceded the tenements, and a leper hospital preceded them). Knowing the high-rises were next on the demolition list, he wanted to create a physical memorial to them. Whilst this would mark the community the high-rises housed, it would also serve to forge a bridge between the old and new Gorbals. Never built, it included towers that mapped out an imagined route one person would take from the street to their flat within 487 Cumberland Street. And a massive space cut out in the ground in which one high-rise flat would be buried: with a glass roof, this flat could be walked over; like a grave it would mark the passing of time and the changing environment.

In 2003 the *Highlights* project began. This was a response to both the physical and communal regeneration of the Gorbals; it was also an attempt to bind these two elements together. Culminating in a two week light installation which turned the face of 487 Cumberland Street into what one passer-by described as a massive 1970s computer, the project began with 16 Gorbals children between seven and 11 years old and one depopulated tower block. Secondary school art students from the Gorbals, who attend Holyrood, King's Park and Shawlands Academy, were also invited to design images and sequences for the light display, but the majority of the development process happened with the 16 primary school pupils.

In association with GAP (Gorbals Arts Project), a series of workshops were designed to ensure that the children took an active role in the creation of an art installation that would impact on their community's space and on their community's sense of itself. Firstly, each of them was equipped with a disposable camera, and taken to explore and photograph the empty building. The trip yielded interesting results: a series of child's eye views of and from the building.

Observing the children negotiate the space enforced the fundaments upon which the project was based: regeneration affects people in ways that aren't quantified. One of the younger girls, on seeing the vacated homes, worried that the occupants would now be homeless, without the means to buy another flat. A nine-year-old boy explained to her in detail the process by which each tenant would be offered potential homes before being ultimately ejected from this one. Would, I wondered, a child from Glasgow's leafier suburbs understand so precisely the impact

of blowing up a building? If the girl hadn't voiced her concerns would she have carried that fear around with her, worried and scared that her family could be the next to randomly lose their home? Such a landscape forces even children to understand the politics of place.

The children's photographs were subsequently used as inspiration for their designs for the light installation: the hat from a *South Park* poster left on a wall, a rocking chair to refill the empty space, wallpaper patterns, a boot. The photographs themselves were finally displayed on 40 cubes exhibited in a community centre during the fortnight of illumination. Placed in a tower-like structure that represented the high-rise, the cubes appeared as the structure's windows, they were removable and interchangeable; an inside-out of the space as the children perceived and documented it.

Edwin Morgan, Scotland's Makar and Glasgow's then Poet Laureate, has written about Glasgow and its residents throughout his career. Processes of regeneration and change have often been explored in his poetry. We asked him to write a poem for *Highlights* and for the Gorbals people—the result was "Old Gorbals". Some sequences in the light display were influenced by this poem: a death-like figure in a long cloak 20 storeys tall turned his head and looked across the city and turned away again.

ide the vacated homes
87 Cumberland Street,
rbals. Photographs taken
ocal schoolchildren for the
hlights project, 2003.

Highlights, 2004. Photo: Anthony O'Doibhailen.

lamp placed in each window of the west-facing side of the building, each lamp individually connected to dimmer racks that were, in turn, connected to a central control panel. For one week, Peter programmed the panel to generate the images and sequences designed for *Highlights*: every frame individually programmed to animate the building. On 25 March 2004 the project moved into its final stage: each night for 14 days, the light sequences repeated themselves for two hours, illuminating, celebrating and commemorating the end of a Gorbals era.

IDENTITY AND REGENERATION

The Gorbals is currently undergoing its third facelift in less than 200 years. First there were the tenements. They housed the Gorbals' growing community; and when they became run down, over-populated and under-sanitised, they were labelled slum and razed to the ground. Then came the glorious new dawn: the ultimate modern experience wrapped up in one towering package. The high-rises. An ingenious way to resolve all the area's housing problems. Except they did not, because the plan to create glittering new homes with all mod cons failed to include the amenities a community pivots around. Pubs and clubs and shops were ripped out with the tenements to make way for these giant structures and were never truly replaced. The utopia became a strange kind of wasteland—buildings dropped from the sky onto barren plains. Eventually, those buildings became damp: their air moist with condensation, and many of them fell, like their predecessors, into disrepair.

Communal identity is marked by the double binds of belonging and ownership. Buildings and roads and parks transform a barren landscape into a social space, but it is people who, in the act of belonging to somewhere (connecting a visual landscape to an emotional one), transform space into place. This process develops and deepens over time, forging a sense of communal ownership. But the concept of belonging is essentially illusory (subject to the imagination), and regeneration reminds us of that.

Then there were the sequences created by Peter: the whole building lit up, then one by one the lights went out, a wave of light that swept across the building and swept back, lights changing frequency so that each pulsed to its own rhythm—each light, an ode to those who occupied its room. 23 storeys of illumination. The more playful game of space invaders, the falling snow, the question mark.

And then the theory became practice: the high-rise was illuminated with 220 500-watt spotlamps. One

If the visual landscape acts as a shorthand to the social one, then regeneration disrupts this by vigorously changing the visual landscape. And, because it is urban planners and architects that decide what the new facade of a space will look like, the process appears to disempower the community itself. By sweeping aside the visual shorthand to its history, regeneration creates an interstice between the appearance of a space and the emotional resonance of it as a place. This disruption may be transitory, but it does reinforce the underlying lack of control that the people have over the perception of their community and, ultimately, their own homes.

The fact that the tenements were wiped out with no trace and without any attempt to commemorate their passing bolstered the negative associations surrounding them. And whilst commemorating or celebrating the demise of tenement living may not have prevented the negative perception of them, it would perhaps have challenged the discursive construction of the Gorbals as a place where poverty, slum living and violence prevailed. The flip side, rarely acknowledged, is that Gorbals is where wave upon wave of immigrants first called Scotland 'home'. Irish, Russian, Indian and Jewish communities all bustled in this melting pot, establishing roots and businesses, creating new lives and identities. Gorbals was—and for many of today's refugees, still is—a place from which to seek your fortune, turn over a new leaf, start a newer, safer life. For them it's not about violence and degeneration, but about hope and regeneration.

For the Gorbals, the sense in which outside sources enforce a shape and identity onto the community is linguistic as well as physical. Through books, photography and reportage, the Gorbals has become a notorious place. So much so that it is rarely referred to by its proper name alone: Gorbals. 'The Gorbals' became Glasgow's synonym for violence, slums and poverty. The current regeneration process, whether consciously or not, has sought to redefine both the linguistic and physical identity of Gorbals. Renaming it 'New Gorbals', its name now imposes a shiny reinvigoration onto it. Nevertheless, its new title remains tied to its past: New Gorbals has, by and large, become 'The New Gorbals', so, rather than shunning the definite article and the negative connotations it attaches to the place, it both subverts and contains them.

Whilst the physical and linguistic regeneration of the Gorbals changes the look and feel of the space, it also involves a level of repopulation: many old Gorbals families are re-housed out-with the Gorbals, and new people buy and invest in the area. Each new generation develops out of a relationship with preceding generations—this is problematic in a place that's wiping out much of its history. Remembering the people and places of old Gorbals is just as integral to building the future as redesigning the lived environment, and that is something architects and urban planners cannot do alone. An interstice exists between what makes a space materially successful and what makes a community identify itself as such. It is within this space, this potential void, that the impact of art in regeneration comes: in the gap between the physical and the felt worlds, where the borders of both can be negotiated and interlinked.

COMMEMORATION

The *Highlights* project negotiated the borders of physical and emotional identity and, in some way attempted to bridge the gap that regeneration creates.

By getting the younger generation involved in the design of light sequences, the project tried to negotiate the relationship between physical space and the intellectual sense of belonging to a community. In many respects this aspect of the project reinforced popular motifs linked to the Gorbals—one girl designed a shoe as part of the sequence, actively alluding to the Oscar Marzaroli image of three young boys in their mothers' high heels, whilst another used a heart, which points to the popular belief that part of St Valentine's remains are in the church of Blessed St John Duns Scotus. Others found new associations, or took as their influence the high-rise experience itself.

Whilst constructing images which reflected their identity as Gorbals people was a relatively simple process, it served a more complex role: to bridge the emotional and physical concepts of the Gorbals by transforming the materiality of the high-rise into an animation of their concepts of identity. And, as the physical landscape is drastically changed by demolishing high-rises, the bridge was doubled by binding notions of identity up with the regeneration process. In this sense the project did not alter the fate of the building, but it did—like a palimpsest—reinscribed the building (and, by association the visual and emotional landscape) with a positive memory of its demise. •

DEUS EX MACHINA

THE DEMAND for standardisation is nothing new. The story of Procrustes comes to us via the heroic deeds of Theseus. Procrustes' predilection involved guests spending the night in his wondrous bed. No ordinary bed, this one demanded physical uniformity. Each sleeper was required to meet its dimensions exactly. So a short guest, according to Procrustean logic, necessitated hammering and stretching into shape, while a tall guest would lose his legs in Procrustes' pursuit of perfection. A strange, pre-Vitruvian man, this.

IN LANGUAGE THERE ARE ONLY DIFFERENCES [1]

The urge to categorise, to pigeonhole, to standardise our existence is ultimately defeated when it comes to language. The differences de Saussure points to are not between one language and another, but are part of an internal tension: "Within the same language, all words used to express related ideas limit each other reciprocally." [2] Definition not by what something is, then, but by what it is not.

There is a longstanding desire to re-enter a mythical Golden Age in which sameness exists as the norm — a naturally occurring homogeneity free from the accusations of ethnic cleansing or even 'gentrification'. This brief period, for the great Western religions, ends in Babel.

Behold, the people is one, and they have all one language; and this they begin to do: and now nothing will be restrained from them, which they have imagined to do. [3]

God's response is clear and, characteristically, dramatic. His 'final solution' for a people building the first skyscraper in order to meet their maker, is to divide them irrevocably through the punishment of multiple languages. From this point on, we are destined to fear difference. The rationale for the 'curse' is to divert humanity's ability to assimilate new ideas through the distractions of petty in-fighting and clan-like hatreds. Gone forever are the days of harmony and understanding, replaced with rivalry and discrimination. The original Ground Zero: an aspirational city shot down not by domestic aircraft but by Heaven-sent fire and brimstone.

David Cotterrell, Visualisation of The Debating Society, St Francis Centre, Cumberland Street, Gorbals, 2006. Courtesy the artist.

Borges' "The Library of Babel" reveals the universe as a potentially infinite collection of seemingly meaningless books. Untold generations have lived out their existence in the library, each man charged with a 'hexagon' filled with indecipherable texts. There exists no catalogue of catalogues, no divine key with which to read the scriptures. Over the centuries, men have launched various efforts to discover the 'truth' concealed in their universe, but none have succeeded. The death of a librarian is marked by the throwing of the corpse over the edge of his hexagon — falling forever through the airshafts, the body decomposing as it moves.

"By the end of the twenty-first century, between 50 to 90 per cent of current languages will have become 'extinct'."

Language is experienced as a riddle to be solved: its potential solution offers the promise of a kind of human omnipotence. De Saussure's assertion that without language, thought exists as a nebulous, indistinct form, is echoed by Foucault:

Because he is an empirico-transcendental doublet, man is also the locus of misunderstanding — of misunderstanding that constantly exposes his thought to the risk of being swamped by his own being, and also enables him to recover his integrity on the basis of what eludes him. [4]

Our languages define our identities. We are gendered, aged, named, welcomed and rejected by them, native speaker or asylum seeker. They tell us who we are, who we are not, and how we fit in to the larger schema of our civilisations. Foucalt asks how man can

… be the subject of a language that for thousands of years has been formed without him, a language whose organisation escapes him, whose meaning sleeps an almost invincible sleep in the words he [uses], and within which he is obliged to lodge his speech and thought, as though they were doing no more than animate?

Like Borges' librarians seeking their answers, or Babel's engineers aiming skyward, periodic attempts to rise above our pawn-like status as language users

1
de Saussure, Ferdinand, *Course in General Linguistics*, W Baskin trans., London: McGraw Hill, 1966, p.120.

2
de Saussure, *Course in General Linguistics*, p.116.

3
Genesis 11.6, *The Holy Bible*, King James Version, 1616.

4
Foucault, Michel, *The Order of Things*, London: Routledge Classics, 2002 (first edition 1966), pp.351–352.

are to be expected; taking control of language, reining it in and tidying it up a bit.

The early fifteenth century rise of Chancery Standard English (the 'style' used by London-based scribes) was a bid to develop a 'colourless' tongue, free from the distinctive dialects throughout the rest of Britain. But Chancery Standard contained its own anomalies, which marked it rather clearly as a southern vernacular. The Enlightenment voraciously embraced the standardisation and classification of everything it encountered and, in 1712, Jonathan Swift proposed an overhaul of the English language, which could permanently set the rules and regulations for correct usage:

But what I have most at Heart is, that some Method should be thought on for ascertaining and fixing our Language for ever, after such Alterations are made in it as shall be thought requisite. For I am of Opinion, that it is better a Language should not be wholly perfect, that it should be perpetually changing; and we must give over at one Time, or at length infallibly change for the worse.[5]

Swift's interest in hermetically sealing a living language invites comparison with the Victorian collector's obsession with procuring rare species of butterfly: the act of capturing and fixing the subject inevitably kills it.

Nathaniel Bailey, the British lexicographer who published his *Universal Etymological English Dictionary* in 1721, was not the first to construct an English dictionary, but his effort in the application of a consistent etymology influenced Samuel Johnson who, in 1755, published *A Dictionary of the English Language*. Many of Johnson's 42,773 definitions are unashamedly subjective and satiric, with 'lexicographer' defined as "a writer of dictionaries, a harmless drudge". His definition of 'oats' belies the overbearing confidence of an age of southern superiority: "a grain which in England is generally given to horses, but in Scotland supports the people".[6]

A major shift in the perception of English came with the publication of the *Oxford English Dictionary* in 1933. Here, for the first time, was an acknowledgement of the language as evolving and mutable—words obsolete, archaic and technical, as well as those classed as dialect or slang were included. The impetus for the dictionary was the formation in

1857 of the Kafkaesque-sounding 'Unregistered Words Committee', which aimed to locate and attach meaning to words previously undefined. By the end of 2005, the *OED* had compiled and made public definitions for over 300,000 words.[7]

In 1887, Dr Ludovic Lazarus Zamenhof published his *Lingvo internacia*. Zamenhof's Esperanto was to be a unifying force: a constructed, rationalised language, which would ultimately lead to a peaceful and regularised society through its development of a single speech currency. Back to Babel. But this well-intentioned effort is a limp substitute for the subtleties or complexities of naturally evolved dialect. Entering 'minute' in an Esperanto online dictionary gives us the definition of "minut/o = minute".[8] No allowance is made for the multiple meanings offered the word in English: minute as something very small, a coin, something we do in a meeting, etc.. There are no definitions for 'conductor', 'bass', 'treble' or 'clef', though 'violin' is represented as 'violon', for all the good it might do an Esperanto orchestra ('orkestr/o').

D EVOLUTION OF D ENG LNGWIJ [9]

English is a work in progress. While some vernacular dialects are subsumed by more popular modes of expression, new means of communication flourish. The advent of cheap text messaging services has enabled the development of a new, youth-oriented shorthand. Website 'txt' dictionaries abound—even the Collins publishing house are in on the act, with some rather hip deconstruction, though no phrasing translation system as yet.[10] The creation of 'new' pronouns, or ones previously used only in isolated communities, like 'you all', 'y'all', 'all y'all', 'yiz', 'youse', and 'you lot', suggests the rebelliousness of youth.[11] The need to make a mark as an adult is at the heart of much 'New Speak'—there's nothing quite like an oblique, ultra specialised language to define a teenager's posse. But apart from the urge to be different, these new pronouns actually help to bridge the gap left by our collective rejection of subject-specific pronouns like 'thee', 'thou', 'thy' and the more formal 'you'.

For many non-American English speakers, 'z' represents the creeping spectre of cultural imperialism. Electing to spell 'with an s' has become something of a quiet, defiant stance—a way of rejecting things American in favour of a more British demeanour. But historically, Britain accepted the use

5
Swift, Jonathan, "A Proposal for Correcting, Improving and Ascertaining the English Tongue", 1712, www.newark. rutgers.edu/~jlynch/Texts/proposal.html, accessed 24 March 2006.

6
www.wikipedia.org/wiki/A_Dictionary_of_the_English_Language, accessed 22 March 2006.

7
en.wikipedia.org/wiki/Oxford_English_Dictionary, accessed 6 April 2006.

8
wwwtios.cs.utwente.nl, accessed 2 April 2006.

9
www.transl8it.com/cgi-win/index.pl?convertPL, accessed 3 April 2006.

10
www.collins.co.uk/wordexchange/ Sections/TextingWords.aspx?pg=11, accessed 3 April 2006.

11
Hogg, R, "The Standardization of English", 2000, www.phon.uclac.uk/home/dick/SEHogg.htm, accessed 29 March 2006.

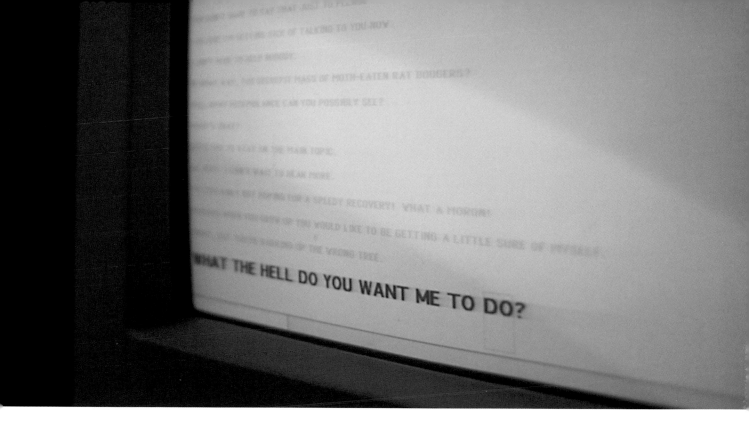

WHAT THE HELL DO YOU WANT ME TO DO?

of both consonants interchangeably, and it wasn't until Noah Webster's attempt to create a standardised American English in 1806 that a preference for 'z' was declared.[12] The Webster lexicon elected for a number of definitive spellings: removal of 'u' in words like humour and the reversal of 're' to 'er' in words like theatre. But again, it was only after American English had declared its preferences that non-American English resolutely sat down on the opposite fence.

The metatextual world, image saturated and full of hyperlinks, offers users the opportunity to view, define and edit new codifications for many fast-evolving languages. *OED* online provides a lineage of preceding volumes for direct comparison. It has renewable pages that can update you on recently admitted words. Wikipedia is now one of the most popular websites accessed on the Internet, and is distinguished by its reliance on contributions from users. Here, the democratic process is pushed to its limits, with many pages dealing with issues like abortion and Intelligent Design hotly disputed and, in some cases, sabotaged, by those with opposing views. The Urban Dictionary also allows users the ability to develop their own definitions of 'new' words, and is a great resource when looking for the roots of 'chav', 'pikie' or 'brokeback' (anything of questionable

masculinity: a brokeback man-purse, for example).[13] Again, the democratic urge comes up against issues of freedom of speech, with definitions as 'humorous' as dead nigger jokes littered throughout the site.

Neal Stephenson's *Snow Crash*, 1992, reveals a late twentieth century America in chaos. Hyperinflation and the demise of central government have led to the privatisation of most of the country, and the Metaverse, a sort of virtual reality successor to the Internet, allows people to play out their existence via online avatars. The recent glut of MMORPGs (massively multiple player online role-playing games) owes a great debt to Stephenson, with *Second Life* and *Uru* both inspired by his Metaverse. The zeal with which these games have been embraced by players, coupled with the programs' ability to offer new modes of expression to users who create avatars quite different to their 'real' personalities, evidences an evolving sense of self, and with it, a new use of language.

As our physical world is usurped by the growth of virtual space in the form of communication technologies, our range of choices for everything from languages to supermarkets is being reduced. Over the past decade, Hollywood has been concentrating its efforts on the development of films for international

David Cotterrell, *TDS (after Joseph Weisenbaum)*, early prototype using custom software and sound, 2002. Courtesy the artist.

12
www.askoxford.com/ asktheexperts/faq/ aboutspelling/ize?view=get, accessed 30 March 2006.

13
www.urbandictionary.com, accessed 6 April 2006.

audiences: sparse, easily translated dialogue, with story lines that deliver a minimum of offence to other cultural mores characterise this new type of Blockbuster. Think of the increasingly insipid *Star Wars* franchise, or the now *de rigueur* inclusion of martial arts inspired fight sequences in everything from *The Matrix* to *Charlie's Angels: Full Throttle*.

The code written for everything from MMORPGs to word processors continues the journey of English, both as a spoken and written language. Like a new Wild West, this is an area as yet unregulated: these languages are full of coding anomalies and idiosyncrasies. The development of XML, or Extensible Markup Language, has enabled the use of a metalanguage, which can describe other languages. Perhaps here we are starting to come closer to Borges' catalogue of catalogues?

A LANGUAGE IS A DIALECT WITH AN ARMY [14]

Estimates suggest there are approximately 6,000 known languages spoken throughout the world today. 2,000 known languages are currently spoken on the African continent.[15] But with English, French, Spanish and Arabic the official languages of two thirds of the world's nation states, the survival rate for less popular idioms is low. In China, Mandarin is outstripping Cantonese as the first choice for foreign communications, and Cantonese is openly

acknowledged to be a 'dying' language. By the end of the twenty-first century, UNESCO estimates that between 50 to 90 per cent of current languages will have become 'extinct'. Languages have an acknowledged 'lifespan' and this is not a new phenomenon, but the widespread and fast-paced subjugation of language we are today presented with has a great deal to do with an unspoken interest in development of cost-effective homogenised markets. The Yiddish linguistic community has long proclaimed, "A language is a dialect with an army". To the victor the spoils: the erasure of difference.

The spread of global capitalism is slowly eroding choice. With multinational conglomerates overtaking nation states as the arbiters of freedom and individuality, the limitless options suggested by the spin of new media and information technologies are not the reality of a New World Order in which the unique is usurped by the uniform. For difference to continue to exist, it must be cost effective, it must be bought in bulk.

Language is not complete in any speaker; it exists perfectly only within a collectivity [16]

This systemic urge to create uniformity from difference is challenged by much of David Cotterrell's work. He deliberately enlists off the shelf technologies to create works that subvert their original design

14
Yiddish proverb, source disputed.

15
Online Atlas of the Word's Languages in Danger of Disappearing, http://portal unesco.org/, accessed 5 Ap 2006.

16
de Saussure, *Course in General Linguistics*, p.14.

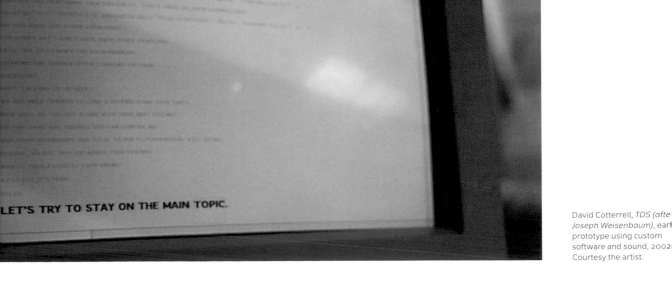

David Cotterrell, *TDS (afte Joseph Weisenbaum)*, ear prototype using custom software and sound, 2002 Courtesy the artist.

LET'S TRY TO STAY ON THE MAIN TOPIC.

use. *The Debating Society* deals with a lexicon of specialisation—the Glaswegian 'patter' spoken in the Gorbals. Using five computers, state of the art software and bespoke programming, the project acts as a reflection of the vernacular speech of a neighbourhood in transition. But there is more to this work than a simple mirroring of people and the area they live in: *The Debating Society* extends discussion about the nature of choice, hierarchy, difference and independent thought. Cotterrell's computers work in real time, self-selecting words and meanings in the ongoing evolution of a potentially limitless five-way conversation. Local voices recorded during chats most often in a sitting room are reassembled as sonic groupings and uploaded as tri–bi and uni-grams, as in, "The elision in Jane's speech is represented by 'dya' for 'do you', which occurs in her most frequent expression, 'dya know what I mean?'"[17]

Cotterrell's work exists as five distinct voices, each programmed with a set of 'preferences' that make up a prototypical personality. Artificially intelligent in the sense that the programmes are able to self-select information, the voices carry on an endless banter of their own creation. Each program bolts together phrases in response to information received from one or several of the other programs attempting the same task. Unpredictability has been predicted and accounted for—using shifting probabilities based on both internal logic and information received externally, Cotterrell's programs demonstrate innovative responses, which may at times seem 'out of character' to those who know them well.

What must I be, I who think and who am my thought, in order to be what I do not think, in order for my thought to be what I am not?[18]

Foucault's treatment of Descartes' *"cogito ergo sum"* suggests that once the 'I' is established, there are to be more questions than answers. For Cotterrell, the establishment of a forum in which non-humans are allowed the luxury of thought-based language is an intriguing possibility.

Cotterrell's practice finds interest in both the nature and mechanics of intelligence. Illusions of intelligence reflect back on themselves as each computer attempts discussion with one or more of the others— the disturbing, hyperreal image caught by a lens filming a monitor reveals the limitations of this closed system. This is perhaps an inevitable feedback loop, but equally, this is an introduction to new possibilities.

The Debating Society is a work that seeks to explore the nature of thought, and by necessity, language. Condillac's sensitive statue, made of marble, but possessing a soul, comes to understand the world around it through the evolution of its senses:

A whiff of jasmine is the start of the statue's biography; for one moment there is nothing but this odour in the whole universe—or, to be more accurate, this odour is the universe ... the consciousness of being the odour of carnation and of having been the odour of jasmine, the notion of the I.[19]

Cogito. Like Condillac's statue, Cotterrell's machines have an intelligence that exists in a limited domain. Here, there is a limited range of parameters, a limited vocabulary from which to select and, perhaps most importantly, as in Babel, the finite intelligence of the programmer.

Like the *Deus ex Machina*, the ancient Greek theatrical device in which, literally, 'God descends from the crane' in an unlikely, perhaps slightly ostentatious, manner to resolve a problem, *The Debating Society* lands in the Gorbals. This endeavour offers past and future residents of the area something unique to them. The Glaswegian 'patter' is now found on novelty mugs in the town centre. Being Scottish can be big business. Books given at Christmas, destined for the loo, work to translate the dialect in a humorous fashion. Here, in response, is a living lexicon of real voices, augmented and made unreal by the very technology that threatens the difference the 'patter' represents. This work is externally updatable—this is not the freeze-dried legacy proposed by Swift or Johnson.

If the changes we fear be thus irresistible, what remains but to acquiesce with silence, as in the other insurmountable distresses of humanity? It remains that we retard what we cannot repel, that we palliate what we cannot cure. Life may be lengthened by care, though death cannot be ultimately defeated: tongues, like governments, have a natural tendency to degeneration; we have long preserved our constitution, let us make some struggles for our language.[20]

"Palliate" the death-throes of the English language? Now there's a thought. ●

17
Fraser, M, "Speech Synthesis with the Gorbals Jane Voice", Edinburgh: Centre for Speech Technology, University of Edinburgh, 2003.

18
Foucalt, *The Order of Things*, p.354.

19
Borges, Jorge Luis, "Two Metaphysical Beings", in *The Book of Imaginary Beings*, NT di Giovanni trans., London: Random House, 2002 (first edition 1967), pp.144–145.

20
Johnson, Samuel, *Preface to A Dictionary of the English Language*, 1755.

CULTIVATED WILDERNESS

All good things are wild and free.[1]

THE TERM wilderness calls to mind uncultivated land, virginal territory untouched by human hands. It has the connotation of being slightly dangerous, foreboding, and unpredictable. If one goes into the wild there is always the chance of not making it out, for it is the place where natural forces preside over mankind, where animal presides over human. Wild or untamed nature has been an abiding theme in literature and the arts for centuries, from the poems of Emerson and Wordsworth to the Swiss Family Robinson.

The idea of cultivation is seemingly anathema to wilderness, which signals a pristine, raw state, unfettered by human intervention. In this sense the wild also connects to political ideology. What price comes with the cultivation and colonisation of land? The idea of the indigenous, be it plants, animals, or people, is relevant here. Today it is difficult to find anything authentic. The idea of origins and the impossibility of pure ethnicity are concepts that have been problematised by many postmodern and postcolonial theorists.[2] Is it possible to cultivate indigenousness? How can the wild be used as a means of cultivation? The terms 'wilderness' and 'cultivation' seem strangely at odds in the first instance, but perhaps less so in the heterotopic space of the city.

The notion of converting urban wilderness into useful public sites is a current one in British policy. The United Kingdom is known for hosting a plenitude of such barren sites given the extent and history of its industrial activity. With the decline of heavy industry, many UK cities are being reconceived, gentrified and subsequently rebranded.[3] Britain's current policy aims to build 60 per cent of new housing developments on brownfield sites, and Glasgow is no exception to this rule.[4] With the decline of the shipbuilding and steel industries in the last century, derelict areas such as the Docklands are being transformed into luxury residences and shops.[5]

Cultivated Wilderness is a project created by artist Matt Baker in collaboration with Sans façon (a collaborative practice between environmental artist, Tristan Surtees, and architect, Charles Blanc), as part of The Artworks Programme in the Gorbals.[6] Its

"What price comes with the cultivation and colonisation of land?"

physical incarnation consists of a 120-metre stainless steel serpentine trellis containing indigenous weeds and plants, which forms a border between what is now called The Rose Garden and a new social housing development around Queen Elizabeth Square. *Cultivated Wilderness* runs alongside The Rose Garden, a square of green land, which was formerly known as the Gorbals Burial Ground. This was established in the eighteenth century in what was then the periphery of the town. As the population and size of the Gorbals village grew, the burial ground occupied a more central location, and was eventually turned into a park.[7]

Cultivated Wilderness is much more than a serpentine trellis or boundary. Ideologically, it represents the result of the artists' abolition of an ill-fated plan of the developers to build a two and a half metre high yellow brick wall, as well as the outcome of collaboration on a number of levels and the possibility for sustainable public art. Rather than a monumental or spectacular intervention, *Cultivated Wilderness*, similar to other projects in The Artworks Programme, represents a subtle and modest approach to urban change.[8]

Baker is an artist who works mainly in response to sites, ranging from inner city urban locations to remote landscapes. He says his work is interested in the way that "memory and identity can inform the spaces that we inhabit".[9] His practice ranges from responding to public contexts in the form of a temporary event or installation to permanent sculpture, or at a strategic level, for example his role as Lead Artist of The Artworks Programme. His sculptural work often engages with the human figure.[10] Baker studied architecture and from 1998 to 2002 he worked as part of the Heisenberg studio collective, a partnership with architect Dan Dubowitz. Like Sans façon, Heisenberg existed to find new ways of working with the public beyond what was available to either practitioner through the usual channels in their roles as artist or architect. A concentration on action or activity in forgotten places in the city was central to Heisenberg's practice.

1
Thoreau, Henry David (1817–1862).

2
Homi Bhabha, Stuart Hall, Gayatri Chakravorty Spivak and bell hooks, among others.

3
e.g. Liverpool's Albert Docks, Manchester and Gateshead.

4
See http://www.urbanmines. org.uk. They define a brownfield site as "any land or premises which has been previously used or developed and is not currently fully in use, although it may be partially occupied or utilised." *Journal for Environmental Planning and Management*, vol. 43, no. 1, January 2000, pp. 49–69. *Cultivated Wilderness* was funded through a brownfield grant to the developer to assist in overcoming 'problems' left on site from previous uses.

5
The Albert Docks in Liverpool and Docklands in London are among the many other British industrial areas to have been gentrified.

6
The artists would like to acknowledge the title of Paul Shepheard's *The Cultivated Wilderness*, Cambridge, MA: MIT Press, 1997.

7
Tipton, Gemma, unpublished essay, July 2004.

8
e.g. Daphne Wright's *Home Ornaments* and Kenny Hunter's *Untitled. Girl With Rucksack*.

9
http://www.mattbaker.org.uk.

10
e.g. *Journeyman*, a project during Glasgow's City of Architecture and Design festival in 1999, consisted of ten installation works inserted into overlooked spaces in the city. The project focuses on sites such as the Winter Gardens, Kirkhaven, and the Springburn Public Halls, which played roles in significant moments in Glasgow's history.

Research phto: tree eating fence. Photo: Charles Blanc.

Sans façon, *Cultivated Wilderness*: parallel trellises weave over existing boundary wall to form seating niches. 2005. Photo: Charles Blanc.

11
Sans façon information booklet, December 2001, unpaginated.

12
See Marc Augé, *Non-places: Introduction to an Anthropology of Supermodernity*, John Howe trans., London: Verso, 1994.

13
In this aspect they work similarly to curatorial or cultural agencies, for example Artangel in the UK, or Public Art Fund in New York. See http://www.artangel.org.uk; James Lingwood and Michael Morris, *Off Limits: 40 Artangel Projects*, London: Merrell, 2002; http://www.publicartfund.org; and Tom Eccles, Anne Wehr and Jeffrey Kastner, *PLOP: Recent Projects of the Public Art Fund*, New York: Merrell, 2004.

14
Wentworth's *Making Do and Getting By*, begun 1974, is an ongoing photographic ode to this London neighbourhood. See *Richard Wentworth*, London: Tate Publishing, 2005.

Baker invited Sans façon to participate in the project. Surtees and Blanc began working together in 1998 out of a similar desire to expand a dialogue between disciplines. Their practice often consists of subtle, fleeting interventions in the city:

Exposing a place, its workings, and its structure, by the slightest intervention can create a shift that suddenly reveals a condition and allows the site to be seen anew. We wish to give an awareness of the otherwise hidden qualities of a site, to give it a sense of place. The places we choose to work with are mostly forgotten, left aside, mundane places seen as uninteresting economically or culturally….[11]

Sans façon's interest in mundane spaces calls to mind what the postmodern philosopher Marc Augé has termed 'non-places', or the sites where we spend increasing amounts of time in today's fast-paced culture. For example, Augé considers airport lounges, highways or superstores as 'non-places'.[12] These are eventless, transitory spaces, devoid of serious human interaction. Sans façon transform Augé's theory of peripheral 'non-places' into disused urban sites in the centre of the city.[13] They create experiences

or interventions using the spatial refuse of cities, seeking inspiration equally in what is left behind as what is present.

For example, their audio pieces *Terra Incognita*, 2004, act as alternative audio guides for unassuming spaces in Glasgow. Here the viewer/participant is incorporated into the work of art and becomes a player in the drama. Strapping on a listening device, the visitor is taken for an unconventional tour through the eyes and ears of the artists. Instead of concentrating on the spectacular or traditional historical elements of the city, they focus on the unassuming, unglamorous and forgotten spaces of urban life. The only physical manifestation of the piece is the audio disc, which can of course be infinitely reproduced. This paradigm of art practice, which one might call archaeological or anthropological, finds a context in international contemporary art, particularly in the work of Richard Wentworth and Igor and Svetlana Kopystiansky. Wentworth is an intrepid explorer of his own local neighbourhood, the quite unfashionable and seedy King's Cross area.[14] Sans façon's project has a similar ethos to Wentworth's work: both focus on the overlooked and fugitive elements of city life, which are often unspectacular in nature. Similar to Sans façon, Igor and Svetlana Kopystiansky are Russian-born artists who collaborate to investigate disused spaces and the effluvia of cities.[15] Their work almost always involves historical research and has taken place in defunct libraries and botanical gardens, which they reinvigorate through an artistic intervention. Sans façon's work fits into the context of such contemporary practice, with its focus on the history of urban sites, and the transformation of disused urban spaces.

Sans façon and Baker met when Heisenberg was working on a project in Berlin and Glasgow in 2000 called *Sounding Vessels*. Heisenberg's invitation to participate became the start of an ongoing discussion and collaboration. The three artists share an obsession with the contextual relevance of their work and the idea of art as something that happens through public interaction rather than through a studio-based practice.[16] Their discursive methodology moves beyond their triumvirate: the project for The Artworks Programme is also the result of previous discussions with the local community, as well as negotiations with the developers, the council's landscape team, architects, and to a limited degree, property purchasers.[17]

When the artists joined the project, there was a proposal in place to build a brick wall as a boundary between the park and the adjacent housing complex, and thus create a border between the public and private space. This would have involved the removal of the Old Burial Ground Wall, which almost blends into the surroundings in its unobtrusiveness. The removal of this wall, which is literally embedded in the history of the local area, seemed unnecessary to the artists, who felt that this plan was inappropriate. Their research revealed that the wall, like the city, had been morphed and altered over time. For the artists it became a symbol for 300 years of life in the Gorbals.

Baker and Sans façon stated their case to the developer and architects who were surprisingly amenable to the idea of keeping The Old Burial Ground Wall and adapting it into a new infrastructure, as long as the process did not cause them any inconvenience.[18] The team's brief then became a way to create an impenetrable barrier between the new housing development and the park without creating

Sans façon, *Stock: Muster*, bronze, cast stone and steel. Photo: Anthony O'Doibhailein.

an obstructive intervention. The resulting design consists of the stainless steel trellis, which warps and curves around the existing stone wall. Baker and Sans façon's curved trellis allows it to straddle the public park and the private housing development. It forms an almost transparent boundary, blurring the distinctions between the public and private. It creates what one might call a permeable boundary between the sites. While it is impossible to pass through or climb over, it is possible in places to crawl underneath.

The stainless steel trellis, which allows for sustainability, works well within the urban context of the site. The artists planted shrubs and foliage within the trellis which are indigenous to the local environment.[19] The idea was that the garden would not require maintenance, and would be encouraged to expand beyond the structure in time. This strategy finds its context in artworks that use nature or landscape as material, from Robert Smithson's land art to Andy Goldsworthy's environmental pieces. Permanent installations such as Smithson's *Spiral Jetty*, 1970, and Walter de Maria's *Lightning Field*, 1977, use the landscape, as well as the indigenous vegetation of their sites, for inspiration as well as material. Both

15
For more information see Svetlana Kopystiansky, *Workers Library*, Second Johannesburg Biennale, October 1997; Igor Kopystiansky, *Exhibition of Paintings*, Second Johannesburg Biennale, Johannesburg Art Gallery, October 1997; Svetlana Kopystiansky, *El Jardi*, *Barcelona, Institut Botanic Barcelona, Parc de Montjuic*, Barcelona: Institut de Cultura, Ajuntament de Barcelona, 1999; and http://fridericianum-kassel.de/kunsthalle.html.

16
Email from Matt Baker to the author, 13 January 2006.

17
Email from Matt Baker to the author, 16 January 2006.

18
The developer was Dawn Homes Ltd; the architects were Hypostyle Architects.

19
The artists gratefully acknowledge the assistance of Greg White (Loci Design) in the design and specification of the planting.

of these projects change slowly over time, as the lake and/or land erodes and evolves. *Cultivated Wilderness* finds its heritage in such projects, but transfers the ethos into the dense urban centre of Glasgow.

Baker and Sans façon, at the time of developing their project, researched the effects of plants that overgrow and meld with their structures—for example, trees that grow around fences and other street architecture, literally devouring them in time. The concept for *Cultivated Wilderness* is that the wild plants will occlude the trellis, transforming it into a dense and opaque wilderness, which eventually takes on a life force of its own, a metaphor for the heterotopic city. Thus, the artists cultivate an interstitial space beyond human control and subject to the flux of the city. Since its construction in 2004, the plants have indeed begun to overgrow the trellis. In time this will become even further overgrown and wild, occluding the view of the trellis itself.

Small bronze sculptural elements punctuate the trellis, breaking up the monotony of the structure. They were conceived as "buttons on an upholstered sofa", which contrast with the vegetation that grows up and around the trellis.[20] These are a conscious reference to the niche sculptures one finds in pleasure gardens of the Romantic tradition. Thematically they also reference graveyard art (particularly of the Scottish variety), in that the sculptural reliefs

meditate on mortality and human characteristics. Structurally the 'Lego' block appearance of the bronzes on the trellis is also a conscious parody of the modern building techniques the sculptures find as their context.[21]

The ideas implicit in *Cultivated Wilderness* may also be considered a parody of the traditional concept of pleasure gardens, where exotic plants and trees are inserted into an alien environment. This is the equivalent of enclosing animals in a zoo: it both protects and exploits its inhabitants. Botanical gardens, like zoos, create a constructed reality, which has little of nothing to do with the local or indigenous wildlife. Those such as the Royal Botanical Gardens, Kew, or the Jardin des Plantes in Paris, were creations of Victorian society, when colonialism and the expansion of empire made such collections possible. Baker and Sans façon replace the classification of the botanical garden with the untamed and unregulated in *Cultivated Wilderness*. Where pleasure gardens were meant to instil awe, their Artworks project for the Gorbals avoids the spectacular or exotic. Instead it offers a quiet intervention into the fabric of the site. Also, where the Jardin des Plantes and Botanical Gardens at Kew occupy a hermetic space outside of the entropic and untidy realm of the city, Baker and Sans façon's project locates itself within the centre of it, embracing the chaos, litter, and unhygienic elements of urban life.[22]

20
Email from Matt Baker to the author, 17 January 2006.

21
Email from Matt Baker to the author, 17 January 2006.

22
For more information on the history of hygiene and cities see Dominique Laporte, *History of Shit*, Nadia Benab and Rodophe el-Koury trans. Cambridge, MA: MIT Press, 2000.

Research photo: fenced vacant plot in central Glasgow. 20 Photo: Tristan Surtees.

In its sculptural form, *Cultivated Wilderness* provides a backdrop for human activity. Its design offers several possibilities: while it acts as a boundary, you can sit enveloped in it on the old cemetery wall, which serves as a bench transforming it into furniture in its new incarnation. In this sense, one can consider *Cultivated Wilderness* a work of 'relational art'. Coined by Nicolas Bourriaud, this term applies to art practice that is informed by artists who resist creating objects for contemplation, and rely on social interaction as the material of their aesthetics.[23] Bourriaud refers to artists who "refuse to buy into the 'slipstream of historical modernity'" and avoid repeating its forms and devices.[24] In his book he writes of relational art as "an art taking as its theoretical horizon the realm of human interactions and its social context, rather than the assertion of an independent and private symbolic space".[25]

Sans façon and Matt Baker's project for The Artworks Programme embodies the ethos of relational aesthetics. At the most basic level it provides a conversation piece. Why the curvilinear form of the trellis? A trellis is normally not shaped that way. Why those ragged and scruffy plants instead of more beautiful vegetation? One can imagine the discussions of the local community or casual passers-by. Or perhaps they don't even realise that it is a work of art. Wouldn't this be the ultimate achievement of a work of relational art? The artists left the cemetery wall to act as a seat, encouraging conversation and a casual response from the viewer. In fact, the team used S shaped Victorian love seats as inspiration for the curvilinear shape of the design. These love seats feature an infinity symbol, which poetically relates back to the idea of the weeds and plants, which will survive in perpetuity. The creation of a place to sit and contemplate or gossip subverted the brief/idea for a boundary. Instead of creating a wall that would repel, Baker and Sans façon fashioned a boundary that attracts people to linger and enjoy the site.

In this sense, *Cultivated Wilderness* represents more than its physical manifestation. It also symbolises the negotiations that occur between public artists, developers and architects, as well as the interaction of the local community, who are in fact the primary audience and users of the piece. The project will provide a platform for future generations of the Gorbals to sit on the graveyard wall and to continue to enjoy the rose garden as the city ebbs and changes over time.

Aerial view of *Cultivated Wilderness* (public space to the right and housing to the left) 2004. Photo: Anthony O'Doibhailein.

Cultivated Wilderness, though subtle and quiet in its transformative qualities, avoids being a decorative or monumental sculpture; instead it provides a necessary function, and even moves beyond this pragmatic level. What do projects such as *Cultivated Wilderness* and The Artworks Programme on the larger scale contribute to the urban fabric? Though artistically of merit and in some cases visually pleasing, what long-term impacts are they providing to their respective cities? Do per cent for art schemes pay lipservice to new social agendas, or do they really make an impact? Projects such as London's Tate Modern and Guggenheim Bilbao have made cultural regeneration a key word in current legislation around government funding of the arts. However, how much do these projects, which admittedly have a tremendous impact on the economic growth of the local community, engage or affect the local resident? Are the more grassroots, subtle interventions a more realistic method of regeneration? However they engage with visitors, either through formal, guided tours, or perhaps by walking past unaware, each work of art makes an impact on its environment and questions the role of art in our culture. Can art renew and regenerate? Should it be expected to? *Cultivated Wilderness* represents a response to such questions and an invitation for the public to respond. •

23
Bourriaud is editor of the journal *Documents sur l'art* and co-director (with Jérôme Sans) of Palais de Tokyo in Paris.

24
Bourriaud, Nicolas, *Relational Aesthetics*, Simon Pleasance, Fronza Woods, and Mathieu Copeland trans., Dijon: Les Presses du Réel, 2002, p. 14.

25
For an interesting challenge to Bourriaud's theories, see Claire Bishop, "Antagonism and Relational Aesthetics", *October*, no. 110, Fall 2004, pp. 51–79, and Liam Gillick's response to this piece, in "Letters and Responses", *October*, no. 115, Winter 2006, pp. 95–107.

Streets are a primary ingredient of urban existence. They provide the structure on which to weave the complex interactions of the architectural fabric with human organisation. At once the product of design and the locus of social practice, streets propose rich questions.[1]

THINKING OF the street brings forth a myriad of conflicting perceptions. Whether romanticised as the site of political action, demonised as the haunt of whores and teenage tearaways, or celebrated and solemnised as a host of ritual processions and parades, the street is a fundamental and yet problematic constituent of the city. Where there are streets, there are also street corners, and they have, similarly, been subject to changing perceptions. To play upon a bodily metaphor like those so often reserved for the urban condition, they are the joints of the skeleton, the linking nodes, which meet at various angles and in various configurations. Those more technologically minded may prefer to consider the corner as an interface, a common point or boundary between things or, more interestingly, able to link one location with others. As, although the corner itself is the junction of two streets, it often meets other corners and opens out a network of possibilities.

The prominence of the street corner was recognised, particularly, by the Victorians, who often decorated the corners of their buildings with sculpture, architectural embellishments or, especially for retail establishments, elaborate doorways. A heady mix of civic pride, promotion, commerce and a boasting of wealth and supposedly good taste has left a legacy of such corners in the contemporary urban environment, if at a considerable height. For a city such as Glasgow, which still prides itself on its Victorian architectural heritage, this is perhaps truer than for most. As the emphasis on the aesthetic implies, street corners were also of social consequence and, problematically, still are. The corner was once a prime meeting point for old friends or young courting couples, a playground for children, the place where neighbours would linger and have a chat whilst surveying and commenting upon the 'goings-on' in adjacent streets, and a prime location from which traders could sell their wares. Increasingly, however, the 'street', and, by association, its corners, have taken on negative connotations. Rather than playing home to a vibrant public realm, some streets are seen as stalked by shadowy figures

up to no good. Fear of the street, of being outside, particularly at night, has led to an increased divide between public and private; a divide which is, arguably, being exacerbated by the embarrassment of technological riches now available.

"The purpose of the artwork is not to bring about an ideal, utopian community."

For those wishing to reinvigorate the life of cities, streets may "propose rich questions", but they also pose significant problems. Rightly or wrongly, the demonised street corners and their shadowy inhabitants have become unpalatable and, along with the graffiti and rubbish that frequently accumulate there, are taken as evidence of the social deprivation that the regeneration of areas like the Gorbals seeks to eradicate. The deployment of public art or landscape design in urban regeneration schemes geared to change the fortunes of downtrodden areas is now almost *de rigueur*, in its re-imaging of the space it can offer an alternative experience of the place and thereby appeal to different users. The nature of that art, however, varies considerably, as does the manner in which it addresses its social and physical context.

The Glasgow-based artist Stephen Hurrel is currently creating a work for the Gorbals' Queen Elizabeth Square redevelopment. At the time of writing, the site was little more than a mound of rubble beside a substation, but when the abutting building is finished it will resemble an archetypal street corner. For a landscape designer, it lends itself to being made into a 'passing through' space, with people encouraged to walk, rather than amble, along directionally designed paths with little to distract them into lingering. Some artists may be tempted to place a large sculpture or similar artwork in the space which would, arguably, make it physically, socially and conceptually 'undwellable', inaccessible in many ways for those to whom such a space might have previously appealed. For Hurrel, however, it presents a different proposition. In pondering the changing nature of the street as a social and physical space and considering its relationship with technology, it is possible to resituate the notion of 'public art' and to argue that both the imaginative and the technological can have a key role to play in reviving truly public spaces.

1
Çelik, Zeynep, Daine Favro and Richard Ingersoll eds, *Streets: Critical Perspectives on Public Space*, Berkeley, CA: University of California Press, 1994, p.1.

Aerial view of site.

STREET CORNERS

Making a playground of every street, swarming in and out of the close-mouths, clattering up and down the stairs, moving in gangs from court to court, the children of the Gorbals made the most of a sunny day.[2]

Ironically, whilst here McArthur and Kingsley Long's *No Mean City* demonstrates the vibrancy of the Gorbals tenement-lined streets of the 1930s, the sensationalist image of a neighbourhood overrun by gangs engaging in razor fights portrayed elsewhere in this novel had significant consequences for perceptions of the Gorbals' streets. Elsewhere, the streets were portrayed in a more positive light. For example, another classic Gorbals novel, *Growing Up in the Gorbals* by Ralph Glasser, although not overlooking the unsanitary living conditions, describes the sociability and cultural diversity of the streets, with one language merging into another as people congregated around shop fronts and shared public spaces, like that around the monument that once stood at Gorbals Cross.[3] Whilst it is partly true that the streets were so attractive because the insides of the tenements were not, the communal was an unavoidable but not necessarily negative aspect of tenement life, with shared closes, privies and backcourts increasing neighbourhood conviviality. Although the experience of living in the Gorbals was undoubtedly perceived differently by inhabitants, the 'No Mean City' reputation was so prevalent that, in 1944, a ballet was devised by Arthur Bliss and somewhat incongruously set in the heart of the Gorbals slums. Entitled *Miracle of the Gorbals*, it told the 'miraculous' story of being able to find love in the "slumland community in its dark cavernous dwelling".[4] This was symptomatic of a growing fear of the streets and strangers in urban crowds that has its roots in the Victorian era and their division between public and private. The street no longer seemed a viable social or communal space and culture, alongside profound social and economic factors, has to accept its part in condemning it as such.

In order to eradicate the problems of social deprivation and, significantly, re-image the area, the Gorbals was ear-marked to become an exemplar of Modern(ist) living. After a visit to Marseilles, city councillors had become seduced by the sleek-lined minimalism of Le Corbusier and introduced a high-rise policy in Glasgow. The community was dispersed into peripheral housing estates while the Gorbals area underwent whole-scale redevelopment. Modernists tolled the death-knell for the street, which was seen as a means to get from A to B, designed as a "machine for traffic", rather than a communal, social space.[5] Nicholas Fyfe, commenting on Brasilia, the city with the infamous claim-to-fame of having been built according to Le Corbusier's principles, explains that it is "a city without 'street corner societies' where people might gossip informally and exchange information because there are no street corners and people therefore rely on more domestic and private spaces for social information".[6] Therefore, it could be said that Modernist planning and the dispersal of the long-standing Gorbals community had the combined effect of sealing the fate of communal, lively public spaces and further segregating public and private. Contrastingly, and contemporaneous with the Modernist redevelopment, Jane Jacobs, reacting against the negative perception of people hanging around on streets, was arguing that multi-functional, used streets were a vital component in building a communal city life and that this sense of community was key to promoting safety:

Most of it is ostensibly utterly trivial but the sum is not trivial at all. The sum of such casual, public contact at a local level—most of it fortuitous, most of it associated with errands, all of it metered by the person concerned and not thrust upon him by anyone—is a feeling for the public identity of people, a web of public respect and trust, and a resource in time of personal or neighbourhood need. The absence of this trust is a disaster to a city street.[7]

This sociability cannot be institutionally imposed, it has to be lived, and the want of such contact and the community it builds is seen as devastating for streets and their neighbourhoods.

These different experiences of streets, as planned, imagined and lived were theorised by the French sociologist Henri Lefebvre, who, writing in the 1970s, conceived of a "conceptual triad" when contemplating the production of space.[8] There were the "representations of space", the spaces of scientists, planners and urbanists which often dominated the "spatial practice" of everyday life which, in itself, could not be fully experienced without 'representational' or 'lived' spaces of the imagination, which were fostered and indeed sustained, against the forces of capitalist society by arts and literature. Lefebvre argued that this imaginative, lived space had the

2
McArthur, Alexander and H Kingsley Long, *No Mean City*, London: Corgi Adult Paperback, 1992, (first edition 1935), p. 10.

3
Glasser, Ralph, *Growing Up in the Gorbals*, London: Chatto and Windus, 1986.

4
As cited in Rudolph Kenna, *The Heart of the Gorbals*, Ayr: Fort Publishing, 2004, p. 95.

5
Le Corbusier, *The City of Tomorrow and its Planning*, Frederick Etchells trans., Cambridge, MA: MIT Press, 1929, p. 123.

6
Fyfe, Nick ed., *Images of the Street: Planning, Identity and Control in Public Space*, London and New York: Routledge, 1998, p. 3.

7
Jacobs, Jane, *The Death and Life of Great American Cities*, New York: Random House, 1972, p. 56.

8
Lefebvre, Henri, *The Production of Space*, D Nicholson trans., Oxford: Blackwell Publishing, 1990.

potential to unsettle the hierarchy of the everyday perceived and institutionally conceived spaces. The experience of the three spaces was linked, although neither simple nor stable, and, as Lefebvre notes, in the relationship between subject and space, the body was essential.[9] Lefebvre himself questioned "… what intervenes, what occupies the interstices between representations of space and representational spaces. A culture, perhaps? Certainly—but the word has less content than it seems to have. The work of artistic creation? No doubt…."[10] The exact nature of that artwork, however, and its relationship to physical and social context, requires further deliberation.

CORNERING COMMUNITY

This notion of an embodied experience of space and an art which subverts the rigidity of the planned environment is echoed in the work of Stephen Hurrel. In 2003 Hurrel completed *Constellation*, an artwork for the Citadel housing development in Ayr, on the west coast of Scotland. The area, once the site of a Cromwellian Citadel, castle, barracks and industrial port, was being redeveloped into a residential neighbourhood with retail and leisure facilities according to a masterplan by the then Kyle and Carrick Council and Enterprise Ayrshire, advised by London architects Patel Taylor. Hurrel's work was for Carrick Housing Association (CHA) who, within this development, built a complex of 78 modern-style flats and houses for rent in a standard, grid-like configuration. CHA was eager that the artist should engage with their tenants, who were not only moving to a new home but also an entirely new community, and try to create a talking point which might foster a sense of community.

Hurrel interviewed the new residents and found a common link in the act of travelling, which had further resonance for the site itself as it was once a port. *Constellation* comprised a series of poles, painted in colours reminiscent of the ships that once journeyed through the harbour, embedded in which were either small model landscapes or windchimes. The poles were arranged in a random order in the public spaces throughout the development and subtly referenced the configurations of stars by which mariners once navigated. In the process of making the work, Hurrel had photographed items that residents always took with them when they travelled and created postcards, themselves indicative of journeying and of

communicating about that experience, which were given to each resident. The landscapes within the poles had a resonance with these smaller items as they were something residents could look at but which would take them on a further, mental journey perhaps to far off places. The landscapes themselves were viewed through a small peephole, akin to peering into a periscope or telescope and experiencing a sense of discovery, and illuminated with a torch, which was kept in the foyer of each housing block. The experience of interacting with the poles echoed the sensory nature of the port environment which, whether through sight or sound, created the sense of being in one place but at the same time alluded to many others. In this, Hurrel recalled an earlier art event, *Zones: an audiology of the River Clyde*, which intertwined personal histories with those of the river and which heightened, as well as disturbed, sensory experience of place. Like *Zones*, *Constellation* was at once public and private: the poles were visible to all who passed through the area and yet knowledge of the landscapes and the choice to share the experience of viewing with others was reserved for the residents.

Standing on street corners and gazing up to the stars, the concept of constellation seems obvious and yet it is more involved. On one hand it implies

9
As Nicholas Fyfe has argued with reference to Glasgow poetry, the post war planning in Glasgow allowed the conceived spaces of the planners to be projected onto the concrete, lived spaces of the city and this had an impact on the imagined. Fyfe, Nick, "Contested Visions of a Modern City: Planning and Poetry in Post-War Glasgow", *Environment and Planning A*, no. 28, 1996, pp. 387–407.

10
Lefebvre, *The Production of Space*, p. 43.

11
Lacy, Suzanne ed., *Mapping the Terrain: New Genre Public Art*, Seattle: Bay Press, p.19.

12
Bourriaud, Nicholas, *Relational Aesthetics*, S Pleasance and F Woods trans., Dijon: Les Presses du Reél, 2002.

13
Bourriaud, *Relational Aesthetics*, p.14.

14
Bishop, Claire, "Antagonism and Relational Aesthetics", *October*, no.110, Fall, 2004, pp.51–79.

15
Bourriaud, *Relational Aesthetics*, p.13.

16
Bishop, "Antagonism and Relational Aesthetics", p.65.

17
Young, Iris Marion, "The Ideal of Impartiality and the Civic Public", in *Justice and the Politics of Difference*, Princeton: Princeton University Press, 1990, p.227.

predetermination, the position of the stars at the time of birth and the paths and turns of life determined by fate thereafter; on the other it suggests something altogether more random—arbitrary connections between disparate elements seen to have something shared, however tenuous. After all, stellar constellations are made by the viewer who perceives the arrangements of stars to resemble an animal or mythological character, and it is through communication and acculturation that they are commonly recognised as such. *Constellation* resonated with personal and place history, but it was left to the residents to perceive any linkages between themselves or with the artwork. In the random placement of the poles Hurrel subverted the planned, regular space of the housing scheme and through the artwork tried, imaginatively, to forge links that would enrich the lived spaces and spatial practice of everyday life. While *Constellation* was ultimately of place, it was not restricted to place, and it encouraged a looking beyond to an imaginary or real distant realm. In that it required the residents to 'enact' the work and tried to encourage these points of discussion, there was a sense of attempting to cultivate a sense of community amongst the new residents but in a way that was unforced.

In this emphasis on community engagement it is tempting to read Hurrel's art within the practice of 'new genre' public art as outlined by Suzanne Lacy: "Unlike much of what has heretofore been called public art, new genre public art—visual art that uses both traditional and non-traditional media

Stephen Hurrel, *Constellation*, Ayr, 2003.

to communicate and interact with a broad and diversified audience about issues directly relevant to their lives—is based on engagement."[11] Despite the importance of community and engagement, Hurrel's practice does not dovetail neatly within this paradigm. For Lacy, engaging the community in the process of creating a work seems to be about engendering a sense of togetherness. For Hurrel the notion of both engagement and community is more intricate. In the case of *Constellation* this was partly because there was no existing community and thus the process continues once the work is in place and as the community begins to form and engage with one another. There is no prescribed form of engagement and the purpose of the artwork is not to bring about an ideal, utopian community.

In this notion of community, Lacy's new genre public art has parallels with Nicholas Bourriaud's 'relational aesthetics', a term coined from his 1997 book of the same title in which he seeks to highlight and characterise artistic tendencies of that decade.[12] Bourriaud believes that: "The possibility of a *relational* art (an art taking as its theoretical horizon the realm of human interactions and its social context, rather than the assertion of an independent and *private* symbolic space), points to a radical upheaval of the aesthetic, cultural and political goals introduced by modern art."[13] He points to a fundamental shift in the contemporary art scene since the 1990s and advocates a critique unfettered by the shackles of Modernism and that moves beyond art as representation to art as relational. Bourriaud sees this form of practice as art establishing a direct and meaningful relationship with contemporary life and culture, albeit, mainly, from the institutional basis of the gallery. Moreover, through this engagement with the contemporary there is an attempt to actively create a community. As Claire Bishop has noted, however, Bourriaud's concept of community is built around that notion of a community as a coherent, bonded body of people to which Lacy also seems to subscribe.[14] He sees art as trying to create 'microtopias' in the present.[15] Critiquing Bourriaud's text, Bishop points out that the qualities of relationships produced in the artworks are never examined and there seems to be an assumption that all artworks that engage in this kind of dialogue are good.[16] However, there are dangers in pursuing this ideal of community, which "denies and represses social difference".[17]

In terms of public art, these varying characterisations of community are of some consequence. For, if art practice, as Lacy and Bourriaud suggest, is turning toward this engaged method it raises questions as to exactly *who* artists are trying to involve, *why* that particular group, *how* this process of engagement is being enacted and, fundamentally, whether this is worthwhile or a successful way of working. There is also a tension between the terms 'community' and 'public' in the discourse surrounding public art, where community art is generally seen as artists working with a certain group of people within a particular locale to encourage their own creativity, where aesthetic quality of the work is secondary to the process, and public art, an artist either working independently or engaging with the community to create a work which retains the artist's vision. Lacy's 'new genre' public art sits somewhere in between. The varied methods of engagement and differing opinions in exactly what the relationship between the artwork and the community should be has implications for considering exactly what form of artwork should be put in a space and to which notion of 'community', if any, that artwork should appeal.

Creating a work that will appeal to the multifaceted public is not straightforward and wading through the bureaucracy that it entails has led to, some contend, the prevalence of a "minimum basic standards" mentality, resulting in bland and generic artworks.[18] Walking through the urban environment, turning corner after corner, and repeatedly seeing similar artworks deadens experience and disinclines imagination. As Rosalyn Deutsche succinctly expressed in *Evictions*: "Critics often treat both art and the public as universal spheres that, harmonized by a common human essence, stand above the conflictual realm of atomized individuals, purely private differences, and special interests. In these cases, 'public art' … comes doubly burdened as a figure of universal accessibility."[19] Arguably this is a consequence of the regeneration and gentrification which, Neil Smith has suggested, is designed to domesticate urban space and thereby make it safe and more assured for investment.[20] Public art is a recurring feature in regeneration schemes, as in the Gorbals, and, if as Smith suggests, the goal is to make an urban space that is appealing and yet uncontroversial, then there is a danger that artworks will suffer as a result. In terms of process, Deutsche argues that including the community in the creation of the work with a

Stephen Hurrel, *Zones: An audiology of the River Clyde*, 1999.

view to creating a 'democratic', and by implication uncontroversial, work "is to presume that the task of democracy is to settle, rather than sustain, conflict".[21] This suggests that there is a need to revisit the process of creating public art, its form and the very nature and purpose of public spaces.

The corollary of this perceived deadening of public space is the increasing amount of time spent in the home, which is partly attributable to technological advancements. Although in support of the technological, Manuel Castells warned of a dystopian America where "secluded individualistic homes across an endless suburban sprawl turn inward to preserve their own logic and values. Closing their doors to the immediate surrounding environment and opening their antennas to the sounds and images of the entire galaxy."[22] More people now work from home and technology is increasingly cornering the market for shopping, travel and leisure. In this identities and communities have been dispersed, fragmented, and made more complex through technology and technoculture. Face-to-face contact has been replaced by an interface that reaches beyond the immediate space. 'Virtual Communities' have formed, drawing together constellations of people who share some common interest from all corners of the globe. The way people interact has been transformed by new media. Likewise, technology has profoundly altered the experience of public space. City streets and squares are often dominated by large screens trying to sell alternative lifestyles and luxury goods, and buildings undergoing renovation are enveloped in large and elaborate wrapping paper promising

18
Philips, Patricia C, "Out of Order: The Public Art Machine", *Artforum*, vol. 4, no. 27, December 1988, pp. 92–97.

19
Deutsche, Rosalyn, *Evictions: Art and Spatial Politics*, Cambridge, MA: MIT Press, 1996, p. 281.

20
Smith, Neil, *The New Urban Frontier: Gentrification and the Revanchist City*, London: Routledge, 1996.

21
Deutsche, *Evictions*, p. 270.

22
Castells, Manuel ed., *High Technology, Space and Society*, Beverley Hills, London, New Delhi: Sage Publications, 1985, p. 19.

Stephen Hurrel's proposal for corner site, 2005 (night-time visualisation of temporary projection system).

more comfortable shoes to tired city feet or enticing passers-by with perfumes they cannot smell. Street corners, once elaborate with sculpture, are now elaborated by neon billboards. Technology has played a key role in intensely commercialising streets and public spaces.

It is not as simple as a binary opposition between public and private, however, as, with technology, these boundaries are beginning to dissolve: via mobile phones people are permanently accessible, web-cams take intimate scenes from everyday lives and broadcast them to complete strangers, surveillance like CCTV in public spaces means that movements are forever watched and via the internet personal information and images are perpetually available. Stephen Hurrel reflected upon this in a *VideoPhoned Dialogues/Television Intervention* in Munich, 1994, where four 'videophoned-dialogues' between a man and woman were broadcast on television, unannounced. The effect was as if there had been some cross-media-cross-wiring and somehow the private had been made public.[23] The dialogues reflected upon the illogical nature of the world and also on the prevalence of media—people being filmed unawares—and, by broadcasting these into the home questioned the nature of television itself. Through television, public events can be viewed from the privacy of the home and yet, with millions doing the same, whether the act of viewing is private or public is a moot point.

Put simply, technology is a powerful force in shaping lives and modes of interaction. As WJ Mitchell has argued: "Computer networks become as fundamental

to urban life as street systems. Memory and screen space become valuable, sought-after sorts of real estate. Much of the economic, social, political and cultural actions shift into cyberspace. As a result, familiar urban design issues are up for radical reformation."[24] By extension, so are our conceptions of the nature of public art and public space.

STREETS AHEAD

In 1992 Stephen Hurrel, in collaboration with Matthew Dalziel and the local people of Wester Hailes in Edinburgh, illuminated two multi-storey flats over a five night period which coincided with the European Summit. In conjunction with the summit, buildings of 'cultural importance' such as the castle and cathedrals were being floodlit across Edinburgh to show dignitaries the best of the capital's architectural heritage. For the people of Wester Hailes, the tower blocks were of as much significance as, say, the castle in terms of their cultural identity, perhaps more so and therefore this afforded the opportunity to highlight their importance. Over 80 projections of local people commenting on the EU were screened on the facade of the blocks and thereby, through technology, the local, cultural identity was considered in relation to the wider world. Not only did this challenge preconceptions of what might be considered a building worth highlighting, but it also used technology as a means to bring people into public space and, in that space, to engage in a meaningful dialogue about personal and local identity in a more global context.[25]

Although it is tempting to berate technology as a prime cause for the dissolution of the public realm, as Hurrel's work suggests, it is perhaps worth considering what can be done by placing technology in public spaces. If it is accepted that technology plays a considerable role in shaping public life, behaviour in public spaces and modes of interaction, and if public art is truly to engage with contemporary society and communities, then it seems worthwhile considering the potential of using new media in public spaces. Lefebvre spoke of the need for an embodied appreciation of spaces and technology, as a medium, is modelled on exchange and interplay. It appeals to participants rather than simply an audience. In keeping with the disruption of the hierarchy between planned and lived spaces, interaction with technology tends to be more random and unsystematic. Rather

23
In 1971 Peter Hall carried out a similar project for *Locations Edinburgh*, devised by Alistair Mackintosh and funded by the SAC.

24
Mitchell, WJ, *City of Bits: Space, Place and Infobahn*, Cambridge, MA: MIT Press, 1995, p. 107.

25
Hurrel has also produced architectural/light-based interventions in Hobart, Tasmania (*Light and Text*, 1999), Canberra, Australia (*Activating ACTEW*, 1999) and in artworks created in conjunction with Glasgow's Year of Architecture and Design, 1999.

sen, Mark, *New Philosophy*
New Media, Cambridge,
MIT Press, 2004.

ng, Iris Marion, "The Ideal
ommunity and the Politics
fference", in *The Blackwell*
Reader, Gary Bridge
Sophie Watson eds,
rd: Blackwell Publishing,
33–434.

nett, Richard, *The*
science of the Eye: Design
Social Life of Cities,
don: Faber and Faber, p. xiii.

ovre, *The Production of*
ce, p. 26.

than seeing technology as a disembodied experience, Mark Hanson, drawing on the theories of Henri Bergson, argues that new technologies alter the very basis of sensory experience and that the convergence of media brought about by the digital age actually increases the role of the body as the selector and processor in the creation of images.[26] This positive engagement of the body with technology has been explored by Hurrel in his work *Rings*, 2004, an installation in the Buchanan Galleries shopping centre in Glasgow. The light-based installation in the shape of a coil responds to noise levels on the city streets below and therein is an interaction between body, senses and technology. This incorporation of the body emphasises the real, sensory, direct experience of the space. In a more immediate, individual installation, Hurrel placed headphones in public places in one of Glasgow's principal shopping centres. When the public placed the headphones over their ears, the soundtrack transformed their perceptions of their immediate space. Along with *Zones*, this highlights technology's potential to emphasise the sensory and embodied nature of public spaces.

As well as being able to bring people into the space and to enhance, alter or challenge their embodied and sensory perception of that place, technology also has the potential to reach beyond the geographical limits of that particular place. Whereas communities were traditionally considered to be geographically bounded groups of people, it is now recognised that multifarious forms of communities exist beyond the residential, including virtual communities. As Iris Marion Young has explained:

> The normative privileging of face-to-face relations in the ideal of community seeks to suppress difference in the sense of time and space distancing social processes, which material media facilitate and enlarge .... For all social interaction takes place over time and across space. Social desire consists in the urge to carry meaning, agency, and the effects of agency beyond the moment and beyond the place.[27]

Technology need not dissociate people from spaces but can encourage people to reconsider the purpose of public space and the nature of community. Rather than walking headlong down a street toward a centrally located sculpture or to a square with a plinth-led procession of civic dignitaries, it is perhaps time to turn the corner and encounter the unexpected.

TURNING THE CORNER

In *The Conscience of the Eye*, Richard Sennett suggests that "Our urban problem is how to revive the reality of the outside as a dimension of human experience."[28] In order to do this, however, the nature of contemporary urban communities, spaces and public art needs to be critically considered. Following Lefebvre's thinking, there is a need to revive the imagination of the outside as a means to reinvigorating life on the streets and in planned urban spaces. As, if people are responsible for the production of spaces, and thereby the city, getting people to use those spaces both physically and imaginatively is, potentially, the key to a re-engagement with urban life. Central to this is the embodied, sensory experience—the human *being* in the space, but that is not to say that it is limited to that space for, recognising the role of technology in shaping society and the potential it offers, suggests new media as a means of creating a public art that is directly in dialogue with contemporary communities and urban life. Lefebvre famously argued that "(Social) space is a (social) product."[29] If Lefebvre is right, an artwork is not enough to create a social, successful space—it needs the engagement of the community. The nature of that community and its mode of interaction, if any, with the artwork cannot, however, be forced.

Stephen Hurrel's work has explored different means of using new media to disturb and encourage a reconsideration of relationships with space. In working with communities yet to be established, he does not force a particular relationship with works or try to appeal to a particular concept of community, ideal or otherwise. His is a community-engaged practice that accepts the mutability of the social terrain. The concept of *Event: Space* is to create a place in the street that could be used for events or performances and which might incorporate new media on some level. The idea is for the space to be looked after by a local community group and so, if a work like *Event: Space* is to succeed, it is reliant upon the formation of complex networks to ensure its continuance and that it remains an open space, accepting of different, perhaps conflicting dialogues. In so doing, the street corner will hopefully once again become an area of sociability, networking, debate and chance encounters. •

THE ARCHITECTURE of Sir Basil Spence is by no means universally controversial. Despite his most productive period coinciding with an era that produced some of the most relentlessly vilified buildings in British architectural history, much of his output appears mild or inoffensive. Outside his native Scotland, Spence is best known for what is arguably the most symbolic building of Britain's post war period of reconstruction. Though massive state intervention during the 1950s and 60s may have provided unprecedented possibilities for architects to introduce modern architecture to a public previously broadly unfamiliar with it through the building of new schools, housing, hospitals and universities, it is a religious building that best represents the complexity of the hopes and aspirations of a beleaguered country considering its future.

Coventry Cathedral was the result of a 1951 architectural competition to rebuild a Gothic cathedral destroyed by Luftwaffe bombing in 1940. That competition saw Spence's proposal win through against a large number of submissions with qualities ranging from the conservative to the distinctly avant-garde. With Modern architecture's recent appearance as a topical issue in the popular consciousness following the Festival of Britain, Spence's victorious design was inevitably bound to attract much attention. Although criticism both at that time and after its completion in 1962 indicated that its architectural hybridity was too modern for the traditionalists and too traditional for the Modernists, it was generally recognised as being the best possible response to a complex situation and has nevertheless weathered a lengthy period of grudging acceptance to emerge as an icon of Britain's post war period of physical and emotional reconstruction. It is also a building in which the formal qualities, visual contrasts and intellectual dichotomies within Spence's work emerge on a large scale for the first time. Here he could indulge his interest in historical context and traditional materials in relation to the ruins of the bombed Cathedral of St Michael and satisfy his desire to employ structure to create dramatic monolithic form. His approach was one of pluralism and was somewhat at odds with the popular image of pre war Modern architecture as austere and ascetic. Spence had a strong sense of the picturesque both in terms of the context within which buildings are placed and their sculptural qualities both internally and externally, but here it is difficult to see where the art (by such luminaries as Graham Sutherland, John Piper and Elizabeth Frink) stops and the architecture begins. This is particularly clear in his own perspective drawings of the Cathedral that indicate a certain romanticism and grandiosity of intention, stated more clearly by the architect in his memoirs of the process of the Cathedral's construction:

"The curious outcome of its erasure from Glasgow's skyline is that Queen Elizabeth Square still exerts a massive influence over Glaswegian consciousness ..."

[My] first visit to the ruined Cathedral was one of the most deeply stirring and moving days I have ever spent .... As soon as I set foot on the ruined nave I felt the impact of delicate enclosure. It was still a cathedral. Instead of the beautiful wooden roof it had the skies as a vault .... I was deeply moved. I saw the old cathedral as standing clearly for the Sacrifice, one side of the Christian Faith and I knew my task was to design a new one which should stand for the Triumph of the Resurrection .... In these few moments the idea of the design was planted. In essence it has never changed.[1]

The position of Coventry Cathedral, and by extension Basil Spence, in the landscape of the post war architectural scene is a curious one. For an individual site to be so charged with emotional symbolism on a national scale is unusual and must surely present an insurmountable challenge to all but the most capable architects and whilst it is undoubtedly an impressive building that seems fit for its religious purpose, there is the nagging sense that the Cathedral is somehow a compromise. From a position more than 50 years on from its conception it is clear that Spence's approach was an accomplished, rich and unique piece of image-making by an architect just beginning to hit his stride, but is there much more evident in this and other of his buildings than mere application of tasteful style and compositional technique?

Spence's Cathedral sits chronologically at the start of two decades of fierce architectural debate and frenetic construction in Britain. In terms of the built

1
Spence, Sir Basil, *Phoenix at Coventry*, London: Geoffrey Bles, 1962, pp. 5–6.

Sir Basil Spence outside the British Pavilion at Expo 1967, in Montreal. Reproduced courtesy of RCAHMS (Sir Basil Spence Archive).

A developmental perspective drawing of Spence's Coventry Cathedral scheme dating from 1952. Reproduced courtesy of RCAHMS (Sir Basil Spence Archive).

2
Esher, Lionel, *A Broken Wave—The Rebuilding of England 1940–1980*, London: Allen Lane/Penguin, 1981, p. 66.

3
Esher, *A Broken Wave*, p. 67.

character of the majority of noteworthy buildings of this extraordinary period, Lord Manasseh provided a useful rule of thumb in 1964. Then president of the Architectural Association, he characterised the polarities of contemporary architectural discourse as being defined by the differing aesthetic and theoretical approaches of the 'Art Boys' and the 'System Boys'.[2] By this period Spence had expanded his practice from Edinburgh to open a London office and was engaged in work on one of "the plum jobs of the sixties", that of the construction of one of Britain's new universities in Sussex.[3] This major project, alongside other university commissions elsewhere, the construction of both public and commercial buildings and a variety of schemes for housing, confirmed Spence's position amongst a select group of what might now be referred to as 'celebrity' architects. Viewed as prima donnas

by those who felt industrialised building systems were the only rational, economic and even moral route to a productive process of regeneration, the likes of Spence, Ernö Goldfinger and Denys Lasdun nevertheless defined in British terms the role of the visionary artist-architect. In Spence's case a desire not to dispense with architectural tradition, an interest in indigenous materials, his early experiences in exhibition design and his heavy reliance on attractive perspective renderings (usually drawn by himself) to promote his plans marked out his stance as a poetic one. His emphatically picturesque approach provides a stark contrast when one views, for example, his work at Sussex against the more prosaic contemporary universities at York and Essex. It seems hard now to reconcile this dominant aspect of Spence's practice, and the critical response to it from many in professional architectural circles that flamboyant oratory and fine draughtsmanship might promote the atmospheric subtlety of a scheme at the expense of an intellectually rigourous design process, with the current popular Scottish view of him as a detached and brutal wrecker of cities and communities.

In Scotland, Coventry Cathedral, the new universities of the 1960s and even the controversy surrounding the construction of monumental buildings overlooking London's Royal Parks are of little consequence to the reputation of Basil Spence. For the last two decades an architect who might otherwise have been considered one of Scotland's more significant twentieth century cultural figures has been held as synonymous with the failure of high-rise social housing in the country. From an external perspective this may seem somewhat at odds with Spence's built legacy in that he designed a proportionately modest amount of housing when compared to his university, school, commercial and religious building. Indeed, what few public housing projects he did participate in were built early in his career and are uncontroversial in their style and construction. What places Spence at the heart of the painful and ongoing discourse surrounding Scotland's trouble with tower blocks is his involvement in the regeneration of the Gorbals.

In the early 1950s Glasgow, Scotland's largest city, faced enormous challenges in providing suitable housing for its inhabitants. At the time, out of the city's population of 1,085,000 people it was considered that 600,000 were occupying sub-standard housing.[4] The 1947 Town and Country Planning Act greatly extended the power of local authorities to compulsorily purchase and develop land and this cleared the way for the phenomenon of the Comprehensive Development Area (CDA). In its housing study published in 1954, Glasgow Corporation designated four large CDAs and of these identified the Hutchesontown/Gorbals area as that most desperately in need of redevelopment. This area had a particularly bad reputation for poor housing, both in terms of sanitary provision and the structural condition of its buildings. A 30 year lack of investment by private landlords and a dearth of maintenance due to the breakdown in the system of factoring had created a slum. The 1954 report was followed in 1957 by a more expansive and ambitious proposal for 29 zones of housing redevelopment with no fewer than 17 of them taking the form of CDAs. At the same time the Housing and Town Development Act

was passed to delineate the practice of population overspill from crowded inner city areas slated for redevelopment into surrounding settlements and the New Towns. This procedure was deemed necessary because the desire to reduce excessive population densities meant that less than half (around 250,000) of those in need of new homes could be catered for within Glasgow's boundaries, a situation compounded by the fact that the city's new peripheral estates at Castlemilk, Drumchapel and Easterhouse could only accommodate 100,000 inhabitants.

This plan was of enormous scope and had at the heart of its rationale situations like that facing the Gorbals. The Hutchesontown/Gorbals CDA covered an area of 111 acres and was massive by any measure. Within this area bounded by the River Clyde to the north, Waddell Street to the East, Caledonia Road

Queen Elizabeth Square under construction as seen from Camden Street, Gorbals in 1964. © Newsquest (Herald & Times). Licensor www.scran. ac.uk.

4
Smith, Ronald, *The Gorbals*, Glasgow: Glasgow City Council, 1999, p. 15.

A perspective drawing of
Queen Elizabeth Square as
seen from ground level, 1958.
Reproduced courtesy of
RCAHMS (Sir Basil Spence
Archive).

to the south and Crown Street to the west only 180 inter war council flats were to be spared demolition whilst more than 7,400 tenement dwellings were condemned and 62 commercial sites were to be moved to locations elsewhere in the city. In line with Glasgow Corporation's aspirations for population density, only 10,179 out of the 26,860 living in the affected area would be able to be re-accommodated in the proposed 3,502 new homes.[5] The Secretary of State for Scotland approved this approach in February 1957 and shortly thereafter, and to a considerable media fanfare, Spence and his then equally prominent contemporary Robert Matthew were appointed as design consultants to Glasgow's City Architect and Planner.

The Hutchesontown/Gorbals CDA was to rise from the site of the cleared slums over the course of 20 years, and in five distinct stages. The first of these stages was the tentative Hutchesontown Area A, a small preliminary group of three- and four-storey blocks containing a total of 96 maisonettes, completed in

May 1958. Designed by Glasgow Corporation architect Andrew Gardner, it is interesting that these modest dwellings went on to win that year's Saltire Award in light of the fact that Spence had received the same accolade the previous year for a series of flats at Newhaven in Edinburgh. Considering this early period in the transformation of the CDA in 1960, the architectural writer Iain Nairn captured a poignant impression of the Gorbals past, present and future;

There are far too many people living (in the old tenements) and the state of the backyards and the communal staircases with their lavatories on the half-landings are intolerable and must be altered.

However, the actual outside appearance, in other circumstances, would be applauded as a splendid piece of urban design. Parts are past repair: the worst bit of all is Hutchesontown, and here the first rehousing schemes are going on—wee maisonettes with a few trees, done by the City Architect's department, decent but a crushing come-down from the potential

5
Eunson, Eric, *The Gorbals—An Illustrated History*, Ayrshire: Stenlake, 1996, p.104.

framework for living of the old work. On the quayside much taller flats are about to go up, by Robert Matthew and by Basil Spence, which may provide the answer, though they may—through the inevitable pre-set conditions—repeat the bad features of Hutchesontown on a huge scale.[6]

Although at this stage Glasgow's planners advocated an approach of CDAs containing no more than 50 per cent high flats, there began an enthusiastic move towards them as a possible way to achieve the desired population density of 165 people per acre. The schemes for Matthew's Hutchesontown Area B and Spence's Hutchesontown Area C would have been under construction when, in 1962, Glasgow's firebrand socialist 'housing crusader' Bailie David Gibson stated that "In the next three years Glasgow's skyline will become a more attractive one to me because of the likely vision of multi-storey houses rising by the thousand …."[7] Gibson was vehemently opposed to the 1957 report's overspill policy, actively pursued a policy of high-rise construction within the city limits and, despite opposition from many quarters, did much to make Glasgow "the new 'shock city' of the Modern housing revolution".[8] Despite some overspill (between 1961 and 1975 Glasgow's population had fallen by more than 20 per cent) and Gibson's initiatives to build on gap sites, there remained within the city's boundaries a shortage of land for housing sites. Although high-rise building was not considered to have been a panacea in the late 1950s, due to the expense of construction and relatively small benefit to population density, as the 1960s wore on it came to be viewed as the solution to Glasgow's acute housing shortage. By 1968 six dwellings were being built in high-rise form to every one in low-rise, and the tower block had become an inextricable presence in the cityscape.[9]

In this hothouse period of Glaswegian redevelopment the Hutchesontown/Gorbals CDA had emblematic status. Its sheer scale, expense (the estimated cost in 1957 was £12,915,000) and much anticipated utopian nature called for a centrepiece and the Queen Elizabeth Square blocks fulfilled that role. Spence and his job architect Charles Robertson designed two 20-storey slab blocks that contained 400 maisonettes with inset communal balconies and an arcade-style shopping centre at their base with a further 42 maisonettes above. These blocks, in contrast to Matthew's Area B and the later Area D, ran parallel to the Clyde as opposed to being orientated on a north/south axis. Incidentally John Paterson, Matthew's project architect for Area B, is credited with the invention of roof-mounted floodlighting during the design process after being inspired by the work of Hieronymus Bosch. This imposing lighting effect came to be employed on many subsequent Scottish high-rises.[10]

The Queen Elizabeth Square slab blocks were to be rugged reinforced concrete monoliths on a colossal scale as yet unseen in Scotland. Despite a 1960 Glasgow Corporation Report's account of a visit to Le Corbusier's first Unite d'Habitation in 1955 concluding that such housing was "not entirely suitable" for Glasgow, the blocks had a distinctly Corbusian flavour.[11] Spence employed various motifs that are central to the form of the iconic Marseille block, including interlocking apartments accessed along internal 'streets' and the raising-up of the slabs on massive sculptural concrete 'piloti'. These buildings fitted in admirably with a fashionable contemporary discourse on social housing that was shot through with Le Corbusier's influence and sat comfortably alongside Goldfinger's slabs, Lasdun's cluster block, the LCC Architects' Department's Roehampton Estate, Alison and Peter Smithson's Golden Lane proposals and Sheffield Corporation's Park Hill. Indeed, Alison Smithson claimed that Le Corbusier's effect on architectural practitioners was such that it was generally felt that "he has had all your best ideas already, has done what you were about to do next."[12] Characteristically, Spence added his own lyrical embellishment to the scheme by claiming he wished to "civilise the tenement" and claiming to the Housing Committee that a resuscitation of working-class back green culture on the communal balconies would mean that "On Tuesdays, when all the washing's out, it'll be like a great ship in full sail!"[13] The architect's romantic and historical pretensions are evidenced further by his hope that green-fingered residents would transform the facades into modern Hanging Gardens of Babylon.[14]

Spence considered Ove Arup the "best engineer to understand the aesthetic point of view" following his lightening of the treatment of Coventry Cathedral's nave columns and vault, and appointed his firm as structural engineers.[15] Arup's Danish engineer Povl Ahm, in contrast with the solutions found at Coventry, helped Spence achieve a monolithic quality. The structure of the blocks was forcefully expressed, the huge piloti "physically and visually transmitting (their)

6
Nairn, Ian, Britain's Changing Towns, BBC, 1967, p. 52.

7
Glendinning, Miles and Stefan Methusius, Tower Block, New Haven, CT: Yale University Press, 1994, p. 220.

8
Glendinning and Methusius, Tower Block, p. 220.

9
Markus, Thomas, "Comprehensive Development and Housing, 1945–75", in Glasgow—The Forming of the City, Peter Reed ed., Edinburgh: Edinburgh University Press, 1993, p. 160.

10
Glendinning and Methusius, Tower Block, p. 169.

11
Markus, "Comprehensive Development and Housing, 1945-75", p. 158.

12
Jencks, Charles, Movements in Modern Architecture, London: Penguin Books, 1973, p. 259.

13
Edwards, Brian, Basil Spence 1907–1976, Edinburgh: The Rutland Press, 1995, p. 82; Glendinning and Methusius, Tower Block, p. 170.

14
Kenna, Rudolph, The Heart of the Gorbals, Ayr: Fort Publishing, 2004, pp. 128–129.

15
Edwards, Basil Spence 1907–1976, p. 72.

OVER: Early perspective drawing of the Queen Elizabeth Square 'Arcade', 1950s. Reproduced Courtesy of RCAHMS (Sir Basil Spence Archive).

J

J P E R S P E C T I V E   O F   S H O P P I N G   A R E A

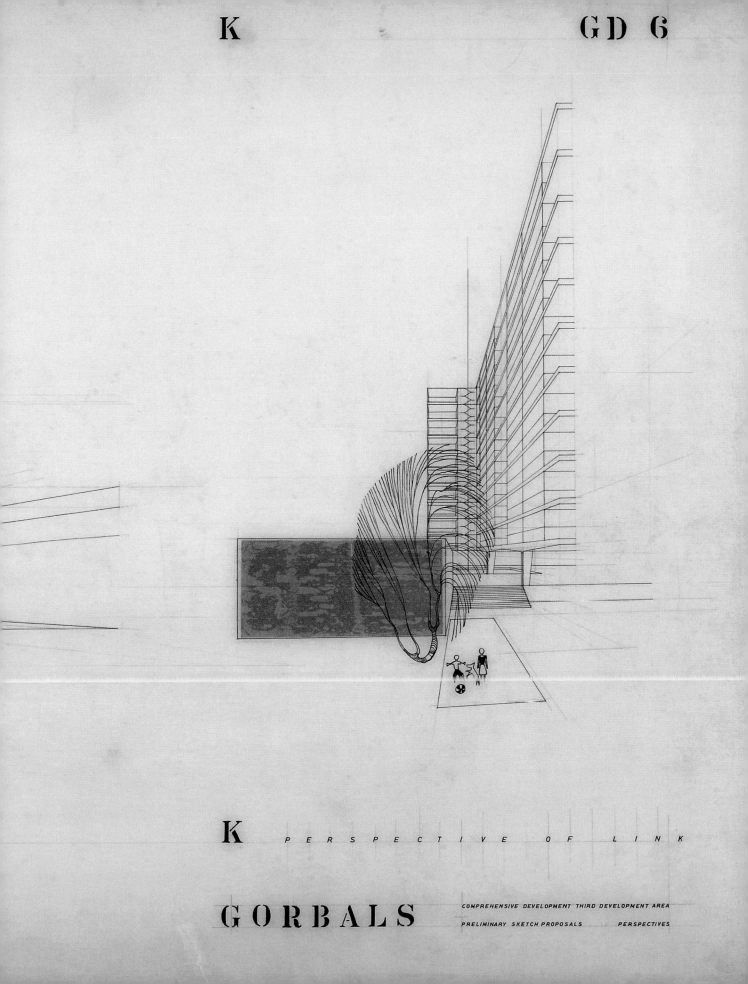

K   *PERSPECTIVE OF LINK*

GORBALS   COMPREHENSIVE DEVELOPMENT THIRD DEVELOPMENT AREA
PRELIMINARY SKETCH PROPOSALS   PERSPECTIVES

panels and apertures created a graphically striking facade image that directly echoed the building's internal layout. The apartments themselves were functional and carefully designed with the fitted kitchens, internal bathrooms and impressive views eager council tenants had come to expect. With Queen Elizabeth Square Spence had created the defining iconic image Glasgow wanted for its housing crusade—majestic yet rational forms, the shallow relief of their facades creating a play of light and shade rising above the rapidly vanishing squalor of the old Gorbals.

Even before Queen Elizabeth Square was completed in 1965, reservations were being expressed about Glasgow's approach to inner city renewal. In 1963 the Scottish Office's Housing Density Report indicated concerns about what effect CDAs, peripheral schemes and the commitment to high-rise construction were to have on the city as a whole and warned that Glasgow was

Producing an image of itself it may regret and which we may regret in relation to what we are attempting to achieve for the Scottish economy as a whole. It would appear that no effort has been seriously made to consider whether the Glasgow housing policies are really suitable to meet the conditions of the latter half of the twentieth century; there would appear to have been no pause to consider whether or not the actual requirements of the population were really being met; there would appear to have been no consideration as to whether this kind of investment would stand the test of time.[18]

These sentiments, understandably unpopular at the time, were sadly to be borne out. It can be said with certainty that, in contrast to much European and even some English experience, Glasgow's policy of high-rise construction was a bitter failure. There proved to be problems with almost all types of construction, not only those using prefabricated systems with their origins in continental areas of more temperate climate. Queen Elizabeth Square was not immune to the social, structural and management problems that would come to bedevil almost every high-rise in Glasgow, and with hindsight its fate can seem sadly predestined. As in many other blocks, it was found that the structures of Spence's buildings were prone to creating 'cold bridges', where structural elements penetrate from outside inwards forming cooling fins and making insulation impossible. Somewhat

The view looking east of the Hutchesontown 'C' development as it was in 1987. The monumentality at the heart of Spence's design ethos is readily apparent. © Royal Commission on the Ancient and Historical Monuments of Scotland. Licensor www.scran. ac.uk.

16
Edwards, *Basil Spence 1907–1976*, p. 84.

17
Glendinning and Methusius, *Tower Block*, p. 171.

loads to the ground" and providing a more dynamic interpretation of Glasgow's housing aspirations than any other high-rise scheme built in the city.[16] This was a bespoke set of buildings, as distinct from the contractors' 'design and build package' system blocks that were to follow in their immediate wake as they were from the tenements they were built to replace. When Sam Bunton, designer of the extraordinarily austere Red Road flats, declared that "housing today is no longer domestic architecture; it's public building. You mustn't expect airs and graces, and things like different-sized windows and ornamental features", he might as well have implicated Spence's approach in the Gorbals.[17] The rhythm of concrete slabs, aggregate

kus, "Comprehensive
elopment and Housing,
5–75", p. 161.

of Glasgow House
dition Survey 1985,
5, Glasgow: Glasgow City
ncil, 1989.

surprisingly, given received views on system-built flats and dampness, the City of Glasgow Housing Condition Survey of 1985 states that "the highest incidence of condensation among tower blocks is in those developments constructed using in-situ concrete or load-bearing brickwork." [19] At ground level piecemeal planning and a poorly structured range of amenities compromised the vision of the open public space within which the blocks would sit. As the shine came off the showpiece, increasingly poor management and maintenance of communal areas, both inside and outside of the buildings, led to inevitable vandalism and criminal activity. In social terms, the dispersal of over 75 per cent of the Gorbals' indigenous population meant that what social cohesion there had been in the tenements evaporated, ruling out any real hope for community self-regulation. This situation was exacerbated further when selective letting policies resulted in concentrations of the Glasgow Corporation's most deprived tenants being moved into the blocks. Attendant to the poverty of these occupants were the inevitable troubles of drink and drug abuse and petty criminality, and as the 1970s wore on many of Queen Elizabeth Square's original tenants must have wondered how the dream could have gone so awry.

By the early 1970s many aspects of Modern architecture and planning were being called into question, the most prominent of these undoubtedly being public housing. Both popular and professional opinion had turned decisively against much of the thinking of the previous decade through an analysis of what that decade had produced. Modern architecture was under attack from almost every angle, the broad Corbusian assertion that 'good' architecture can deliver a better life for its inhabitants being neatly inverted by cultural commentators who claimed that, surely then, 'bad' architecture must debase and dehumanise all who come into contact with it. This simplistic but effective critique has been employed at every level of society when dealing with buildings such as Queen Elizabeth Square. It even forms the basis for the highly entertaining and appropriately dark 1975 novel *High-Rise*, in which author J G Ballard suggests that Modern architecture only finds its true *metier* when it provides the setting for violent social breakdown.

The truth of the situation is somewhat less sensational than this reductive critique indicates as it fails to take fully into account the necessarily complex reasons for which buildings rise and fall. Failures in local and national political processes, town planning, procurement, quality control, social policy, welfare provision, building management, cosmetic maintenance, financial control and letting strategy can all contribute to the rejection of a scheme like Spence's. These, however, are invisible failures. Resentment will inevitably focus upon something

chesontown 'E' deck-
ess flats in a state of
eliction in 1984, three years
r to their demolition.
ewsquest (Herald & Times).
nsor www.scran.ac.uk.

tangible and in almost every case that will be the building itself, and if possible an individual architect on whom to hang the blame.

In 1977 Charles Jencks stated that "happily, we can date the death of modern architecture to a precise moment in time." [20] The demolition by dynamite of Minoru Yamasaki's Pruitt-Igoe slab blocks in St Louis on 15 July 1972 can certainly be represented as that precise moment and it acted as a starter's pistol for the backlash against high-rise building of all kinds.[21] To a public already shocked by the four deaths caused by the collapse of the system-built Ronan Point block in London in 1968, the spectacle of high-rise blocks being demolished in America as a result of social problems even then beginning to emerge in British examples must have been startling. It certainly set the precedent for all the graphic demonstrations of the rejection of Modernism that were to follow. Meanwhile, the redevelopment process in the Gorbals was about to reach its architectural nadir. The first inhabitants moved into the new Hutchesontown/Gorbals Area E, a mixed development of 384 flats in two 24-storey tower blocks and 759 dwellings in seven-storey deck-access blocks, the month after Pruitt-Igoe was flattened. These 'package deal' buildings were constructed by Gilbert Ash Ltd, a subsidiary of Bovis, using the Tracoba system of prefabricated concrete panels developed in France and employed widely in Algeria. Within two years tenants in what became known as "Hutchie E" were suffering severe condensation and water penetration as the Tracoba system's insulation and waterproofing performance was proven to fall well short of what was required in a Scottish climate. As material damage and physical and mental illness caused by the damp atmosphere worsened, the scheme's tenants resorted to undertaking a lengthy rent strike. After its eventual, and almost total, abandonment and dereliction Hutchesontown E was eventually demolished in November 1987; three years after the Council had finally acknowledged its manifest shortcomings and barely ten years after its completion.

The Hutchesontown C development hardly fared any better in the long run. By 1985 the residents of Queen Elizabeth Square had succeeded in their own attempts to make the Council address problems of wind and water ingress, with work being completed in 1987. This costly process was made visible in a most determined manner through the addition of absurd pitched roofs and facade panels in jolly colours, but the reprieve was only a temporary one. The Spence blocks status as an image signifying the end to squalor offered through the application of modern architecture was mirrored by the theatrical gesture of their 'blowdown' on 12 September 1993.[22] The buildings' position as the flagships of 1960s Gorbals redevelopment understandably made the matter of their failure a focal point, despite them not being the 'worst' in qualitative or functional terms. Compounding this partisan approach to the destruction of the Spence blocks is their unjust conflation in the popular memory with Hutchesontown E, to the extent that several inaccurate sources implicate Spence himself in their design. The charismatically creative figure of Basil Spence as author of the blocks, and his very visible public profile, was far more suitable for demonisation than the faceless design teams and convoluted commissioning bodies responsible for the buildings' neighbours. Their symbolic demolition has also proved useful in helping bury the issue of comprehensive social housing in favour of a post Thatcherite model of developments built through public/private partnerships, as was to happen on a huge scale over the next decade. Once again large-scale urban clearance and re-planning is being undertaken in an attempt to provide a panacea for the Gorbals multitudinous and ongoing problems. When bearing current developments in mind it is surely worth considering that with "the mythology of the Gorbals that had developed in the 1930s, it was inevitable that any tabula rasa solution, no matter what its actual quality, would be regarded as salvation".[23] The curious outcome of its erasure from Glasgow's skyline is that Queen Elizabeth Square still exerts a massive influence over Glaswegian consciousness, even inspiring nostalgia from previous tenants in the same vein as the Gorbals slums had done. "History has created a myth that the tenements were loved and the tower blocks were universally loathed, but the truth lies somewhere in the middle. Despite its problems, when Queen Elizabeth Square finally fell in a cloud of dust, there were tears from many former residents." [24]

Ironically, one might say that the blocks' image is now more powerful for their absence, acquiring them a posthumous presence that it is hard to imagine any other demolished high-rise having. With 'iconic' and 'landmark' designs being a prerequisite for any self-respecting property developer's wish-list at the

20
Jencks, Charles, *Post-Modern Architecture*, London: Academy Editions, 1977, p.9.

21
Yamasaki was also the architect of Manhattan's ill-fated World Trade Centre twin towers. Built between 1966 and 1977, the buildings were destroyed in the terrorist attacks of 11 September 2001.

22
As well as being theatrical the spectacle proved fatal, putting an effective end to what Glendinning and Methusius identify as "that most conspicuous ritual of Anti-Modernism". Falling debris caused the death of 61-year-old Helen Tinney and injured three others viewing the demolition from Hutcheson Court, despite them being 20 metres outside the 120 metre exclusion zone. Although there were no prosecutions as a result of the subsequent fatal accident inquiry, the court was told that outdated methods were used to calculate the exclusion zone and that double the specified amount of explosives were used to bring the blocks down. The companies involved in the work, whose tender for the job had been £800,000 lower than their nearest competitor, had failed to bring a klaxon to warn spectators of the imminent explosion and many were taken by surprise after the 'controlled blowdown' had been twice postponed. Kenna, *The Heart of the Gorbals*, pp.190–192.

23
Markus, "Comprehensive Development and Housing, 1945–75", p.162.

24
Eunson, *The Gorbals—An Illustrated History*, p.105.

Aerial View of the
Hutchesontown/Gorbals CDA,
with Queen Elizabeth Square
at its centre, 1965. Reproduced
courtesy of RCAHMS (Sir Basil
Spence Archive)

start of the twenty-first century, and with current regeneration in the Gorbals being as riddled with this language as any of a dozen other developments in Glasgow, such marketing gestures grimly echo the use of Spence's blocks as promotional tools. The fundamental difference being, of course, that Queen Elizabeth Square was largely trading in abstract ideals made concrete in ways that at least temporarily gave a very real improvement to residents' quality of living, whilst our current housing boom is transparently trading only in cold, hard cash. It will be intriguing to see whether private money and the individual ownership of today's rash of symbolic new homes in the Gorbals and beyond will be adequate to save them from an ultimate fate similar to that of Basil Spence's much contested attempt to "civilise the tenement". •

THE GOREY-BELLS
or: "How Childe Roland ... came to the Dark Tower" [1]

19 February 1994: Sun's out. Blue sky grades down to mucky smog. The Kingston Bridge collapses silently into The Clyde. A flight of pigeons rises up.

SOME DAYS I would leave my flat in the Gorbals and it was as if the freaks had decided to take some air all at the same time, bashed-in faces, wasted flesh, toothless gums. The alkies were early risers, up and out around eight to catch the offy, licking their lips in anticipation of that first can of special. The junkies appear around ten, either strung out or gabbling before the nod.[2] Sometimes it seemed like the fabled Gorbals leper colony had never gone away, still on their way to ring the 'gorey-bells' for their supper, still causing a shiver of horror as they pass you in the street more dead than alive.[3] The junkies and alkies were a constant, you couldn't escape the punishment of their faces. These were the pitiable emblems of our crass materialist culture, their metronomic lifestyles a febrile negative to the work, eat, sleep, consume treadmill. One evening around 9.30 my doorbell rang. Immediately I was on guard, as this had happened before—some alky looking to have a party with the former tenant. I crept to the top of the stairs to see three long pale fingers slipping through the letterbox. It was a moment of almost comical horror. I shouted (squeaked) "who is it?" and heard in reply the unmistakable tones of the Glasgow junky, a kind of nasal whine. It was my neighbour from up the corridor, she claimed to be looking for cigarette papers, but I suspect her's was a mission to check my status—was I a fellow traveller? Could I be used in some way? Occasionally I would meet her and her daughter at the lift, the small girl squirming with embarrassment as her mum attempted a 'normal' conversation. Later that week I stopped some kids throwing stones at a nesting swan; they came back soon after and finished the job, smashing all of the eggs except one. After a few days the mother reluctantly abandoned the nest, leaving the one intact egg, which I retrieved and kept on my balcony for years until it began oozing slime and had to be thrown away.

It's really not all that bad in the Gorbals, there were only a couple of instances of threatening behaviour and people were cautiously friendly; my main problem was the daily dose of poverty-stricken, low-expectation culture. You can smell it—its unwashed clothes and cheap fags, the morning vodka breath (Haddows' own brand), the pound shop mentality.

I'd ended up in the Gorbals and got stuck. For eight years. Back to what I'd come from, a solidly working class area and a multi-storey building, but it was close to town and therefore easy to escape. I spent hours, day in year out, sitting at my desk pushed up against the big picture window in my living room, watching the birds, the cloud formations and the banks of rain rushing in constantly from the west. Often I was stoned, dreaming, writing reams of shite in my notebooks and keeping a regular diary for the one and only time in my life, pining for girls I wanted, brooding neurotically about my lack of ambition.

Whether it was warm or not, I'd often stand on one or other of my balconies and watch the comings and goings of Gorbals folk. They had their rituals too. Plenty of people were on the sick or unemployed, like me they had turned their faces away from the world of work, to inhabit a free-floating timeless zone bounded by the TV schedules and the fortnightly trauma of signing on. It was a frugal and exacting existence, zen-lite. I lived on rice, lentils and vegetables, coffee and bread and as much red wine as I could afford.

18 October 1994: It's blowing up a storm out there in Gorbals land. This building has a bit of a dubious shake about it. Too many things move and squeak when the wind hits. Still, the seagulls seem to get some enjoyment. Or maybe it's safer way up there? Sometimes the window goes concave. One morning we will wake up to an endless grey lake, scummy, shitty and full of corpses, with a bit of luck the Christians will have been raptured out of the picture. Vicious wind, shredded concrete. The man in the newsagents resembles some strange species of fish, naked and flapping on the quayside, out of its natural element. Dying.

4.29: The sky is an incredible shade of nicotine yellow, almost biblical. Finely-etched cloud mass.

My flat was high on the top corner, with two large balconies, one at the front and one at the back. It was beautiful, a dream of functional, contained, Modernist living. The front door opened onto stairs that went up to a relatively vast hallway. There was something ridiculously optimistic about that hallway. It took up practically the whole flat, essentially functionless, apart from (critically) adding a sense of spaciousness.

[1]
Chapter heading from
Huntingtower by John Buchan.

[2]
They are briefly lucid and talkative before 'nodding off'.

[3]
Situated on what is now Hospital Street.

All photos and drawings
Jim Colquhoun, Untitled,
1993–2001.

Another set of stairs took you up to the bedroom and the bathroom, there seemed to be no practical way to reach the light fitting on that far away ceiling, nowhere to prop a ladder. The bathroom was large and the bedroom adequate, with plenty of cupboard space. My living room was separated from the tiny kitchen by a sliding wooden door, which I thought neat. Stuck to the wall was a four bar electric fire that was totally inadequate for the job of heating a very draughty space; there was no other heating.[4] On one wall I could just make out the palimpsest of a sprayed gang name—Cumbie.

The views and the river save the Gorbals from being just another blighted inner city shit-hole. Nature is right at hand and amongst the despondent-looking trees and bushes lining the riverbank a pair of mute swans attempted to nest every year. The huge nest was constructed from a bathetic stew of reeds and rubbish. The locals fed the birds their leftover pan loaves then chucked the plastic bags, which the swan would diligently add to the nest. Once I watched a white cockatoo fleeing between my building and another, hotly pursued by two lesser black-backed gulls. It was doomed and by its terrified screams I think it knew it. The local crow family spent hours performing aerobatic displays for each other, only stopping to harass a passing heron. Early one morning, coming home from town, I surprised an otter strolling along the river walkway; it spotted me and leapt through the fence. I heard it crash into the bushes six feet below, obviously a stranger to the neighbourhood. Another time, again in the early morning, I drunkenly watched a man standing on the very edge of the tidal weir, looking intently at something at his feet. He ignored my worried questions, just stared. I thought he was a suicide, but found out later he was counting elvers as they crawled painfully up the weir.

9 January 1995: With concentration camps/hospitals all over the civilised world filling up with the victims of Spongiform Encephalitis or Creutzfeld-Jakobs Disease it seemed inevitable that a 'soft-brain' cult would raise its ugly, malformed and drooling head. House parties and raves are filled with young people doing 'The Stagger', this being a stylised version of the symptoms of this horrifying disease. Dying animals are often introduced onto the dance floor, with the result that getting crushed by a 'mad cow' is now a commonplace weekend injury.

I thought, when I first went to live in the Gorbals, that I would play a full role in the local community. This was my chance to engage in some kind of meaningful way with my neighbours, my locale. What an arsehole. What did I know? I didn't have the stomach or the inclination for local politics. So I became what I should have known I would—a permanent tourist, a *dilettante* prole. None of my neighbours could make me out. I wasn't a junky or an alky. I spoke different. I was friendly but standoffish at the same time. I suppose I was lucky I didn't get my head kicked in, but living in high-rises is curiously impersonal, especially if you are unemployed as I and many of my neighbours were. Most people spend the day indoors watching TV. There is nothing else to do. After a year of this lifestyle (I was actually starting to admire Judy Finnegan, mainly for putting up with Richard), I placed my television in the hall by the lift.[5] It was gone within 20 minutes. I felt heroic and nervous. What the fuck was I going to do now?

The days and weeks and months were spent with friends experiencing a similar stasis or fencing with the Department of Social Security as they tried to send me on yet another useless 'Restart' course, or wandering the city in search of fuck knows what. I'd stripped the embossed white wallpaper from my walls to find a kind of shabby chic putrid yellowness. It was ugly yet appropriate, complementing my state of ongoing psychic distress.

5 April 1995: Greasy Glaswegian weather sits on the city like failed cloud, the monkey on the back of the Scottish psyche. (Or is that our pathetic whining nationalism?)

The view does something to your head. The River. The Green.[6] From my east-facing balcony I could see all the way to Tinto Hill and north to the Campsie and Kilsyth Hills. Closer in I had a panorama of the scrofulous east end. From here I'd watched the men from the Orange Lodges battering each other for want of anyone else to hit (nobody was stupid enough to venture onto The Green on that day), it was working class culture devouring itself. There always seemed to be a column of thick black smoke churning up from somewhere, a pyre of burning tyres or another chip pan fire (an east end speciality). From here I watched what I thought was the head of a drowning man dip below the surface of the river. After calling the police and watching a helicopter and George Parsonage from the Humane Society

4
Everyone in working class areas has power cards now. They are foisted on to those who cannot pay their bills. They have what's called the 'emergency' function, allowing an extra £15 of heat and light before shutting down altogether. This is charged at a higher rate and after it runs out a full £20 has to be found to start the process all over again. That can be a lot of money out of a giro, so, perforce, people cut themselves off, letting the power companies off the moral hook. Everyone lives on emergency now and thinks nothing of it, but it ends up being a default tax on poor people, same as the lottery. I exercised my right to have the device removed as soon as possible.

5
The Richard and Judy Show was the ultimate in homely, anodyne pap. They were surrogate parents to the workshy and the terminally medicated.

6
The Glasgow Green is a large riverside park.

search and find nothing, I realised it was probably a seal mooching around for fish, they came up with the tide looking like swimming dogs.[7] My other balcony looked to the west, the city centre and the south side. If not for the Queen Elizabeth flats the view would have been marvellous. But they sat there like a vast malevolent temple dedicated to a particularly loathsome deity. It was hard to imagine anyone living there, even harder to know where the inhabitants disappeared to once the flats were gone? Perhaps they had decided to retreat underground, like the Morlocks in Wells' *The Time Machine*?

I had a party on the day in 1993 when the flats were summarily wiped from the skyline. As it went down it became obvious the spectators had been allowed to venture too close. People began to run from the rapidly approaching dust storm and Mrs Helen Tinney took a mortal blow from a piece of the building, leading to a fatal heart attack. As a result

the authorities never publicise the erasure of yet another embarrassing bit of Modernist junk, this particular spectacle having been deemed no longer appropriate, Helen Tinney's unsought epitaph.

But Basil Spence's giant folly was not always so reviled. People embraced the notion of concrete decking and sci-fi perspectives as all part of the dream of progress, a dream almost instantly compromised but seductive and powerful all the same. Soon electricity would be cheap or free and vast space colonies would ring the earth. Even the working classes would get a taste, no hint yet of an underclass (those Morlocks again), or the triple whammy of mass unemployment, heroin and daytime TV. We were silkily informed that leisure time would expand exponentially due to the automation of manufacturing processes. A life as contented hobbyists beckoned, everyone working their allotments and becoming part-time astronomers or pigeon fanciers or whatever.

7
George Parsonage is the man who fishes dead bodies from the Clyde and is seen regularly rowing around on the river.

Meanwhile those casting a weather eye around them began to notice little things like military-industrial complexes and mutually assured destruction.

16 February 1996: A roosting pigeon watches me warily.

A pattern quickly formed: I'd get up and go on a usually futile hunt for *The Guardian*. Drink my coffee, have my toast and head into town. Or south side. Or anywhere but where I was. Did I mention that the flat quickly became oppressive? Especially the constant 'friendly' surveillance by the concierge service, who's presence (through no fault of their own) more and more resembled that of jailers. I spent many long days exploring the badlands to the east. The dereliction left by dead heavy industry sometimes seemed to spread as far as the eye could see. Somehow the east end had become *terra incognita*, to be walked and mapped. Discovered. Vast disused railway yards swarmed with Buddleia, Himalayan Balsam and other horticultural escapees. There were huge metal sheds,

like the remnants of some aborted Scottish space programme. Not even kids seemed to come to these rotting places anymore, except that the traces of people were everywhere. Old fires, makeshift shelters and camps, abandoned clothing, the remnants of the sort of desperate parties that always ended in wild kicks and punches. Once I watched a man struggling to remove his trousers while all the time baying like a wolf, he was doing the evostick shuffle.[8] Another time I came across a deep stone well filled with dead fox cubs and fat toads. Then there was my herring gull. For years it came every day to be fed, long after I'd stopped giving it food (because of the awful mess). It had a screeching, piratical, but somehow engaging personality. For hours it simply sat and stared with one mad eye and then the other. A similar thing was happening on my side of the glass I suppose.

12 September 1996: Nice day. Null creativity. Everything is horribly familiar. At the entrance to G's building a girl was shouting rape. "You fuckin'

8
Evostick seems to be the glue addict's brand of choice—any patch of waste ground will turn up several 'used' containers. Oddly, I'd watched identical behaviour years earlier on the south side.

beast", she kept screaming. Not pleasant. Horrible thought—they probably made up, or at least I watched them arguing earnestly by the riverbank. Neighbours are squalling again. Dishing out the verbal beatings. Drink-fuelled.

I'd spent my childhood and teenage years climbing around in multi-storey buildings. Hiding in the stairwells and concrete drying greens, jamming the lifts between floors to smoke joints or have sex, or just sit. But I can remember as a kid the feeling of new horizons opening up, that brief honeymoon period before everybody realised the promises of modernity were essentially empty, the dream faltering and stuttering on a raft of bad planning, shady deals and naked profiteering. But more than that, the buildings just did not work as communities. These were the seedbeds of anomie and spiritual dislocation. They worked as long as they did because the communities inhabiting them were relatively strong and cohesive; the Thatcher years put paid to all of that. It always struck me as odd how heroin made an appearance (in quantity) around about this time? I think my friends and I escaped that fate by the skin of our teeth. I can remember arranging with the local dealer to buy some and watching with a friend from my bedroom window on the 12th floor as they cruised around in their car waiting for us. We had chickened out at the last second, a defining moment for us.

Yet for all the low-level dread, there is something wonderful about being able to see the world roll out before you every morning. From my balcony I would plot my routes into the east. I'd found a lost loop of land cut off by industrial units, dirt embankments and a travellers' encampment. A wilderness of spoil heaps, pits and giant hogweed infestation. On my first visit I noticed that someone had been hacking a path through the hogweed, a dangerous pastime as the 'juice' from this particular interloper is extremely toxic, allegedly causing 'nerve damage'. Then I came across a sunken bath filled with tadpoles and newts; then bird feeders; finally after a chance stumble through a bramble bush, I found a beautifully constructed shed, carefully hidden, its roof camouflaged by vegetation—someone did not want it to be found. I left a note for these latter day levellers and months later received a mysterious phone call describing a secretive alliance, which had laid claim to the loop without bothering to inform the relevant authorities. A kind of quasi-utopian community was flourishing under my nose, careful to disguise itself from the encroaching hordes of suits and vandals. Now it's a mooted site for a new Glasgow zoo, having only just escaped becoming a section of the new M74 extension.

17 April 1997: The Voodoo Enigma of the Filthy Rich and the Dirt Poor. Sun, clouds, pigeons fucking brazenly on my balcony. Springtime. Green shoots. Staring at the wall, waiting to win the lottery, junk food apocalypse. Turin shroud torched. White bread complexions. Radio 4's *Kaleidoscope* arts programme whitters on in its well-bred fashion. In a couple of weeks there will be a general election.

The biggest cemetery in the Gorbals is the Southern Necropolis. A vast bone-yard and *al fresco* drinking and drugging den. I ventured in there one day in

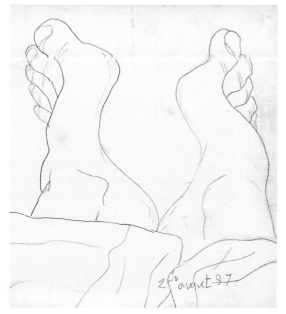

search of some dead Colquhouns and on a whim decided to follow a chaffinch that seemed to be flying purposefully from tombstone to tombstone; naturally it led me directly to a headstone dedicated to some obscure branch of my family. It was here in September of 1954 that the 'Gorbals vampire' made its fleeting appearance, gnashing its scary metal teeth. As a boy I can remember leading a large group of kids into Pollok Park on the south side, to track down 'the murderer', a mythic figure conjured by lurid media reportage and wishful thinking. (I got myself belted by the headmistress for that one.) A similar thing happened in the Gorbals I imagine, with a huge gang forming to seek and destroy 'the vampire', who apparently resided within the graveyard. Nothing came of it of course, but the moral guardians of the day blamed the influence of 'horror comics' (the classic EC series of that era). Most likely it was a combination of youthful imagination, mischief-making and boredom. I like to think that there is a bit more to it than that though. In the absence of any meaningful celebrations in our lives, the urge to get together and do something (anything) will tend to take strange and unlikely forms—like the aforementioned vampire stake-out, or when local girl gang the 'She Cumbie' allegedly head out glammed-up and team-handed, looking to contest the virginal status of the youngest members of the group.

23 April 1997: Saturday night streets slick with pavement porridge. My camera at the ready I wait eager for a sign. At last! Across a crowded Sauchiehall Street a couple play out the final horrorshow of a failed relationship. Improvised street theatre at its sweetest! Click. I catch the grimace of drunken hatred as she hoists her lover's glistening genitals into the night. Kneeling on the filthy pavement as if to receive the host she sinks bared fangs into his ruined crotch. A shudder of almost religious fervour rushes through me. If only every moment were this sweet!

The Gorbals Diehards were the creation of writer John Buchan. In his book *Huntingtower* they embodied a vision of the working classes as honest toilers with a bit of spunk who nevertheless knew their place, always kowtowing to the officer classes and ever ready and willing to go over the top if called upon. I suspect the original inhabitants of what is now the 'New Gorbals' are expected to "just get on with it" in similar fashion, as their community is yet again the proving ground for an experiment in social engineering. As the two camps, one seemingly prosperous, the other still reeling from

generations of economic realpolitik rub up against each other, it's not really surprising that there may be friction. When I was there, just as the initial stages of the redevelopment were taking place, there was an outcry from the new residents about the attendance of the local heroin addicts at 'their' chemist.[9] Somehow these very visible signifiers of urban decay and squalor were just supposed to melt away. Perhaps the 'Old Gorbals' would shake off its blanket despair and taking its cue from its new (Labour) neighbours, pull itself up by its bootstraps, get a job and stop being so bloody embarrassing? If they would just be helped—maybe by turning up at their (privatised) 'Working Links' interviews with a smile on their faces for once? Surely this was not too much to ask? The obvious solutions to the problem never seem to be on the table—i.e. a minimum wage that isn't a slap in the face, decent benefits for those that don't work, and the (re)introduction of ritual slayings and maypole dancing.

30 April 1997: As someone on the radio said: Labour is determined to break all promises before the election instead of afterwards, as is traditional. Vision of an endless motorway clotted with garden centres, retail parks, entertainment complexes, boring architecture and lowest common denominator tat as the populace attempt to hide their fear behind a furious materialism. •

DEDICATED TO HELEN TINNEY

9
Addicts on the methadone programme are given the drug over the counter in chemists.

DAPHNE WRIGHT'S collection of *Home Ornaments* is the result of a commission to mark the redevelopment of Queen Elizabeth Square in Glasgow's Gorbals, a project that was initiated in 1998 and will be completed in 2006. This particular exercise in urban regeneration took the form of a housing development designed by CZWG architects for the Cruden Group, to be executed under the direction of Piers Gough. Wright's contribution is both characteristically idiosyncratic and nonetheless attuned to the sense of community such projects are conventionally designed to affirm or reassert. Each one of her set of five distinctive ornaments is an emblematic distillation of the complex social history of one of Glasgow's most storied locales. Each object is intended to encapsulate an aspect or several aspects of the communal memory of the Gorbals. Wright was acutely aware from the outset of the disparities between the notions of community she set out to explore, and that which necessarily informed the developers' plans. Her extensive research brought her into contact with the physical and social reality of a traditional, close-knit community bound by a common history, shared experiences, intertwined families, a particular material culture, and a rich and self-renewing trove of stories. The developers, on the other hand, inevitably dealt with a more abstract model of an idealised inner city community, as well as the practical strategies best suited to achieve this ideal at the beginning of the twenty-first century. This contrast between the old and the new, the inherited and the fabricated, provides the underlying dynamic of Wright's project of commemoration and renewal.

The written history of the Gorbals acknowledges it as one of the city's oldest neighbourhoods, dating back to the founding of the parish of that name in 1771. It grew rapidly from a small weaving village in the late eighteenth century to an expanding suburb by the mid-nineteenth century. By the end of that century it was a teeming urban centre, the largest and most densely populated district in Glasgow. Having assimilated several immigrant groups, this thriving community was, by the 1930s, home to almost 90,000 people, most of whom lived in packed tenements. By this time it was also largely dependent for local employment on the traditional heavy industries of shipbuilding and ironworks, both of which were in decline and were eventually to collapse, resulting in

massive unemployment and a variety of attendant social problems, including endemic ill health and high levels of violence and squalor. The slum clearances of the 1950s and the local authority's experiments with high-rise housing in the 1960s failed to alleviate these problems. The question of housing remained particularly intractable. Unfortunately, the multi-storey apartment blocks that were built in the 60s proved unsuitable to the wet Scottish climate and these homes became known as the 'dampies' due to severe problems with condensation. The general decline in living standards persisted through the 1970s and 80s. Some indication of the social demographic profile of the Gorbals by the beginning of the 1990s may be seen from the following contemporary statistics: 96 per cent of the housing stock was public rented; 50 per cent of households with children were single parent homes; and 80 per cent of the local population, which now numbered less than 10,000, belonged to the most deprived ten per cent of the Scottish population. Following a period of vigorous activism spearheaded by local community leaders, the 1960s apartment blocks were finally demolished in the early 1990s to be gradually replaced by developments such as the one in Queen Elizabeth Square.[1]

*"**Home Ornaments** gestures backwards and forwards in time, acknowledging a complex set of relations between loss and progress, impoverishment and regeneration."*

The documented history of a neighbourhood like the Gorbals, or indeed of any other locality, can tell us only so much, no matter how rich it may be in incident or vivid in detail. A crucial aspect of Wright's project, therefore, was her willingness to delve into the largely untapped riches of the area's contemporary oral lore. Much of her preliminary research took the form of extensive interviews conducted with a number of long-term locals whose highly personal—and sometimes lurid—recollections of the Gorbals in times past she was eager to solicit. That the stories she unearthed should both complement and at times contradict the 'official' account of the area's evolution is hardly surprising, given the categorical differences between written and oral narratives in the modern world. As

[1]
This brief account of the social history of the Gorbals is derived from http://ensure.org/entrust/cases/glasgow/2.Gorbals-history.

Daphne Wright, Full set of *Home Ornaments*. Courtesy the artist.

early as 1936 Walter Benjamin was lamenting the fact that the traditional art of storytelling was coming to an end in the Europe of his day:

Less and less frequently do we encounter people with the ability to tell a tale properly. More and more often there is embarrassment all around when the wish to hear a story is expressed. It is as if something that seemed inalienable to us, the surest among our possessions, were taken from us: the ability to exchange experiences.[2]

One obvious reason for this phenomenon, according to Benjamin, was that at the dawning of the information age 'experience' itself had fallen in value and the perceived possibility of adequately communicating it was rapidly decreasing. Unlike a traditional story, modern 'information' is required to be 'understandable in itself', so that in a media-saturated world events invariably come to us "already… shot through with explanation". In contrast, half of the art of storytelling is "to keep a story free from explanation as one reproduces it". A story is of enduring value precisely because it "preserves and concentrates its strength and is capable of releasing it even after a long time".[3]

Stories have always been important to Wright, though her work has tended to stress their inevitable gaps, failings and contradictions as much as their more obviously cherishable qualities. Over the years she has insinuated into her work a variety of narrative or pseudo-narrative genres—documentary interviews, personal recollections, songs and nonsense rhymes—generally in the form of subtly modulated soundtracks accompanying large-scale sculptural installations. This aural element has often been crucial to the haunting, destabilising effect of these environments on the viewer. On the whole, Wright's use of language tends to be more ludic than lucid, and her narratives more elusive than informative. As such they tend to confirm Benjamin's contention that, for the most part, we have lost the ability "to tell a tale properly". As Shirley MacWilliam has pointed out, the human voice in Wright's work is more often than not "the vehicle of play in and perversion of language", in the sense that Roland Barthes had in mind when he argued that the activity of play within language frustrates the production of meaning and causes those who read (or hear) it to become aware of the essential instability of their subjectivity. As MacWilliam notes, this has the effect

of "revealing the fundamental fiction of the self as a coherent identity".[4] Wright's *Home Ornaments* work slightly differently. Conceived as modest memorials to the collective history of the Gorbals, they also contrive to call into question the very notion of 'the community' as a coherent identity. This is largely due to the essentially ineffable nature of these somewhat melancholy objects. They are, in more than one sense, 'conversation pieces', mute physical mementos of conversations past, and obscure spurs to conversations that might take place in the future.

Despite her frequent recourse to narrative, Wright is at heart a visual rather than a verbal artist in whose work the word is inevitably subordinate to the image, the object or the specular environment. The myriad stories of the Gorbals she has patiently gathered are therefore honoured indirectly in the five individual sculptures that make up her set of *Home Ornaments*. 'An Architect's Plan' is a white polyurethane cast of the 1960s apartment building that formerly stood in Queen Elizabeth Square, apparently captured in the very throes of its demolition, as dust clouds billow from its collapsing infrastructure. 'Guinea Pig' is a naturalistic cast of a pet guinea pig in blue or white porcelain, accompanied by a small white porcelain drinking-bowl. 'The Cacti Collection' is a set of three small cacti hand-knitted in grey wool, each of which sits in a knitted grey or blue pot. 'Fidelma' is a hand-embroidered silk parrot, set on a white perch, whose face, beak and claws have been meticulously painted by a modelmaker specialising in religious icons. 'Uncle' is an intaglio print of the doleful countenance of an orangutan, framed in an ornate bespoke gesso frame. The set of associations brought into play by these ornaments is complex and various, ranging from the straightforward invocation of well-documented aspects of the history of the Gorbals to obscure and highly mediated allusions to the personal recollections of its disparate inhabitants. Whereas 'An Architect's Plan' is easily the most literal and explicit of these objects, 'Uncle' is arguably the most obscure, with the three other ornaments occupying various points along a spectrum of interpretive accessibility between these two extremes.

The building depicted in 'An Architect's Plan' is the Hutchesontown C scheme, the most widely derided project of Sir Basil Unwin Spence, a notable Scottish architect, possibly best remembered for his association with Coventry Cathedral. Spence

2
Benjamin, Walter, *Illuminations*, London: Fontana Press, 1973, p. 82.

3
Benjamin, *Illuminations*, pp. 88–90.

4
MacWilliam, Shirley, "Playing in the Field", in Daphne Wright, *They've taken to their beds*, Exeter: Spacex Gallery, 1998, p. 46.

was, however, also responsible for numerous other buildings, mostly designed in a Modernist or Brutalist style. The most infamous of these were a number of high-rise housing developments in the Gorbals, which were intended to replace the area's notorious slum developments. Unfortunately, a number of factors, including the insufficient consideration of local climatic conditions and the poor execution of his designs, meant that the developments merely exacerbated the existing social problems. The Hutchesontown C scheme was demolished in 1993. 'Guinea Pig' refers, in the first instance, to the household pet once popular among inner city dwellers, especially those whose domestic circumstances might not readily accommodate a larger animal. It is, however, also intended to refer more obliquely to the well-known 'Wemyss pig' ornaments, which could be commonly found in working class homes as late as the 1960s, but have more recently become rare and valuable collectables. This ornamental pig was the flagship product of Wemyss Ware, first produced in Fife in 1882 by the potter Robert Methven Heron and named after the family that owned nearby Wemyss Castle, who were avid early collectors of these ornaments. (The pottery eventually fell on hard times and was forced to close down in the 1930s, and the rights to Wemyss Ware were subsequently bought by a pottery in Devon.) Guinea pigs are not, of course, indigenous to the British Isles. Of South American origin, where they still flourish in the wild, guinea pigs were most probably introduced to Europe in the sixteenth century. They were not selectively bred until the 1920s, initially by well-heeled fanciers, and only later did they become popular domestic pets.

During the development of the *Home Ornaments* project Wright was involved in various workshops with local children and she quickly came to realise the enhanced significance of the domestic pet as an emblem of affection, intimacy and continuity

ABOVE: Twomax textiles factory, Gorbals, 1950s.

OVER: Daphne Wright, *Domestic Shrubbery*, 1994, plaster and continuous loop tape, 488 × 457 × 366 cm. Sound: Middle-aged female voice imitating a cuckoo, alternating between an intimate term of endearment and that of a bird in the landscape. Courtesy the artist/ Frith Street Gallery, London.

within a context of sundered families and shifting households. When, for instance, they were invited to suggest a suitable subject for a monumental sculpture, quite a few of these children chose to nominate their own pets. Many adult residents of the Gorbals tower blocks in the 1960s also kept pets, often birds of an exotic variety. Parrots, parakeets and macaws tend to be long-lived and, according to local legend, some of these birds survived into the 1990s and, in the end, had to be released into the wild just prior to the demolition of the buildings in which they had lived alongside their owners for decades. Wright's ornamental parrot is called 'Fidelma', a traditional Gaelic name whose manifest Irish roots register the significance of one of the largest and most longstanding immigrant groups in the history of the Gorbals, and of Glasgow more generally. 'The Cacti Collection' calls to mind that mixture of patience and ingenuity required of even the most green-fingered low income flat dweller for whom a tiny, sodden window-box may be the only garden to which he or she can ever aspire. These knitted plants also evoke more indirectly the textiles industry that was such an important facet of the earlier history of the Gorbals. Until quite recently the Twomax textile factory, housed in an old building close to the site of the new Queen Elizabeth Square development, was the major source of employment for local women. There they produced, for minimal wages, a product they could

Daphne Wright, 'Guinea Pig'. Courtesy the artist.

never hope to purchase for themselves: up-market two-piece knitted suits and outdoor wear destined for export, or bound for Glasgow's smarter retail outlets. Finally, the most inscrutable ornament of the whole set is the piece entitled 'Uncle'. This photographic image of a lugubrious primate, reverently placed in its ornamental frame, is more than a little absurd. Yet it manages to exude, however improbably, some of the dignity we associate with a snapshot of a beloved family member, or even that of a holy picture. Many of the stories Wright was told registered a strong desire to bear witness to the origins of the different immigrant communities who made the Gorbals their home, including the Irish community, as already noted. As it happens, the monks of the Franciscan Order, whose only Glasgow Friary was located in the Gorbals, played a leading role in the stories told by the Irish. By way of a roundabout elucidation of this distinctly peculiar ornament Wright mischievously notes the fortuitous resemblance between the orangutan's cowled and tonsured visage and traditional monastic garb. In the more general context of a discourse on origins, the ape can also be read as a sly reference to Charles Darwin's once scandalous take on where we all originally 'came from'.

The specific methods of fabrication and distribution envisaged by Wright were always crucial to her conception of how the *Home Ornaments* might function. While much of her work in the past has had a strong hand-made element to it, clearly registering the artist's sculpturally expressive touch, none of these ornaments were fashioned by Wright herself. The fact that 'The Cacti Collection', though referring to the local tradition of hand-made textiles, were actually made in China pointedly underlines the local demise of such traditional industries in an age of globalised cheap labour. The fabrication of 'Fidelma' and 'Uncle' was dependent on specialist skills that are likewise fast becoming moribund in the developed world. 'An Architect's Plan' is derived from original drawings by Sir Basil Spence produced in an era before computer-aided design had marginalised the skills of manual draughtsmanship; yet the object itself was produced with the aid of the latest digital rendering techniques. Like the *Home Ornaments* project as a whole, it gestures both backwards and forwards in time, acknowledging a complex set of relations between loss and progress, impoverishment and regeneration. The particular mode of distribution chosen by Wright was also important to the project.

One of these ornaments was to be placed in each of over one hundred newly built apartments, there to await the arrival of its new occupants. While the dimensions of the ornaments vary, all five are modest in scale, none of them exceeding 210 millimetres in height. Each work was designed to be installed on an inconspicuous shelf located above the front door of the apartment. There it claimed its place alongside the various domestic appliances and other rudimentary household items that came with the house. Just as the sales representative of the housing development handed over the instruction manuals for the cooker, the fridge and the washing machine to each new owner along with the keys to the apartment, so too did each owner receive a limited edition 'user's guide' to their specific *Home Ornament*. This manual, conceived as an integral part of the work itself, provided specific instructions concerning the care of the individual objects, as well as a general account of Wright's project. It also functioned as a certificate validating the piece as one of a limited edition of potentially valuable artworks. (The fact that one full set of *Home Ornaments* was also gifted to the Gallery of Modern Art in Glasgow, as part of their Recent Acquisitions scheme, provides further validation of their potential value for the more far-sighted homeowner.) The sales representatives were also charged with informing the new occupants

Daphne Wright, 'The Cacti Collection'. Courtesy the artist.

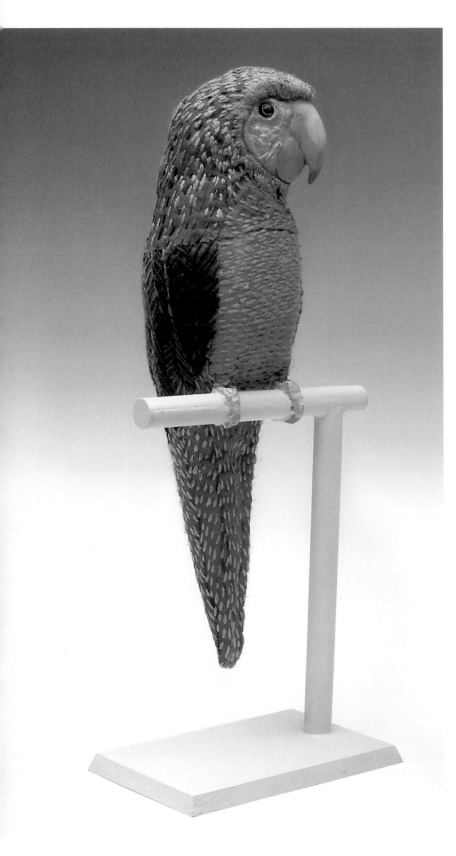

as to the meaning and significance of their specific ornament within the broad context of the history of the Gorbals, alerting their new owners to the various stories that constituted the narrative matrix from which these objects were created. This mixture of legalistic written documentation and informal oral communication fortuitously underlines the ornaments' liminal status (they are, after all, literally sited on a threshold), as they precariously occupy an imaginative space between a traditional culture rich in stories and a contemporary world in thrall to the written word, not to mention electronic media. The reception of the *Home Ornaments* was bound to be affected by the current proliferation of daytime television programmes celebrating the joys of antique-hunting and the rewards to be reaped by the discerning connoisseur of collectables, in the wake of the BBC's remarkably successful, pioneering *Antiques Roadshow*. Given that every 'user's guide' provides information on all five ornaments, Wright always imagined that their new owners might wish to swap their designated ornament for another more suitable to their personal tastes. By sounding their new neighbours out on this matter some sense of community might be spontaneously fomented through the informal mechanism of a decidedly old-fashioned barter economy. Yet such is the power of the printed word that it seems that some of the apartment block's new occupants took considerably more care in preserving the 'user's guide' (along with the manuals for their other appliances) than in caring for the ornaments themselves, which they unceremoniously consigned to a cupboard. (No doubt the contrast between the discreet convenience of the bottom drawer, and the intrusive visibility of the displayed object, was also a consideration here.) Some ornaments were thrown out and turned up later in skips, including a 'Fidelma', which had been removed from her perch and callously 'released into the wild'. Others may yet turn up in one of the charity shops that provided Wright with such invaluable insights into the material culture of the Gorbals during her initial research, thereby integrating themselves into the endless cycle of obsolescence and retrieval common to more conventional bric-a-brac. Many new owners, however, showed sufficient interest in the project to ensure that some of the stories already in circulation concerning the individual ornaments' narrative background show the inevitable signs of creative oral transmission familiar to folklorists the world over.

Daphen Wright, 'Fidelma'.
Courtesy the artist.

The practice of gifting a household item to the occupants of a new home is common in many cultures. These Glaswegian *Home Ornaments* are, in essence, contemporary variants of the traditional 'handsel' (from Old English hand, 'hand' and selen, 'gift'), a ceremonial gift expressing good wishes either at the beginning of a new year or, more pertinently in this instance, at the inauguration of a new enterprise. A handsel is a token of good luck bestowed by a conscientious well-wisher, which promises good fortune to the receiver. As we have already seen, each of these disparate tokens was intended to draw together some narrative threads that might somehow bind the much maligned past of the once notorious Gorbals to a more benign and auspicious future. As such they might also be described as 'souvenirs', albeit of a distinctly unorthodox variety, as Wright acknowledges in a comment on the interests that informed her project from the outset: "I am interested in the idea of the Souvenir, the collection, the common day object ignored in the attic or cupboard that could increase or decrease in value, the egg cup or plate that makes one a fortune or is worthless. I am interested here in the crossover between the personal and the public." As Susan Stewart has pointed out, we do not need or desire souvenirs of events that are 'repeatable': "Rather we need and desire souvenirs of events that are reportable, events whose materiality has escaped us, events that thereby exist only through the invention of narrative."[5]

Stewart suggests that the ordinary souvenir performs a double function, which is to authenticate a past or otherwise remote experience and yet, at the same time somehow to discredit the present by suggesting that it is "either too impersonal, too looming, or too alienating compared to the intimate and direct experience of contact which the souvenir has with its referent".[6] Yet these are no ordinary souvenirs, but artificially forged mementoes, and Wright is conscious of the contradictions inherent in the notion of the fabricated souvenir, its peculiar subversion of the emotional currency of the ordinary souvenir. Her extraordinary souvenirs are intended to provide an intimate connection between their recipients and a past on which they might otherwise have no proper purchase whatsoever. (For the true collector, "ownership is the most intimate relationship one can have to objects", according to Walter Benjamin; but for the inadvertent collector this is hardly the case.) After all, many of the new residents of Queen Elizabeth Square come from recent immigrant communities for whom the rich history of the Gorbals must seem impossibly remote. The 'exchange of experiences' envisaged by Benjamin as the quintessential property of storytelling is bound to be especially tentative and fraught in circumstances such as these.

Grant H Kester's *Conversation Pieces: Community and Communication in Modern Art* is a wide-ranging account of 'dialogical art', work that operates at the intersection between fine art and cultural activism. In imagining how art might play a productive role in salvaging some sense of community from what he describes as "the disaster of modern world history and the scepticism of poststructuralist thought", Kester has recourse to Jean-Luc Nancy's concept of the 'inoperative community'. Whereas conventional models of community are premised on "the concept of centred, self-identical subjects coming into communion through the mutual recognition of a shared essence", the history of the twentieth century provides us with ample evidence of the dangers of an essentialised concept of community. The pressing question for the twenty-first century is:

how can the community without essence ... be presented as such? That is, what might a politics be that does not stem from the will to realise an essence? How can we be receptive to the meaning of multiple, dispersed, mortally fragmented existences, which nonetheless only make sense by existing in common?[7]

For Nancy, the acknowledgment of our decentred, non-essentialist condition need not automatically lead to an overwhelming sense of loss or disconnection. Rather, it can help to bind us to others in a common sense of 'finiteness' and mortality. What we share with other members of Nancy's 'inoperative community' is precisely a common lack of identity, fixity and permanence. Kester invokes this notion of the inoperative community in the promotion of a socially interactive art, an art defined, not in terms of an inspired creator fashioning an exemplary object, but in terms of the discursive relationship a committed art practice might hope to establish with the individual viewer, or with a community of viewers. It may well be that one of the singular achievements of Daphne Wright's *Home Ornaments* project is that it manages to bridge the gap between these two ostensibly opposing models of contemporary art practice. •

5
Stewart, Susan, *On Longing: Narratives of the Miniature, the Gigantic, the Souvenir, the Collection*, Durham and London: Duke University Press, 1993, p. 135.

6
Stewart, *On Longing*, p. 138.

7
Nancy, Jean-Luc, *The Inoperative Community*, Peter Connor ed., Minneapolis: University of Minnesota Press, 1991, pp. xli, xl. Quoted in Grant Kester, *Conversation Pieces: Community and Communication in Modern Art*, Berkeley, CA: University of California Press, 2004, p. 154.

IT IS DECEMBER 2005, and in the premises of Gorbals Arts Project (GAP) on Moffat Street, three life-size bronze sculptures of boys aged between six and ten years old are holed up in the basement. Two of them are bent over in strangely awkward postures, while the third looks up in surprise, apparently clutching his private parts. Nothing very unusual there. What is slightly odd is the fact that all three are wearing stiletto-heeled shoes several sizes too large. Boys will be girls, of course, but that is not really the issue. Clearly some other sort of game is going on.

Gorbals Boys is the work of Liz Peden, a self-taught sculptor on the GAP staff, and it was commissioned as a contribution to the "Public Realm" initiative of the Crown Street Regeneration Project. Modelling and casting were completed by the end of 2004, but delays with the main development have meant it will not be until the summer of 2006 that the three figures will be installed on their intended site in a newly pedestrianised stretch of Cumberland Street. They will be attached directly to the ground, with neither a pedestal nor a plinth to separate them from the pavement, in the process creating the illusion that they are, like any other group of pedestrians, physically engaged in the ongoing life of the street. Part of the original idea was to place a sequence of pairs of empty shoes in a line leading like footprints up to and beyond the figure group, suggesting that the tableau is merely one episode in a longer journey, but this has been shelved for time being and seems unlikely to go ahead. All the same, the importance of the shoes—foot furniture if ever there was such a thing—will be emphasised by the fact that they will be plated with polished chrome, to distinguish them from the regular patina of the main figures.

With or without the supplementary footwear, this is clearly a work with an overt narrative content; and like any narrative that has its roots in the micro-culture of an urban community, its meaning is polyvalent, and therefore capable of generating new stories of its own. First among them has to be the story of its genesis, so we may begin by asking: how did such a work come about?

As a grassroots arts organisation, GAP is committed to providing opportunities for Gorbals residents to participate in a variety of creative activities, including classes and workshops for adult beginners, and projects tailored to the needs of young people. Its identity is defined partly by the outcome of those projects—the work produced by the participants themselves—but also more subtly by the pattern of working relationships that connects what it does to the aspirations of the local community. The staff are all themselves local residents (in Peden's case, "Gorbals born and bred"), and therefore have personal histories that are bound up with the collective history of the area in which they work. Not surprisingly, the invitation to make a major contribution to the Public Realm initiative was seized on as an opportunity to produce a work that would not only promote the values of the new environment that was being created all around, but also act as a link with the historical culture that would inevitably be erased as a result. Early on in the creative process, a vague recollection of a photograph, taken some time in the 1960s, of a girl clomping down a Gorbals street in her mother's high heels suggested the germ of an idea that might work. In this case personal memory proved less than reliable when the girl in question—Oscar Marzaroli's now famous 'Golden-haired Lass'—turned out to be wearing wellington boots. But a quick skim through the plates of *Shades of Gray*, the collection in which she appears, soon threw up the richer possibility of three boys, *all* in high heels, acting out an even more inscrutable narrative of their own.[1] If the image of the girl was cute, this moment of spontaneous absurdity was positively bizarre. It was the perfect pretext for a new work.

"Much of what we think we know about the history of the Gorbals is dependent on the way it has been represented visually ..."

The fact that *Gorbals Boys* owes its origin to a photograph—that it is intended as a three-dimensional realisation of a flat black and white print—is worth reflecting on, as is the choice of a work by Oscar Marzaroli as a visual source. Though primarily a filmmaker, Marzaroli is best remembered today as a stills photographer, and the author of a distinguished body of street photographs that, in the minds of many, provide a vivid and truthful document of the lives of ordinary people in post war Glasgow. He

1
Marzaroli, Oscar and William McIlvanney, *Shades of Grey: Glasgow 1956–1987*, Edinburgh: Mainstream Publishing, 1987, pp. 71 and 73.

Liz Peden, *Gorbals Boys*, awaiting installation in the GAP studio basement, 2005. Photo: Anthony O'Doibhailein.

Oscar Marzaroli, *Children on Street, Gorbals, 1963.* Courtesy the Marzaroli Trust.

2
Annan, Thomas, *Photographs of the Old Closes and Streets of Glasgow 1868/1877*, New York: Dover Publications, 1977, plates 39, 40 and 43.

worked in the 'decisive moment' tradition associated with Henri Cartier-Bresson, and like the great French master relayed his response to the world around him through images replete with insight, humour, and visual grace. *Children on Street, Gorbals, 1963*, to give the photograph its proper title, typifies his flair for catching a live event on the wing, providing just enough narrative detail to make it clear that a human drama of some kind is being acted out, but without enabling us to say for certain what that drama really signifies. Like so much work produced under the rubric of 'documentary' photography, his pictures are in fact deeply ambiguous. While appearing to illuminate how other people live their lives, they in fact merely serve to remind us of how fundamentally inexplicable those lives really are.

Even so, much of what we think we know about the history of the Gorbals is dependent on the way it has been represented visually, and Marzaroli is only one of many photographers who have memorialised its appearance on film. Thomas Annan led the way when he included a small group of Gorbals street scenes in his survey of the Glasgow slums in the 1860s, providing powerful visual evidence that the social problems for which the area later became a byword have origins that extend well back into the High Victorian period.[2] By the middle of the twentieth century its reputation as one of the most chronically deprived suburbs in Britain was such that the magazine *Picture Post*—a leftist weekly publication devoted, among other things, to exposing social injustice—dispatched two photographers, Bill Brandt and Bert Hardy, to

ly, Bert, *My Life*, London:
Jon Fraser, 1985, pp.104
107.

Joseph McKenzie, *Pages
xperience. Photography
7–1987*, Edinburgh:
gon, and Glasgow: Third
Centre, 1987, pp.25–35.

enzie, *Pages of
erience*, pp.34 and 26.

enzie, *Pages of
erience*, p.35.

Glasgow to record it for a special feature. Brandt was apparently so traumatised by the experience that he failed to produce a single useable image, but Hardy proved true to his name and came away with a clutch of what are now regarded as classic shots, including one of a pair of bullet-headed urchins in short trousers grimacing contemptuously at the cameraman as they prepare to dash across the road.[3] By any measure, however, the most powerful photographic critique of the place must be the series made by Joseph McKenzie in 1963–1964 and later published as *Glasgow Gorbals Children*.[4] From the backcourt squalor of *Middens Yard* to the grimy, snot-nosed, bow-legged infant identified simply as *Boy*, it never flinches in its confrontation with the spectacle of social deprivation.[5] McKenzie also took the trouble to revisit the area 20 years later to show how quickly the low-rise housing blocks that replaced the tenements had degenerated into the same semi-derelict condition.[6]

In both content and visual style, Marzaroli's work has none of the incisiveness of McKenzie's, and certainly

lacks its political edge. The children in his photographs are mischievous rather than deprived, and there is throughout an element of whimsy that threatens to descend at any moment into sentimentality. And yet it manages to strike an authentic note. The photographs embody a sense of the meaning of community life that goes beyond the cliché of poverty as an agent of social cohesion, and this was clearly an important consideration for Peden in her choice of *Children on Street* as a source. *Gorbals Boys* is in fact a work of unapologetically nostalgic intent, a bid to reclaim a more affirmative Gorbals history rather than to re-open social wounds that have now been largely healed.

But the place of Marzaroli's image in the context of photographic history is less relevant here than the issues connected to its status as a visual record, and the more general problems that arise when we try to use photographs to situate ourselves within the historical continuum of a particular place. In *Camera Lucida*, Roland Barthes reproduces a print made by André Kertész in Paris in 1931 of a schoolboy named

eden, *Gorbals Boys
il)*. Photo: Anthony
bhailein.

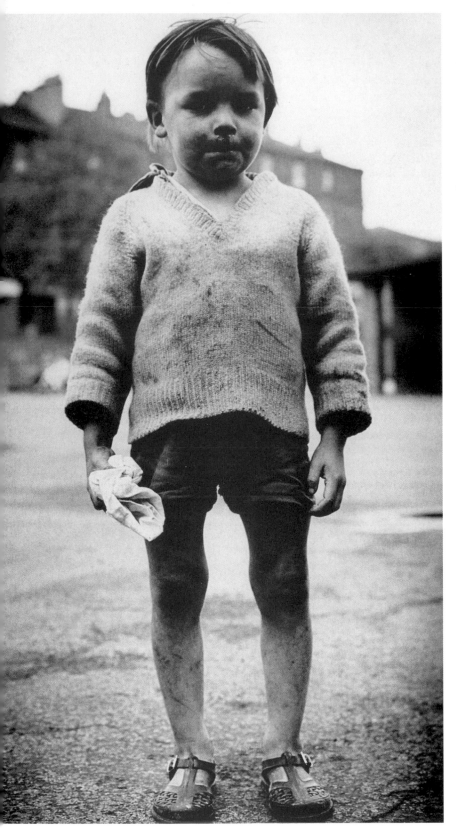

Ernest standing beside his desk.[7] Everything about the boy's appearance—his smock, his heavy boots, the deference of his smile—speaks of remoteness both in time and place; he belongs to another world. Suddenly, however, Barthes makes a rapid computation. If he was writing in the early 1980s, and the boy was standing in the schoolroom in the 1930s, then the time that separates them is in fact no more than the lifespan of an average person. "It is possible", he muses in the caption, "that Ernest is still alive today: but where? how?" And then comes the amazed realisation: "What a novel!" The dramatic telescoping of history precipitated by this act of recognition opens up a dizzying sense of the photograph's capacity to erase the passage of time, with literally an entire life compressed into the space between the two moments. One picture: a multitude of speculative possibilities.

But how, we might ask, can the transition be made from a documentary photograph to a work of art in an entirely different medium? In fact, the idea of taking an historic photograph and using it as the basis for creative invention is not as far-fetched, or as rare, as it may seem. The American writer Richard Powers did precisely that with *Three Farmers on their Way to a Dance*, a full-length novel that extrapolates the events before and after the single moment on a dusty lane in Germany in 1914 when August Sander made his exposure of … three farmers on their way to a dance.[8] Superficially, it would be hard to imagine a more precarious basis on which to compose the plot of a novel, but a moment's consideration of our normal habits of reading photographs will show why this is not the case. It is in the nature of photographs that they combine visual exactitude with an irreducible ambivalence of content. The moment of the event itself is usually clear—the protagonists are quite evidently *there*, doing whatever it is they are doing—and on that basis we can speculate quite confidently what is likely to have happened immediately before and immediately afterwards. It is in fact one of the great paradoxes of still photographs that they encourage us to run a short movie in our heads of the events occurring in the narrow slice of time on either side of the moment depicted. When we look at Marzaroli's photograph we know for sure that the two boys on the right and left have just shuffled towards their companion in the middle and we can almost hear the soundtrack of their heels scraping on the road. As soon as we start venturing beyond that, however, the questions become much

harder to answer. Where did they get the shoes from? What happened to them when the owners/mothers found out? Precisely *why* is the middle boy holding his crotch? On these matters the photograph is much less informative, with the result that the further we stray, the more we are forced to invent a narrative of our own. And such a narrative can take any form we care to give it—literary, historical or sculptural.

I am not sure if Barthes ever inquired into the whereabouts of the boy/man in Kertész's photograph, but an attempt to trace the protagonists of the

original 'Children on Street' was an almost inevitable outcome of the project—inevitable because the primary aim of the work was to bring this moment of recorded history metaphorically back to life. Accordingly, word went out via the press and the BBC and for a short while Marzaroli's photograph was the most widely publicised 'Wanted' poster in Glasgow since the manhunt for Bible John. On the whole the results were disappointing. Only one of the boys—the one in the middle—was identified, and as a blue-collar worker from nearby Motherwell and now approaching 50, he was understandably anxious that his role in the

Children Playing in the Gorbals, 1950s. © Newsquest (Herald & Times). Licensor www.scran.ac.uk.

7
Barthes, Roland, *Camera Lucida: Reflections of Photography*, London: Vintage, 1993 (first edition 1981), p. 83.

8
Powers, Richard, *Three Farmers on their Way to a Dance*, London: Weidenfeld & Nicolson, 1988.

—Three Farmers—
on their way to a Dance

Richard Powers

Cover of Richard Powers'
*Three Farmers on their way to
a Dance*, with the photograph
of the same title by August
Sander, 1914.

leading up to and following on from the alfresco catwalk display remain as mysterious as ever. The difficulties this presented Peden in her attempt to transform the event into three dimensions can readily be imagined: a grainy photograph that tells us less and less the more we look at it, three boys whose faces can barely be made out and an almost complete lack of supplementary historical information. The solution—familiar to many a panicked theatre director whose principal actors have failed to show up—was to use replacements. What the sculpture actually represents is not the event of 1963 but an action replay, with three Gorbals boys of the present century acting as understudies for their predecessors of the last.

Inconclusive though the outcome was, the search for the boys did at least provide an insight into the complexity and unpredictability of the operations that come into play when memory is invoked as a vehicle for understanding history, not least the history of a specific community. Photography is itself a powerful memory system, and the use we make of it, in conjunction with other forms of recollection, largely determines our ability to make sense of the past. On that showing the value of Marzaroli's photograph extends well beyond the simple depiction of the boys themselves, and offers a rich source of information about the conditions in which life was lived at that time in that particular corner of the world. Looking at it from the perspective of today it is hard not to be struck by how empty the streets are. Not only are there no cars to be seen, but the fact that the boys have wandered, with such a cheerful lack of self-consciousness, into the middle of the road suggests there is not even an expectation that a vehicle will pass this way in the foreseeable future. Equally curious is the presence of the two (why two?) "Provisions" shops on opposite sides of the same road junction, one of them with its windows already boarded up in anticipation of wholesale changes soon to come. The story of how this part of the city was ripped out, re-built, ripped out again and is now—hopefully for the last time—being re-built once more, is too well known to be in need of repetition here. The relevant concern, to return to the primary theme of this essay, is to determine precisely what sort of role public art can play within this larger historical process, and the extent to which it can help to shape rather than merely respond to the evolving identity of the place. Now that it has made the transition from a frozen photographic moment

affair should not be too widely broadcast among his workmates. In fact it was his mother who recognised him and came forward with the information, and even she had only the haziest recollection of the event. Of all the puzzles posed by the image only one received a satisfactory explanation. The boy in the middle is not actually holding his crotch but simply buttoning his flies. Other than that, the sequence of events to a depiction of live models immobilised in bronze, the question we should be asking is: what sort of intervention will *Gorbals Boys* be?

To answer this we have to place it in the context of a wider pattern of activities, in which memory is mediated by sculpture and in which urban intervention serves as an embodiment of social concern. Included in the GAP collection is a bronze resin relief depicting the whole area of the Gorbals extending from Aikenhead Road to just north of the River Clyde. Made in 1997, it is designed to do much the same job as the more publicly accessible works of this kind by Kathy Chambers located on Buchanan Street and in the garden in front of Kelvingrove Museum. These have always been works of immense popular appeal, and for good reason. Sculptural relief maps are uniquely seductive objects because they allow us to form a relationship with a place that is simultaneously concrete and conceptual. They combine the information content of a regular map with the realism of an aerial photograph, in the process performing an alchemical transformation in which an entire neighbourhood is compressed onto a metal surface that can be caressed with the hand. Distortions are inevitable ("the map is not the territory") and in this case the licence taken in matters of scale, together with the expressionistic simplification imposed on the tower blocks and tenements, is explained by the fact that the modelling was done by children. If it looks like a toy version of the city it is because that is precisely what it is, complete with exaggerated details like the monstrously enlarged bulldozer squatting on the south-east corner where, at the time, the Oatlands estate was in the process of being smashed to the ground. So here is another record of a city in transition. It includes some landmarks that no longer exist, such as the two Basil Spence tower blocks that were demolished in 1993, as well as others that have only been partially changed, such as Cumberland Street, the future site of *Gorbals Boys*.

Providing a permanent record of the Gorbals as it was in the 1990s was not, however, the only, or even the main purpose of this work: it had another, much more specific function. Dotted around it in various places are a number of small heart shaped motifs that may be identified by the legend in the bottom right corner as "Sara's Markers". The invitation for the children to make the work was prompted by the

death a decade earlier of Liz Peden's own 12-year-old daughter Sara in a road accident in which a worker from the construction site of what would become the Glasgow Garden Festival was speeding in his van on an improvised 'rat run' to his workplace in Shawfield. The incident served to confirm a long-standing anxiety among local parents about the woefully inadequate road safety provision in the Gorbals, and part of

André Kertész, *Ernest*, 1931.

Peden's response to her own personal loss was a determination to use the resources of public art to signal the need for change. The markers shown on the relief are the locations identified by the children, on the basis of their own experience, as places in which they and other children could play without coming to harm, and the intention was that each of these would provide the site for a work of sculpture. In the event, funding restrictions meant that only two of the projected 12 sculptures were completed, but the staff of GAP still regard the project as a piece of unfinished business that may eventually come to full fruition. Of the two that have been completed the most familiar is the small concrete pillar with rhythmically curving sides that stands in the corner of the swing park on Sandiefield Road. Its presence within the fenced enclosure constitutes an understated celebration of the fact that this particular corner of the city satisfies one of the primary requirements of every civilised urban society, that it is a place where children can grow up in safety. There is, however, no plaque to identify it, so its status as one of Sara's Markers is entirely discrete. How, then, can such a work help to bring about change?

The question leads irresistibly to the final narrative generated by this study—the narrative of my own experience as a specialist researcher in the field of public sculpture. Undertaking an investigation into public art—even the driest 'academic' sort in which I specialise—requires that we spend some of our time behaving as an old-fashioned *flâneur*. The process of properly coming to know a place is impossible unless we are prepared to cut loose and drift aimlessly, allowing our itinerary to be directed by whatever comes our way, rather than following a predetermined plan. If we are 'serious' academics we can also read up on it, of course, and in the case of the Gorbals there is an extensive literature for us to consult at our leisure and that will immeasurably enrich our understanding. But this only tells us what others have said about it. To truly know it we need to generate our own private dialogue with the place and listen to what it tells us about itself. Even so, there is no guarantee that everything it tells us will be clear or even intelligible—at least on first encounter. Indeed, we may take it as a rule that under such circumstances we will find ourselves confronted by objects that resist interpretation. Far from being a problem, however, that is just the point when we can really begin to learn. Every physical object, by virtue of the fact that it occupies space, has presence, but a *cultural* object has both presence and meaning. When access to the meaning is denied, it simply becomes another kind of object and assumes the status of an enigma.

The truth of this was confirmed by my own first attempts to get to know the public art of the Gorbals in the late 1990s. Enigmas there were in abundance, but three in particular stood out as presenting the kind of conundrum that was worth making an effort to try to unravel. The first was a small geometric abstract sculpture made of concrete at the foot of the tower block on Adelphi Street; the second was the hexagonal structure in red sandstone with carved panels opposite the Citizen's Theatre; and the third was the curvaceous pillar now identified as *Sara's Marker*. My awareness of all three was a product entirely of my own aimless wanderings; none of them, as far as I could make out, was documented in any way, and nobody I knew at the time could throw any light on what they signified or how they came to be there. How does one proceed in such a situation? The answer is by putting our trust in the strictly non-academic process of serendipity and waiting for the meaning to find us—which it will usually do in the fullness of time. In the case of the fountain, this occurred by means of a chance conversation with a former colleague who happened to know that it had been made by a recent graduate of Glasgow School of Art named Jim Harvey. Apparently he had, while still an Environmental Art student, negotiated an agreement with the City Council to salvage and relocate a disused Victorian drinking fountain on condition he transformed it into a work of art by filling the waterspout recesses with carved reliefs. As it turned out, Harvey died not long afterwards, still a very young man, and so the work became—at least in my mind—an unofficial memorial to him. It remains there to this day. With *Sara's Marker* the process was not dissimilar, though in this case the story, and therefore the meaning, of the work was not revealed to me until I paid my first visit to GAP studio and found myself unexpectedly confronted with the plywood model from which it was cast. And the concrete abstraction on Adelphi Street? Nothing has reached me so far and for the time being is keeping its secrets to itself.

What I suppose I am struggling to suggest here—and should try to clarify before descending any further into a diaristic self-indulgence—is that the haphazard quality of my experience is neither unusual nor a particular cause for concern. This is precisely what we should expect from our engagement with the objects we find on the streets. Negotiating our way through the city is a process of decoding signals that come at us from every direction and in a multitude of different forms. Some we assimilate right away, others we have to work at; some we respond to positively, others we simply pass by without a second glance. But even those we ignore are still inescapably there, making their own contribution to the complex, baffling, kaleidoscopic palimpsest that is the city street, and it is the impulse to make sense of this unique mixture of the coded and the explicit in the objects we encounter that makes urban archaeologists of us all. Those who already know the narrative of *Sara's Marker* will recognise it as both a commemoration of personal loss and an assertion of our collective responsibility as citizens to make our streets safe. Those who do not must come to terms with it in their own way—or sit tight until its meaning eventually comes to them. To risk what might be perceived as an inappropriately trite analogy, public sculptures are like the windows on an advent calendar. We are not obliged to lift the flap, but when we do we should not be surprised if a new picture—and therefore an opportunity for new readings—opens up. Even when they are concealed from us, the stories are all there; they are merely waiting to be activated.

Gorbals Boys is an attempt to intervene in this process by setting in motion a more specifically historical narrative and re-inserting it into the domain of contemporary experience. Only the most hardened cynic will fail to respond to its humour or to recognise the affection it embodies for the Gorbals' rapidly vanishing past. It is almost certain to be a popular success, even if some sectors of the public art community will doubt the wisdom of trying to address contemporary needs through a practice as rootedly conservative as figure sculpture. If, as part of a pedestrianisation programme, it helps make the streets safe for flesh and blood children to flourish in, so much the better. If not, the value of its presence will have to be judged in other ways.

When the bronze boys at present languishing in the basement at the GAP studios finally make their appearance on Cumberland Street in the summer of 2006 more than 40 years will have passed since the three rascals in Marzaroli's photograph trooped out into the street in high heels for reasons, and with consequences, that we will probably never know. In 40 years' time, the boys who volunteered to stand in for them will themselves be middle aged. How many novels there? •

The following chapter will briefly visit each of the other projects which were commissioned by The Artworks Programme: Gorbals as part of Queen Elizabeth Square's regeneration.

01. OATLANDS NEEDS PAKORA
HEISENBERG, JUNE 1999
The old red sandstone tenements in the Oatlands area of the Gorbals were among some of the last to be built in Glasgow from this material and their demolition in 1996 left an expanse of waste ground with its parameters marked by contrastingly grey rows of housing. It was this seemingly ownerless space that was identified by Matt Baker and Dan Dubowitz's collaborative enterprise Heisenberg as a potential site for inclusion in their *Journeymen* 1999 project as part of Glasgow's year-long reign as UK City of Architecture and Design. In total ten sites were chosen throughout the city that seemed to be residual or forgotten spaces and in each Heisenberg developed actions and installations aiming to explore this condition.

Oatlands Needs Pakora, which takes its name from graffiti sprayed across the walls of the last chip shop standing in the area as the demolition began, was initiated by inviting the local residents to produce maps recalling the arrangement of the buildings in the area prior to 1996. These personal cartographies became the source for an evolving installation over two weeks in summer 1999, which borrowed the form of a cultural heritage operation where public information markers or 'memory posts' installed by Heisenberg delineated the Oatlands estate as it had once stood. The positioning of these posts proved hugely contentious and a great deal of public debate was stimulated provoking Baker and Dubowitz to modify their arrangement and include additional markers.

Other sculptural actions also produced a very vocal response, with residents leaving their houses *en masse* in one instance to protest against the lengths of washing line that had been hung across the vacant space. The project culminated in a street party with an open invitation to the community; Pakora were distributed and the Oatlands' bar Chancers was resurrected for the day.

The speculative and experimental nature of *Oatlands Needs Pakora* invited input and engagement from the local population and through this dialogue the ownership felt over this neglected areas of the Gorbals was publicised. Particularly apt in this case perhaps is Heisenberg's choice of the title *Journeymen*, humbly presenting themselves as craftsmen developing their trade under superior supervision with dependence upon external guidance.

Oatlands Needs Pakora involves the ghost of a Glasgow tenement, 30 eight foot tall orange men, and Heisenberg's Uncertainty Principle, as well as pakora. Not easy concepts, we know, but that's Glasgow 1999 for you … As Physicist Karl Werner Heisenberg postulated "the very act of observation distorts that which is being observed" They speak of little else in Oatlands except, perhaps, pakora and disappeared tenements.
"IT'S BEST TO CURRY FAVOUR", *THE HERALD*, 17 JUNE 1999

02. LAST ORDERS AT THE QUEENS
DAN DUBOWITZ, JULY 2001
Anticipating some of the questions that would emerge from the debate surrounding urban regeneration in the Gorbals, Dan Dubowitz identified the area's Queens Bar as an establishment of particular importance. Impossible as it is to quantify and effectively evaluate the impact of the presence or absence of community hubs such as bars and cafes, Dubowitz's stark photographs of the Queens' pews, booths and snugs, left empty a week prior to its demolition, offer an insight into the alienating, dehumanising possibility of the destruction of such spaces.

One accusation levelled at the area since its redevelopment is that the absence of structures and venues for interaction and socialising hinder the formation of a collective identity for the new Gorbals. The open, continental boulevard design of much of the redevelopment offers spacious streets without, it has been suggested, the cafes or other social spaces one might expect for this imagined progressive, civilised identity to be forged. In the notion of removing with the bars the social degradation and moral decay with which they were believed to be associated, to be replaced by the utopian designs of a continental model, can be seen a potential friction between the intentions of town planners and the interests of residents.

In Dubowitz's photographs we see pregnant spaces, grubby and flawed, but with an indicated desolation which might accompany the removal of a crucial human element. The stillness and vacancy of the images that comprise *Last Orders at the Queens* highlight the necessity of a social dynamic whilst offering a subtle warning of a controlling influence that may not hold a community's wishes as a priority.

… the success of the new Gorbals depends upon maintaining a tangible link with everything positive about the old Gorbals. The only way to achieve that… is by involving the community itself, a notion urban planners overlooked in the Sixties.

… The story of the pub is just one of many reflecting the Gorbals spirit, a sensibility that can't be quantified by council statistics, or factored into an architectural blueprint. It is that spirit of camaraderie which Dubowitz and his Heisenberg company wanted to put at the centre of their public art projects for the new Gorbals.

"LAST ORDERS AT THE QUEENS", *SCOTLAND ON SUNDAY*, 19 AUGUST 2001

03. TESTIMONIES
DAN DUBOWITZ, JULY 2001

In this video work for the *Stirring the City* exhibition at the Lighthouse in June 2001, an uprooted park bench becomes a mobile stage for pedestrians moving through the Queen Elizabeth Square Arcade, empty and boarded in anticipation of demolition. Dan Dubowitz offered the opportunity to sit and share memories of the area prior to the significant removal of this final monument of Basil Spence's architectural legacy in the Gorbals.

Framed by the arcade's faceless, red-shuttered avenues and seated on the long wooden bench, which could have been plucked easily from any town in the UK, the image on the video screen becomes theatrical. It is a set indicating any modern urban place but one in which personal narratives very specific to the site are delivered offering opportunities for potentially tangential and forgotten histories to be written through a coincidental encounter. The video's presentation for viewing in the gallery on an aging 1970s TV monitor provided another anachronistic context for the discussion of outmoded culture long eclipsed by the zealous forward motion of commercial progress.

Eglinton Congregational Church is demolished.

Plans to demolish the remaining tower blocks in Gorbals is prematurely lea to the press.

A five and a half metre (18 foot) replica of Michelange *David* is unveiled on the ro of Gorbals business Cosmo Ceramics.

The annual Gorbals Fair is resurrected after 15 years.

Heisenberg (Matt Baker an Dan Dubowitz) issue a call artists to submit proposals "process-led" projects whi would be carefully integrat into the overall regeneratio approach to the area.

Dan Dubowitz, *Last Order the Queens*, 2001.

Dubowitz showed the film to Tom Macartney, who heads the regeneration project. Although the whole art project would have been a non-starter without Macartney's support, he watched the film with some surprise and unexpected emotion. The project director had not got the measure of public affection for the centre. "Macartney said: 'I had no idea people cared about it. I saw it, thought it looked like s**t, was trying to clean up the area, so I wiped it out.'"

"TESTIMONIES", *SCOTLAND ON SUNDAY*, 19 AUGUST 2001

04. HARRY AND JANET
VINCENT GOUDREAU AND KAI HILTON, JULY 2001

Harry and Janet, the 20 minute film by Vincent Goudreau and Kai Hilton screened at the *Stirring the City* exhibition, is a peculiar and protean document of the Gorbals in the months leading up to the major phase of demolition in summer 2001.

It is a record of a social dialogue between the two young American filmmakers and Harry McPhilemy and Janet Moore, residents of a soon to be demolished Cumberland Street tower block in the Gorbals. Harry and Janet's shared love of country and western music provides an apparent cultural to link to Kai and Vinnie albeit through an abstract and idyllic notion of Americana which the film examines and deconstructs. This becomes apparent when Harry articulately describes the dependency of the Native Americans upon buffalo, the numbers of which European colonisation of the continent had dramatically reduced, as a key factor in the displacement of the indigenous peoples. It is possible to read the film as simply a microcosmic representation of a similar displacement of the local inhabitants of the Gorbals but there is certainly greater depth to its content.

Harry and Janet is an exploration of attempts to understand a distant and unknown culture while navigating a route through expectation, prejudice, stereotype and their various fictive representations. One key example is Harry's monologue describing his love of country star George Jones as the camera records the video played on his television of a live performance. The TV screen flickers making it hard to decipher what exactly we're viewing beyond the blonde-headed, grinning countenance of the apparently healthy, tanned American entering an auditorium to almost religious adulation. We can see how such illusory notions of culture—Jones in fact

was a mentally ill cocaine addict who started each day with a bloody mary—become hugely powerful and enduring, perhaps simply operating as theatrical demonstrations of what is desirable by virtue of being exotic and unattainable. There is a disconcerting parallel here to Janet's description of the house she has been promised and the dilemma she is faced with waiting for it to be built or simply giving up on the Gorbals altogether and moving away.

Goudreau and Hilton resist a dangerous tradition in documentary making to assume a passive, innocent role in order to win the confidence of the subject and steer their input. There is none of the trite obsequiousness exemplified by the precedents of Theroux, Bashir and Broomfield; instead a genuine attempt by the two parties to understand and speak to one and other. Kai and Vinnie do not present themselves as commentators, they play active roles in the discussion their film documents handing the camera over to Janet to film them chat and struggle to understand her thick Glasgow dialect. Goudreau and Hilton offer no conclusions but give an intimate insight into the social and cultural complexity of life in the Gorbals. There is no condescending gesture as artistic benefactors rather testament to an active and personal engagement.

Vincent Goudreau and Kai Hilton, *Harry and Janet*, 2001.

Alberto Duman, *Gorbals Boys*, 2001.

05. THE PETER PAN EXPERIENCE
STEPHEN HEALY, JULY 2001

Stephen Healy makes tacit reference to the great contest for the golden ticket at the opening of Roald Dahl's *Charlie and the Chocolate Factory* in his itinerant work *The Peter Pan Experience*. At the Gorbals fair in July 2001 teenagers were invited to enter a raffle with the prospect of winning the opportunity to view their home from the air in a flight by helicopter.

Just as Dahl's protagonist's life is changed for ever by his journey across the sky, looking down at his house from the great glass elevator, Healy's work aims to make an indelible mark on the memories of five young residents of the Gorbals in the wake of a dramatic shift.

The event took place just months before the final major phase of demolition, giving the fortunate winners the chance of a final glimpse down onto the area prior to redevelopment. Existing both as an philanthropic gesture for a lucky few and symbolic closure of a social, cultural and political era for the area beheld by the generation to inherit it, *The Peter Pan Experience* addresses the community as a local event and a broader audience as a poetic conceptual act.

06. GORBALS BOYS
ALBERTO DUMAN, JULY 2001

As part of the Gorbals Fair Alberto Duman drew on the nostalgia and tradition of the Victorian seaside with an enlargement of Bert Hardy's famous photograph *Gorbals Boys*. This image, which has become a ubiquitous visual reference for the area's infamous slums, depicts two grubby urchins striding down a street with roguish expressions on their faces. Scaled up beyond life size and supported to stand independently the faces of the boys in the photograph were removed allowing visitors to insert their own. Becoming ludicrous, disembodied mutations of the iconic infants participants committed themselves to history as Duman took their pictures.

The air of temporarily liberated hedonism at a town fair is not unlike that of the traditional seaside jaunt and whilst offering good old-fashioned fun, Duman's work also indicates the deception and falsity of nostalgic exercises. The jolly ritual of *Gorbals Boys* highlights a futility in attempts to convincingly activate representations of history in a contemporary setting. Any deception produced by his construction is immediately confounded by its presence in three dimensions; naturally, one need only walk around it to expose how it functions.

Playful as it is, the work also becomes a self-aware revival of social and cultural heritage and we can view it as a symbolic reminder of how the excessive expansion and development of seaside resorts in the wake of a momentary potential left desolate, failed attempts along the coastline. With the last phase of demolition imminent residents had the opportunity to catch a final glimpse of the surrounding buildings framed in the photograph's vacant faces.

07. FRIARY PROJECTION
DAVID COTTERRELL, JULY 2001

Also conceived to coincide with the Gorbals Fair in 2001, David Cotterrell's *Friary Projection* was among some of the first projects commissioned by The Artworks Programme. It was borne out of sensitive research into the Gorbals and its community, which identified the local Franciscan order as one of the oldest surviving threads in a turbulent, constantly shifting historical and social fabric.

The upheaval caused by the building programme's dramatic changes to the area had forced the relocation of the order to a new site on the fringes of the community, and visiting them Cotterrell set up a temporary studio where he could document the daily rituals of the friars on video. On the day of the fair the edited footage became a moving projection

of these silent devotions and everyday duties, progressing around the exterior of the recently opened St Francis Community Centre and erstwhile home of the Gorbals Friary.

In developing the work Cotterell approached local groups to discuss concerns about the regeneration, and it was the commitment of the Franciscan order to a life of humility and service to the community which seemed to embody many of the virtues felt to be absent in the mechanical process of demolition and reconstruction. The visualising of these humble motions around one of the area's oldest surviving buildings provided a pertinent reminder of the services of the friars. As a well-known facet of the local social structure, in *Friary Projection* the spectral apparition of the order suggested a fleeting and disembodied continuity with their spiritual and local history.

08. ATTENDANTS
HEISENBERG, DECEMBER 2001

It is interesting to note that, at the point when the Glasgow College of Nautical Studies was expanding its range of courses (under the pressures of modernisation which come with a lessening of national focus on seafaring), a sculptural enterprise a short journey down the road was embracing the antiquated maritime art of the figurehead.

Calum Stirling, *The Wanderer*, 2003. Photo: Anthony O'Doibhailein.

Situated a few hundred yards south of the college, 12 protruding aluminium figures comprising the *Attendants* hang above each doorway along the main elevations of the Crown Street Gardens development in the Gorbals. The project is the work of Heisenberg in collaboration with Hypostyle Architects, a commission by Tay Homes (Scotland) and Redrow Homes (Scotland). With arms stretched back, elongated to spindles, and heavy lidded eyes staring solemnly forward, the figures draw the blank facades of the building out into the street whilst looming over the entrances as symbolic overseers of the new residents.

Though somewhat foreboding, the *Attendants*' solemnity seems an appropriate mark of respect in remembrance of the rich history of immigrants who, having travelled great distances, sought sanctuary in the Gorbals. Unselfconsciously decorative, with the supervisory distance of ecclesiastic statuary, the figures are an emotional response to the diasporal flux of people through the area over the last 200 years. Mysterious and commanding, they indicate a place of significance to those arriving while suggesting a reverence for the struggle of their journey.

09. TRAIL OF THE CLAY PIPES
ANNE-MARIE MURRAY, ONGOING

Trail of the Clay Pipes is an ongoing project that began in 2001 following the initial demolitions in the final major phase of regeneration in the Gorbals. Anne-Marie Murray was invited to investigate the foundations of the imminent Dawn Homes development, the site upon which Basil Spence's Queen Elizabeth Square had previously stood. It was here an amateur and speculative archaeological operation yielded the surprise discovery of over 100 clay smoking pipes.

Unsure of how to act upon this discovery but convinced of the objects' potency, Murray began a process of research which carried her through Glasgow's libraries and museums in search of details which might give any indication of their origins.

The frailty and fragility of the broken bowls and stems carried echoes of the hollow calcium of human remains as well as existing as remnants of a predominantly working class pastime, becoming symbols for a forgotten social strata which she felt warranted an almost academic scrutiny.

Evidence of a pipe factory upstream as well as the possibility of a landfill were gradually unearthed but it became clear that any definitive history for the pipes was impossible beyond speculation. Murray identified the significance of the pipes as traces of histories largely forgotten, prompting questions about whether the histories of local residents of the Gorbals today might not suffer a similar fate as the redevelopment took place about them.

Anne-Marie Murray is currently seeking a means of returning the pipes to the community and is designing a work in stained glass inspired by her research.

Local artist Anne-Marie Murray, who originally comes from the Gorbals, was called in to rescue the treasured pipes, and will now return them to the site as a piece of art … After weeks of researching the pipes' origins, Anne-Marie found out that they were made by the city's William White and Sons and McDougals, the two foremost pipe-makers in Glasgow during the nineteenth century.

"THRILL OF THE PIPES AS PIECE OF HISTORY FINDS A NEW LIFE", *EVENING TIMES*, WEDNESDAY, 25 SEPTEMBER 2002

10. THE WANDERER
CALUM STIRLING, DECEMBER 2003

Martians have become the perennial alien beings, stock icons of the distant and otherworldly. In much the same way residents of the Gorbals have become representatives of the standard, impoverished populace of the British slums in the mid-twentieth century. Remote and inaccessible in the eyes of much of the world, both stereotyped parties occupy their cultural niche through their numerous fictive representations in art thanks to exponents such as Raymond Bradbury and Joseph McKenzie.

December 2003 saw the Earth's nearest approach to Mars in 60,000 years and with it came a flurry of activity from the astronomy community to capitalise on this. The temporary astrological arrangement spurred the launch of a number of high profile and exuberantly titled exploratory missions including Mars Express, Spirit, Opportunity and Beagle 2.

Calum Stirling's itinerant work for The Artworks Programme, *The Wanderer*, identified in the climate of the Gorbals a similar atmosphere of potential and anticipation. The 16 by ten metre banner stretched across scaffolding surrounding the partially constructed skeleton of the Piers Gough designed Paragon Building bore an image of the Martian landscape from the Pathfinder mission of 1996. Carrying with it the implicit suggestion of a speculative and intangible venture into the unknown, the banner, which hung between December and March, also spoke the desolate language of the photographic documentation of the demolition of the Basil Spence's Queen Elizabeth Square in the early 1990s, as well as the famous depictions of rubble-strewn middens of the precedent tenements from the early 60s. Dominating the surrounding area and eerily lit at night the bleak facade of *The Wanderer* proposed a vacant site for potential colonisation whilst threatening to be subsumed by its appropriated form of giant civic advertisement.

In the 1960s, when eminent architects like Sir Basil Spence were hired to build the "new" Gorbals, the urban landscape they made was likened to life on Mars—a "Utopian" wasteland that never worked.

"THE WANDERER", *THE SCOTSMAN*, 17 DECEMBER 2002

11. THE BIRDCATCHERS
DAVID RALSTON, SEPTEMBER 2004

Chronometry is one of the oldest human technologies; the desire for regulation and structure a seemingly fundamental component of human society. From the earliest sundials and water clocks to digital measurement of time, man has devised systems to provide a means of maintaining a rigorous schedule.

The clock as an architectural component of central civic monuments is a widespread phenomenon. Famous large-scale timepieces such as Big Ben provide commanding icons of ordered civilisation, in addition to the service of regulating the city's timetables. David Ralston's sculpture for the Dawn Homes development in Queen Elizabeth Gardens, *The Birdcatchers*, is a unique example that playfully embraces abstract notions of time measurement. In this integral project, produced in collaboration with Hypostyle Architects, four one and a half metre tall birds crafted meticulously from stainless steel, copper and bronze take their turn to shift position each hour in such a way as to allow residents and passers by a means of telling the time. These idiosyncratic avian forms perform their protracted choreography through the day, playing the role of the civic place-maker with their oblique chronometry concealed

2003

'The Cumbie', the infamous Gorbals gang of which convicted murderer turned sculptor and novelist Jimmy Boyle was once a member, launch a website.

Residents of the Gorbals housing development by Redrow Homes gatecrash the offices of the company's directors to protest of incomplete gardens, faulty heating and leaking pipes.

Local politicians voice plans to 'breath new life into Oatlands' with a £100 million investment plan.

Glasgow's Science Centre enters its final phase of construction. Designed by Piers Gough's partnership CZWG Architects this new central science and technology district for the city promises to attract £60 million worth of private sector investment and create more than 1,600 new jobs.

The BBC report a "Show of Force by Police" as the Gorbals is identified among other areas in Glasgow as a 'trouble hotspot', with Strathclyde police concentrating their biggest division on controlling gangs of youths.

Glasgow is identified by a London-based broadsheet as murder capital of Western Europe.

10. THE WANDERER

Contact is lost with Beagle 2, the British landing craft which formed part of the European Space Agencies Mars Express mission. The loss of the craft is officially declared two months later.

Richard Holloway, the former Gorbals priest, 1963–1968, and Bishop of Edinburgh 1986–2000, is appointed as Chair at Scottish Arts Council.

Looking Backwards, a video work by Ross Birrell, is shown at the New Gorbals Library for two weeks. The video shows Birrell reading the utopian novel by Edward Bellamy, *Looking Backward: 2000–1887*, in the Disney town of Celebration in Florida.

Architect Zaha Hadid wins the competition to design Glasgow's new Transport Museum on the River Clyde.

The Scottish Execcutive announce that an estimated £2.4 billion will be invested over three years, 2005–2008, in programmes which directly support regeneration.

until their motors whirr into life with each hourly reformation. Ralston's engineering background is the root of *The Birdcatchers*' evident delight in the craftsmanship and charm of the mechanical, each of their distinct characteristics allowing them to watch over the residents like gargoyles as much as public time-keepers.

The Bird Catchers can be read like a clock, to the nearest hour—a bird changes pose every 60 minutes—but instead of indicating time past, present or to come, they represent the passage of time itself.
"BIRDCATCHERS", *HOMES AND INTERIORS MAGAZINE*, OCTOBER 2004

12. COMMUNITY ROSE
GAP, MARCH 2005

Community Rose was a project borne out of dialogue between older community members and local councillor James Mutter as a memorial to those from the local area who had served in times of conflict. Included in this was to be special mention of Private James Stokes, posthumous recipient of the Victoria Cross after his valiant actions in the final months of the Second World War. Providing a perfect icon for aspiration in the face of adversity, Stokes was identified as an exemplary figure worthy of commemoration and attention from all ages of the

community. The reverently bowed head and fallen leaf of the bronze rose was realised by Liz Peden of Gorbals Art Project, developed from the winning design in a competition by local schoolgirl Emma Porter. Red bulbs installed in the convolutions of the petals illuminate the head, while lights in the base play green up the stem, maintaining the sculpture's visibility for passers-by after dark.

The memorial is a timely link between the older population of the Gorbals who have lived through the bulk of the dramatic cultural and social shifts which have come with the different phases of regeneration, and the young who are to inherit its legacy. Rather than a project attempting to overwrite an undesirable history, as one might interpret the cycles of demolition and reconstruction that come with urban reinvention, acknowledgement of the horrifying impact of war through this memorial weaves threads between the generations and provides a solemn recognition of the need to keep such memories alive.

Almost 60 years to the day after [James Stokes] fell in battle, relatives of the soldier paid tribute to his bravery at the memorial, which acts as reminder to all from the Gorbals who fell in battle, designed in the shape of a dying rose.
"MEMORIAL ROSE", *THE HERALD*, 11 MARCH 2005 ●

David Ralston, *Birdcatchers*, 2004. Photo: Anthony O'Doibhailen.

ry, Charles et al, *The
tive City*, London:
o-German Foundation
cations, 1995.

r and Dubowitz worked
her as artist partnership
enberg, 1998–2002.

contributions of Juliet
ey, Project Manager, and
a Warwick, Co-ordinator
editor of *Arcade*, deserve
al mention in this regard.

SUDDENLY, IT SEEMS hard to find any sort of initiative, physical or theoretical, that does not have an artist on the team. The wider world wishes to learn from the artist's unique ways of engaging in situations. The aim appears to be that of adding an indefinable magic seen to be lacking in the deterministic functionalism that has dominated our approach to thinking since the birth of Modernism.

'The Creative City' is the goal, and 'Cultural Planning' its method; projects at all levels of society are looking to artists to spearhead delivery on these promises.[1]

As Lead Artist, my role was to oversee the artistic vision of the Queen Elizabeth Square regeneration programme. In practical terms this meant selecting the highest calibre artists, creating a climate for them to engage in the changes to the area, ensuring that the cultural agenda is a priority for the design team, looking out for unexpected opportunities for further artist involvement, and making artworks personally.

For me, the last seven years have raised fundamental questions about the ways that artists inhabit the political, economic and social structures of urban change. Are they genuinely contributing to the character of change or are they merely the latest weapon in the marketing armoury? Is cultural thinking at the heart of relevant and useful new places, or are artists just adding the décor to gentrified areas that reinforce already embedded ideas?

Central to the discourse is the notion of 'process'—common to all the projects explored in the New Gorbals is the way in which an artist's approach has created a momentum, which then continues to reverberate within the situation. Projects do often create 'objects', but it is important to understand that such objects should be viewed as mechanisms to support the momentum of an idea, rather than ends in themselves to be deciphered and understood by any brand of logic external to the situation.

My own involvement with the Gorbals began by an accident of such an artistic process. In Spring 1999, myself and Dan Dubowitz visited Tom Macartney (then Director of the consortia responsible for the redevelopment of the area) to request £500 sponsorship for a street party, planned as a conclusion to a site-specific project we had been working on called *Oatlands Needs Pakora*.[2] Macartney listened to our pitch (disconcertingly conducted over the book of *Nazi Architectural Masterpieces* that he used to provoke sensitive 'artistic types'), and told us about the clause inserted in the contract of all private investors in the Gorbals, which directed that they must spend one per cent of their total building budget on art. He asked us how we might advise using such funding. Our response was to imagine a strategy for the area with the same process that we would apply to any artwork. Pooling the contributions of the investors we drew up a programme that supported temporary and permanent interventions over the whole area (i.e. not just individual buildings).

A process of open-ended enquiry has been at the heart of the way I have made work and supported fellow artists in the Gorbals; the 'masterplan' that Dan Dubowitz and I conceived was an idea to facilitate and resource a conversation between a group of artists and a place, in a situation that we found utterly compelling. Part of the idea was the creation of the organisation The Artworks Programme: Gorbals, which took an active part in that conversation and adapted to take new risks and create new opportunities.[3]

Whenever I am asked about my role as an artist in a particular public space, I have noticed that I find myself attempting to describe the identity of that place and define myself as a human being in relation to it. After seven years working with the Gorbals, I have come to accept that this is in fact my definition of the role of the artist in public: to have the courage to point at the heart of the place, in the knowledge that the heart is an unstable, constantly changing entity, and that very public gesturing will say as much about yourself as it does about the place.

Claiming the right to take the time necessary to both speak and listen to the place before 'making anything' has been a keynote of the Gorbals approach. That approach requires courage from the artist; the temptation is always to have a ready-made answer hidden up your sleeve, rather than having the confidence to take the time necessary for work to suggest itself. In order to do our job, artists must maintain a position of distance; our difference is that we do not promise to contribute anything conventionally useful. By inviting artists back into the public realm we are revisiting a crucial debate about the use of the 'use-less' in society.[4]

The Gorbals artists were chosen for their commitment to taking a personal journey through the community, and their ability to draw projects from that experience, making work that ultimately added to the story of the place. This artistic process in both temporary and integral projects has left a legacy of works that form a series of 'cultural time bombs', or questions posed by artists in response to the paradoxes of the Gorbals. When I began in the Gorbals I was unsure of the artist's position in relation to this community; personally I was someone needing to belong and be part of something lasting—and the Gorbals rejected me at every turn. This is a place founded on being 'on the outside'—sited just beyond the original city limits, the Gorbals built its formidable reputation on the ability to accommodate migrants from around the world, give them a start, and then watch them leave to make way for the next arrivals. A tight community that paradoxically eulogises those that were 'determined enough to get out' but who are the people who belong to and stay in such a place? They are those who remain to look after the stories and the myths, and welcome new arrivals, a little bitter about being left behind perhaps—understandably mistrustful of anyone who wants to join them and partake in the myth-making.

But there is another story—that of the physical place designed from outside. Each new rebuilding has been heralded as a new paradigm or model that could be redeployed on a wider scale. And yet the 'designed

communities' have all failed spectacularly. The reality of a culture physically planned on generalised 'utopian foundations', and yet defiantly non-conformist, is one of the core paradoxes that has informed the work of artists in the Gorbals. Somehow, we all know that the Gorbals as imagined by the newest masterplanners will be very different to the reality experienced 20 years into the future—this insight has influenced artists and contributed to the sense of 'delay' inherent in many of the works.

When the current rebuilding began, the plan depended on private finance from the investment of large house-building companies. For these developers the reality of the Gorbals was a negative selling point. They aimed for a cultural *tabula rasa*—a squeaky clean inner city neighbourhood of aspirational penthouses and residents who shopped at the designer stores in the city centre rather than the local store. The desire (from the outside) to erase both physically and culturally was a reality impossible to ignore artistically.

This then is the position of the artist in contributing to the imagining and making of new places, weaving an individual path through constant negotiation with professional interests intent on a new 'brand', and a community mistrustful of outsiders and certainly of attempts to represent 'their' culture. From this viewpoint we come full circle, and the artworks made in the Gorbals from 2000 to 2007 reveal their aims as a series of suspended question marks that gradually add a colour and atmosphere, provoke discussion, or contribute to the ever evolving story of the area as a place where people live. •

4
At the time of writing the Scottish Parliament announced a major cultura policy initiative which inclu the right of every Scottish to experience culture as pa their development.

LEFT: Basil Spence's visio presented to Queen Elizal II in the Gorbals, 1960. Courtesy of Glasgow City Council.

RIGHT: 474 Old Ruthergle Road and 487 Cumberlan Street, Gorbals; Blowdow 26 February 2006. Photos Toby Paterson.

INTRODUCTION

Rhona Warwick is an artist who has also worked as Project Co-ordinator for The Artworks Programme since 2004. She studied at the Glasgow School of Art under David Harding where she received a BA (Hons) in Fine Art (Environmental Art) in 2001. Previous publications include *Moving Dust*, which she co-edited in 2003 following an artist residency in the Department of Archaeology (Modern Material Culture), at The University of Glasgow. She presently lives and works in Glasgow.

FOREWORD

Piers Gough has lectured extensively in Europe, North and South America, Australia and China. He has taught at Middlesex Polytechnic and the Architectural Association School as a Final Year Unit Master and in the Graduate School, and has been a visiting professor at both the Mackintosh School in Glasgow and the University of Wales Institute of Science and Technology. He is a regular contributor to the architectural press, newspapers, magazines, radio and television including presenting the *Shock of the Old* series on Channel 4. He has judged a number of architectural competitions, including the Stirling Prize in 2005. He has been the president of the Architectural Association and on its Council from 1990–1999, and is on the Advisory Committees for the London Docklands Development Corporation and the Commission for Architecture and the Built Environment. He is currently a Commissioner of English Heritage and on its Stonehenge Board, Design Champion for Kent and a Trustee of Trinity Buoy Wharf. Gough was appointed a CBE for services to architecture in the 1998 Queen's Birthday Honours List. He was elected a Royal Academician in 2002.

www.czwgarchitects.co.uk

SOMEWHERE NOWHERE: MONIKA SOSNOWSKA'S GORBALS

Moira Jeffrey is a writer and broadcaster based in Glasgow, specialising in the visual arts. She studied art history and politics at the University of Glasgow and has also trained in Scots law.

MONIKA SOSNOWSKA

Born Ryki, Poland, 1972
Lives in Warsaw

Represented by The Modern Institute, Glasgow.
www.themoderninstitute.com

SELECTED SOLO EXHIBITIONS

2006 Galeria Arsenal, Bialystok, Poland
        Museum of Contemporary Art of Castille and Leon, Spain
        Lounging Balloons, Berlin, Germany
        Sprengel Museum, Hanover, Germany
        Museum of Modern Art, New York, USA
2005 Gisela Capitain Gallery, Cologne, Germany
        The Sigmund Freud Museum, Vienna, Austria
        OPA, Guadalajara, Mexico
        Foksal Gallery Foundation, Warsaw, Poland
2004 Stella Lohaus Gallery, Antwerp, Belgium
        The Modern Institute, Glasgow, Scotland
        De Appel Gallery, Amsterdam, The Netherlands
        Kunstlerhouse Bethanien, Berlin, Germany
        Serpentine Gallery, London, England
2003 Laura Pecci Gallery, Milan, Italy
2002 Foksal Gallery Foundation, Warsaw, Poland
2001 *Little Alice*, Laboratorium Gallery, Warsaw, Poland
2000 *Non-existent Room*, Rijksakademie, Amsterdam, The Netherlands
        The Additional Illumination, Rijksakademie, Amsterdam, The Netherlands
1999 *The Shift*, Rijksakademie, Amsterdam, The Netherlands

ORCHARDLAND

Dr Nina J Morris is a Lecturer in Human Geography at the Institute of Geography, University of Edinburgh, Scotland. Research areas include: cultural geography, creative geographies, art and sculpture, natural landscapes, embodied practices, sensory perception, human-environment relations, and experiences of space and place.

AMANDA CURRIE

Born Burnley, Lancashire, 1970
Lives and works in Glasgow

SELECTED EXHIBITIONS/EVENTS

2006 *Responding to Rome*, The Estorick Collection, London, England

2005 *The Lament of the Clyde*, River Clyde, Glasgow, Scotland

2004 *The Gorbals Orchard*, The Artworks Programme, Gorbals, Glasgow, Scotland
New Work, Glasgow Project Room, Glasgow, Scotland

2003 *It's a Wonderful Lie*, WASPS, Glasgow, Scotland

2002 *Alessi/Bradbury/Currie*, Change Studio, Rome, Italy

2001 *Stirring the City*, The Lighthouse Gallery, Glasgow, Scotland

2000 *Oeuvre d'etre*, Temple Gallery, Rome, Italy
Viatico di Arte & Critico, The Change Gallery, Rome, Italy/Frankfurt, Germany

1998 *The Sows Mooring Facility*, Hospitalfield Trust Residency, Arbroath, Scotland
Hampstead Local Post Camden Arts Centre Residency, London, England

1996 *Vendesi*, Public Artwork, Rome, Italy
Heliport Base, Public Artwork, Livorno, Ferraris, Italy

2003 *Feedback Loop*, Centre for Contemporary Arts, Glasgow, Scotland
Freestyle Monumental!, Talbot Rice Gallery, Edinburgh, Scotland

2000 *Man Walks Among Us*, St Mungos Museum of Religious Life and Art, Glasgow, Scotland
Invisible Republic, Glasgow Print Studio, Glasgow, Scotland

1999 The Scottish National Portrait Gallery, Edinburgh, Scotland

1998 Modern Art, London, England
Leeds Metropolitan University Gallery, Leeds, England
Arnolfini, Bristol, England

1996 *Churchill's Dogs*, Norwich Gallery, Norwich, England

PUBLIC ARTWORKS

2005 *Youth with split apple*, King's College, Aberdeen, Scotland

2005 *Lamb*, Whitefriars, Canterbury, England

2004 *Girl With Rucksack*, Gorbals, Glasgow, Scotland

2001 *Citizen Fire Fighter*, Central Station, Glasgow, Scotland

2000 *Calf*, Graham Square, Glasgow, Scotland

1997 *Cherub/Skull*, Tron Theatre, Glasgow, Scotland

SCREENING OFF: KENNY HUNTER'S *UNTITLED. GIRL WITH RUCKSACK*

John Calcutt is Senior Lecturer on the MFA Programme at Glasgow School of Art. A former art critic for *Scotland on Sunday* and *The Guardian*, he has written extensively on contemporary Scottish art. He is also currently Associate Curator for Visual Art at the CCA, Glasgow.

KENNY HUNTER

Born Edinburgh, 1962
Lives in Glasgow

SOLO EXHIBITIONS

2006 *Natural Selection*, Yorkshire Sculpture Park, England

2004 *Works in Colour*, Conner Contemporary Art, Washington, USA
Animal Virtues, Art Connexion, Lille, France
Gates of the West, Aberdeen Art Gallery, Aberdeen, Scotland

THE GATEKEEPER

Dr Julia Lossau is Assistant Professor for Cultural Geography in the Department of Geography at Humboldt-University Berlin. Between 2001 and 2003, she was a postdoctoral Marie Curie Fellow (European Commission) at the Department of Geography and Topographic Science at the University of Glasgow. Her research examines the symbolic production of places and spaces, focusing particularly on postcolonial and aesthetic contexts. Books and articles include "Die Politik der Verortung. Eine postkoloniale Reise zu einer anderen Geographie der Welt", Bielefeld: transcript, 2002; *Themenorte. Produktion und Durchsetzung von Raumbildern*, Münster: LIT, 2005 (co-edited with Michael Flitner); "The body, the gaze and the theorist: remarks on a strategic distinction", in *Cultural Geographies*, no. 12, 2005.

Heisenberg began in 1998 as a collaboration between artist Matt Baker and architect Dan Dubowitz. The core principles of Heisenberg were to create an ambiguous public identity that would allow the exploration of working with public spaces not previously available to artists or architects through the usual channels. A consistent theme was the technique of 'direct action' used in potent but often forgotten areas of the city (see the timeline chapter for other Heisenberg projects).

SOMEWHERE BETWEEN UTOPIA AND REALITY

Simon Sadler is Professor of Architectural and Urban History at the University of California, Davis. He is author of *The Situationist City*, Cambridge, MA: MIT Press, 1998; *Archigram: Architecture without Architecture*, Cambridge, MA: MIT Press, 2005; and co-editor of *Non-Plan: Essays on Freedom, Participation and Change in Modern Architecture and Urbanism*, Burlington: Architectural Press, 2000.

Ross Birrell is an artist and writer who has exhibited nationally and internationally. Publications include *The Gift of Terror: Suicide-Bombing as Potlatch, Art in the Age of Terrorism*, Graham Coulter-Smith and Maurice Owen eds, London: Paul Holberton Press, 2005; *Justified Sinners: An Archaeology of Scottish Counterculture*, 1960–2000, Edinburgh: Pocketbooks, 2002 (co-edited with Alec Finlay).

ROSS BIRRELL

Born Glasgow, 1969
Lives in Glasgow

Represented by Ellen de Bruijne Projects, Amsterdam.

SELECTED EXHIBITIONS/PUBLIC WORKS

2006 *Port Bou: 18 Fragments for Walter Benjamin* (with David Harding), Kunsthalle Basel
2005 *Adam*, Smartspace Projects, Amsterdam
Humo Ludens: Works from the Envoy Series 1998–2005, The Friesmuseum, Leeuwarden, The Netherlands
Legend, The Artworks Programme, Gorbals, Glasgow, Scotland
Looking Backwards, Celebration, Florida, USA
2004 *Documentary Evidence*, Chez Valentin, Paris
Copy Cat, Mess Hall, Chicago

2003 *Between the Lines*, Apex Art, New York
Greyscale/CMYK, Royal Hibernian Society, Dublin
Envoy, BüroFreidrich, Berlin
Utopia Station, Staatgalerie, Sindelfingen, Germany
2002 Gwangju Biennale, Gwangju, Korea

SOURCE

Ellie Herring is presently studying at the Royal College of Art on the MA History of Design course. She has contributed texts to *Untitled* and *Art Review*, and to various artists' publications.

CHRISTINA MCBRIDE

Born Glasgow, 1963
Lives in Glasgow

SELECTED EXHIBITIONS/PUBLIC WORKS

2006 Artist residency, Banff Centre of the Arts, Banff, Alberta, Canada
2006 Public art commission, Peterhead, Scotland
2005 *Source*, The Artworks Programme, Glasgow, Scotland
2004 *Appropriate Place*, Miller/Geisler Gallery, New York, USA
2003 *Knowing and Not Knowing*, Hunter Gallery, New York, USA
Group show, Fairfield University Gallery, Connecticut, USA
Group show, Temple Gallery, Tyler School of Art, Philadelphia, USA
2002 *Boarhills*, public artwork, Fife, Scotland
2000 *East International*, Whitefriars Bridge, Norwich, England
Urban Facades: Faith, public artwork, Dundee, Scotland
1998 *Mostyn 10*, The Oriel Mostyn Gallery, Llandudno, Wales
Urban Facades: Cultivation, public artwork, Wakefield, England
1997 *F200*, California Institute of the Arts, Los Angeles, USA
Artist Flags for Scotland, Stirling, Scotland
1996 *Solo Time*, Pierce institute, Govan, Glasgow, Scotland
1995 *The Art Lotto*, The Collective Gallery, Edinburgh, Scotland

Window Dressing, public artwork, Castlemilk, Glasgow, Scotland

1994 *New Art in Scotland*, Centre for Contemporary Art, Glasgow, Scotland
Super-8 Moments, London Film Makers Co-op, England

1993 *Projecting Gorbals*, public artwork, Queen Elizabeth Square, Gorbals, Glasgow, Scotland

HIGHLIGHTS

Kirsty Williams is a Radio Producer at the BBC where she works across a range of genres, including documentaries and drama. She has a doctorate in contemporary Northern Irish poetry and has also written and published essays on Scottish literature. Kirsty collaborated with Peter Smith on *Highlights*, developing and running workshops with Gorbals' children and liaising with secondary schools to encourage young people to submit designs for the light display. Peter Smith is an architect currently working in Glasgow; having trained as a joiner in Germany where he built wooden houses, he hopes to develop sustainable housing in the UK.

DEUS EX MACHINA

Jordan Kaplan is a writer, curator and part-time Lecturer in Cybercultures at the University of Hertfordshire. She is a founding member of Parabola, a London-based commissioning body established in 2003, and dedicated to the production of exceptional contemporary art practice for non-gallery spaces.

DAVID COTTERRELL
Born Ilford, 1974
www.cotterrell.com

Represented by Danielle Arnaud, London
www.daniellearnaud.com

SELECTED EXHIBITIONS AND PUBLIC COMMISSIONS

2006 *The Debating Society*, The Artworks Programme, Gorbals, Glasgow, Scotland
Searchlight, Civic Works, Sunderland, England

Barton Hill Regeneration, CABE public commission, Bristol, England

2005 *The Unicorn*, The Unicorn Theatre for Children, South Bank, London, England
South Facing, Danielle Arnaud Contemporary Art, London, England
Guardami—Percezione del video, Palazzo delle Papesse, Centro Arte Contemporanea, Siena, Italy
Flux, alternative space, London Bridge, London, England
Artist in Residence for Greater Ashford Area, Kent, England
Fathom, Hatton Gallery, Newcastle, England
Handluggage 2005, Café Gallery Projects, London, England
Latitude, "Dead Reckoning", at the Museum of Garden History, London, England

2004 *Grey Goo*, Flaca Gallery, London, England
Scope Circle, Scope, London, England
Tempered Ground, Museum of Garden History, London, England
Fresco, Great Ormond Street Hospital, London, England
Tape291, 291 Gallery, London, England

2003 *East Wing Collection No. 6: Urban Networks*, Courtauld Institute of Art, London, England
Exhumed, The Museum of Garden History, London, England
Foreign body: Palazzo delle Libertá, Palazzo delle Papesse, Centro Art Contemporanea, Siena, Italy
Lead Artist, Avon and Wiltshire Mental Health Partnership NHS Trust
Reference Frame, Danielle Arnaud Contemporary Art, London, England
Hand Luggage, K3 Project Space, Zurich, Switzerland
Video Invitational, FA Projects, London, England
Ashford Art and Heritage Trail, an alternative mapping for the area, Ashford, Kent, England

2002 Beck's Futures 2002, ICA, London, England; The Mappin Gallery, Sheffield, England; Centre for Contemporary Arts, Glasgow, Scotland
Diversion, Museum of Garden History, Danielle Arnaud Contemporary Art, London, England
Public House, The Establishment, Brixton, London, England
Group show, K3 Gallery, Zurich, Switzerland

2001 *Car Culture*, The Hart Festival, Hull, England
Stirring the City, The Lighthouse Gallery, Glasgow, Scotland
Aquaduct, The Portobello Film Festival, Bay 67: The Westway, London, England
Reliquary, site specific installation, Gorbals, Glasgow, Scotland
High Fidelity, The Red Gallery, Hull, England
Plastic Sheet, AA Silva Gallery, Tel Aviv, Israel
Inefficient Machinery, The Mafuji Gallery, London, England
2000 *Defying Dog*, The Round Chapel, London, England
Summer Agglutinate, 291 Gallery, Hackney, London, England
VoiceOver, sonic public artwork, Hull Time Based Arts in association with Yorkshire Arts, Kingston Upon Hull City Council, and the Millennium Festival, England
Seoul/London, Total Museum of Modern Art, Seoul, South Korea
1999 *A Celebration of Regeneration*, Shillam & Smith 3, London, England
The East Wing Biennial, Courtauld Institute of Art, London, England
Canal, The Birmingham Rep Theatre, Birmingham, England
1997 *Game Show*, Belt Gallery, Hackney, London, England
The Ladies Smoking Room, St Pancras Chambers, Kings Cross, London, England
Beck's New Contemporaries 1997, Camden Arts Centre, London, England
Chelsea '97, Paton Gallery, London, England
Closing Down, Hidden Art of Hackney, London, England
Inaugural Show, Gallery Tu, London, England
1996 *Drawing and Beyond*, Angelus Gallery, Winchester, England
Bunker, Civil Defence Emergency Control Centre, Eastleigh, England
Krajina Zivlu, Mezinarodni Vytvarni Symposium, Czech Republic
Moulding History, alternative space, Vauxhall, London, England
Paranoia of a London Attaché Case, London Transport Museum, London, England

CULTIVATED WILDERNESS

Dr Kathy Battista recently completed her PhD, *Women's Work: Feminist Artists in 1970s London*, at the London Consortium. She writes and lectures on contemporary art and architecture and is co-author of *Art New York*, London: Ellipsis, 2000; *Recent Architecture in The Netherlands*, London: Ellipsis, 1998; and is a contributing author to *Surface Tension 2*, Copenhagen and Los Angeles: errant bodies, 2006 and *Surface Tension: Problematics of Site*, Copenhagen and Los Angeles: errant bodies, 2003. Battista is also on the editorial board of *Art & Architecture Journal*. She founded the Interaction programme at Artangel and was a Research Fellow at Tate Modern. She is a lecturer at Sotheby's Institute of Art London, Birkbeck College and Kings College and a Course Leader at Tate Modern.

SANS FAÇON

Charles Blanc: Born Saint Etienne, 1974
Tristan Surtees: Born Leeds, 1977
www.sansfacon.co.uk

SELECTED EXHIBITIONS AND PUBLIC COMMISSIONS

2006 *Urban Parterre*, permanent public art commission, Bristol, England
Lead artist, Peterhead, Scotland
Millennium Walk, public art commission, Bristol Harbourside, Bristol, England
Lead Artist, Building Schools for the Future programme, Durham, England
Sidekick, curating artists Craig Barrowman, Martine Myrup, Kevin Pollock in a non gallery venue for *Sideshow*, Nottingham, England
2005 *Limelight*, temporary installation for *Radiance*, Glasgow Light Festival, Scotland
PROJECT, art and landscape commission, Peterhead, Scotland
You Are Here, National Waterfront Museum, Swansea, Wales
The distance between us, temporary installation, Birmingham, England
Parks & People, public art commission, Newcastle, England
Sand Garden, International Garden festival, Chaumont-sur-Loire, France
Kielder Observatory, RIBA Art & Architecture competition, Northumberland, England

2004 *Depósito elevado*, temporary installation for Madrid Abierto
Cultivated Wilderness, permanent installation, Gorbals, Glasgow, Scotland
Viewing Platforms, permanent installations, Devon, England
True stories, Magnetic North Theatre Company
Terra Incognita, temporary installation, Glasgow, Scotland
Glasgow Landscape, map, Glasgow, Scotland

2003 *Sea view*, temporary installations, Tyne & Wear, England

2002 *Private view*, temporary installation and solo exhibition, Dun Laoghaire, Ireland
En passant, temporary installation and solo exhibition, Sacy-le-Petit, France
Traces, group exhibition, RK Burt, London, England

2001 *Stirring The City*, The Lighthouse Gallery, Glasgow, Scotland
Desire lines, map, Glasgow, Scotland
Cats, Dundee Contemporary Arts, Dundee, Scotland
Views of the West Coast of Scotland, temporary installations, Argyle and Bute, Scotland

2000 *Samples*, temporary installation, Gorbals, Glasgow, Scotland

***EVENT: SPACE*: A WORK IN PROCESS**
Dr Venda Louise Pollock is currently a Research Fellow in Urban Cultural Regeneration in the Department of Geographical and Earth Sciences at the University of Glasgow. Her research focuses on the relationship between art and the urban environment, particularly within the areas of public art, contemporary practice in public space, urban photography and visual representations of cities.

STEPHEN HURREL
Born Glasgow, 1965
www.hurrel-visual-arts.com

SELECTED EXHIBITIONS AND COMMISSIONS
2006 *Event: Space*, public commission, Gorbals, Glasgow, Scotland

Signal, QE3 Building, River Clyde, Glasgow, Scotland

2005 *Colour memory*, GSS Gallery, Glasgow International, Scotland
City Dreaming, Mitchell Library, Glasgow International, Scotland

2004 *The Rings*, public commission, Buchanan Galleries, Glasgow, Scotland
TGOZ, SAC Travelling Gallery, Scotland

2003 *The Sound of the Wind Looks Like This*, public commission, Blackpool, England
Constellation, public commission, Ayr, Scotland
State Circle, National Gallery of Contemporary Art, Canberra, Australia

2002 *One Hundred Books*, public commission, Leeds Metropolitan University, Leeds, England

2001 *Here and Now Scottish Art 1990–2001*, Dundee Contemporary Arts, Dundee, Scotland

2000 *Continuum 001*, Centre for Contemporary Arts, Glasgow, Scotland
Vauxhall Cross, temporary public artwork, London, England
Infinitude, Gallery of Modern Art, Glasgow, Scotland

1999 *Zones*, an audiology of the River Clyde, Tramway, Glasgow, Scotland
Activating ACTEW, Festival of Contemporary Art, Canberra, Australia

1998 *From Here*, High Street Project, Christchurch, New Zealand

BASIL SPENCE AND THE CREATION OF AN AFTER-IMAGE
Toby Paterson is an artist with a particular interest in architecture and urban design. He lives and works in Glasgow.

www.themoderninstitute.com

GOREY-BELLS
Jim Colquhoun is an artist and writer. He lives in Glasgow.

HOME ORNAMENTS

Caoimhín Mac Giolla Léith is a critic, occasional curator and Senior Lecturer at University College Dublin. His art criticism has appeared in *Afterall*, *Artforum*, *Modern Painters* and *Parachute*. Recent publications include catalogue essays for Franz Ackermann, Cecily Brown, Ellen Gallagher, Jaki Irvine, Karen Kilimnik and Michael Raedecker.

DAPHNE WRIGHT

Born Ireland, 1963

Represented by Frith Street Gallery
www.frithstreetgallery.com

SELECTED EXHIBITIONS AND PUBLIC COMMISSIONS

2006 *Sires*, Limerick City Gallery of Art, Limerick, Ireland

2005 *Sires*, Sligo Art Gallery, Sligo, Ireland
The Witness Tree, Castlebar Courthouse, County Mayo, Ireland
Home Ornaments, Paragon, Gorbals, Glasgow, Scotland

2003 *Sires*, Frith Street Gallery, London, England
Anonymous, Essex University Gallery, Essex, England
These Talking Walls, Crawford Gallery, Cork, Ireland

2002 *Lots Wife 2*, London Artforms, London, England

2001 *These Talking Walls*, The New Art Centre Sculpture Park and Gallery, Roche Court, Wiltshire, England
Nonsense and Death, Sligo Art Gallery, Sligo, Ireland

2000 *Where Do Broken Hearts Go?*, Douglas Hyde Gallery, Dublin, Ireland

1998 *They've taken to their beds*, Spacex Gallery Exeter and Temple Bar Gallery, Dublin, Ireland
New work, Aspex Gallery, Portsmouth and Frith Street Gallery, London, England

1995 *Domestic Shrubbery*, Castlefield, Manchester and The Model Arts Centre, Ireland

1994 *Still Life*, Cornerhouse, Manchester, England
Ballymun Project, public commission, Dublin, Ireland

BOYS AND GIRLS COME OUT TO PLAY

Ray McKenzie is Senior Lecturer at Glasgow School of Art, where he specialises in the history of photography and sculpture. He is the author of *Public Sculpture of Glasgow*, Liverpool: Liverpool University Press, 2002, which won the Saltire Award for Research Book of the Year in 2002, and is co-editor of *The State of the Real: Aesthetics in the Digital Age*, London: Palgrave Macmillan, 2006. He is currently preparing a book on the public sculpture of south west Scotland.

Gorbals Arts Project is a locally based project committed to working in partnership with local communities to produce artwork in the development of arts-led regeneration. They have worked for the past 20 years within the Gorbals area, providing tuition and workshops to local people as well as working in partnership with local groups and statutory agencies to provide artwork that improves the local area, giving people a sense of pride and ownership of their own communities.

www.gorbalsartsproject.org

PROJECT SYNOPSES

Giles Bailey is an artist and writer based in Glasgow.

AFTERWORD

MATT BAKER

Matt Baker was Lead Artist for The Artworks Programme, Gorbals 2000–2006

Born Devon, 1965
www.mattbaker.org.uk

Matt Baker originally studied architecture before working as a trapeze artist and then as assistant to sculptor Bryant Fedden. For the last 11 years he has concentrated his art practice full-time on work in the public domain. During this time Baker has developed participatory and collaborative techniques through projects ranging from temporary events/installations to large-scale permanent artworks and cultural strategies for programmes of urban change. Major sculpture projects include: *Shinglehook*, Scottish Borders; *Cultivated Wilderness*, Glasgow; and *Gatekeeper*, Glasgow. He was appointed as Lead Artist for the City of Inverness in 2006 and was Lead Artist in the Gorbals, Glasgow, from 2000–2006. He has exhibited across Britain and Europe and his work is held in several Scottish public collections. Matt Baker works from his studio in south west Scotland.

ACKNOWLEDGEMENTS

Anthony O'Doibhailein
Anderson Bell & Christie Architects
Bellway Homes
Communities Scotland
Cooper Cromar Architects
Crown Street Regeneration Project
Cruden Group
CZWG Architects
Dawn Homes Ltd
Elder & Cannon Architects
Glasgow City Council
Holmes Partnership
Hypostyle Architects
Kelvinclyde Greenspace
Maclay Murray & Spens
Miller Homes
New Century PR
New Gorbals Housing Association
Ogilvie Homes
Page & Park Architects
Scottish Enterprise Glasgow
Stewart Milne Homes
Turner Townsend Project Management Ltd

This book is part of the artwork strategy initiated and managed by The Artworks Programme, funded by a "Percentage for Art Scheme" of private contributions from seven housing developers appointed by Crown Street Regeneration Project for Queen Elizabeth Square, Gorbals: Tay Homes, Scotland (now Redrow Homes, Scotland), Stewart Milne Homes, Ogilvie Homes, Dawn Homes, Miller Homes and the Cruden Group. The Artworks Programme was appointed by Crown Street Regeneration Project (Tom Macartney) and is part funded by Scottish Enterprise Glasgow.

THE ARTWORKS PROGRAMME

The Artworks Programme was founded in 1999 by artists Matt Baker and Dan Dubowitz to respond to the process of regeneration in the Gorbals, Glasgow. An artwork strategy was developed with and alongside the overall architectural master plan, placing artists at the beginning of the design process to work with architects, housing developers and the community. Juliet Sebley joined the project in 2001 to manage administration and develop community liaison, becoming Project Manager in 2003. Over 20 high-calibre local and international artists were commissioned for both temporary and permanent public artworks, with some projects still to be completed in the next two years. Artists were selected for their approach to exploring fundamental questions about the character, interpretation and expression of place while applying a 'process-led' methodology. Emphasis for the overall artwork strategy pivoted on the role of social history in shaping the community and the recognition of cultural continuity within a context of dramatic change. The Gorbals regeneration is due for completion in 2008, and The Artworks Programme continues to deliver projects under the direction of Juliet Sebley with Matt Baker as Lead Artist.

www.theartworksprogramme.org

Black Dog Publishing
Architecture Art Design Fashion History
Photography Theory and Things

www.bdpworld.com

Edited by Rhona Warwick for The Artworks Programme
Design by Robert Johnston

Black Dog Publishing Limited
Unit 4.4 Tea Building
56 Shoreditch High Street
London
E1 6JJ
Tel: +44 (0)20 7613 1922
Fax: +44 (0)20 7613 1944
Email: info@bdp.demon.co.uk
www.bdpworld.com

The Artworks Programme
1149–1151 Cathcart Road
Glasgow
G42 9HB
Tel: +44 (0)141 632 6735
info@theartworksprogramme.org

theartworksprogramme

British Library Cataloguing-in-Publication Data.
A CIP record for this book is available from the British Library.

ISBN-10: 1-904772-54-4
ISBN-13: 978-1-904772-54-5